Verse by Verse Commentary on

PSALMS
41-80

Enduring Word Commentary Series

By David Guzik

The grass withers, the flower fades,
but the word of our God stands forever.
Isaiah 40:8

Commentary on Psalms 41-80

Copyright ©2019 by David Guzik

Printed in the United States of America or in the United Kingdom

Print Edition ISBN: 978-1-939466-50-1

Enduring Word

5662 Calle Real #184

Goleta, CA 93117

Electronic Mail: ewm@enduringword.com

Internet Home Page: www.enduringword.com

Contents

Psalm 41 – Prayer for Help in Sickness and Against Traitors 7

Psalm 42 – Honest Prayer from a Discouraged Saint 15

Psalm 43 – From Depression to a Procession of Praise 24

Psalm 44 – Accounted as Sheep to the Slaughter 28

Psalm 45 – The Anointed King and His Bride 36

Psalm 46 – Confident in God's Protection and Power 46

Psalm 47 – Praising the King of All the Earth 52

Psalm 48 – The City of the Great King 59

Psalm 49 – What Money Can't Buy 65

Psalm 50 – Judgment Begins Among the People of God 74

Psalm 51 – Restoration of a Broken and Contrite King 83

Psalm 52 – Praying About the Man Who Loved Evil 93

Psalm 53 – The Faithful God Delivers His People from Fools 99

Psalm 54 – Help When Abandoned and Betrayed 106

Psalm 55 – Trusting God Against a Treacherous Enemy 111

Psalm 56 – Faith in the Midst of Fear 119

Psalm 57 – From the Cave to Above the Heavens 125

Psalm 58 – Words to and Against the Wicked Judges 132

Psalm 59 – Praise to My High Tower Against Assassins 138

Psalm 60 – From Defeat to Victory in God 146

Psalm 61 – Hope and Help When My Heart is Overwhelmed 151

Psalm 62 – My Only Rock, My Only Salvation 156

Psalm 63 – Love Better than Life 163

Psalm 64 – Secret Plots and Sudden Shots 170

Psalm 65 – At the Temple, In the Earth 175

Psalm 66 – How Everyone Can Praise God 182

Psalm 67 – A Missionary Psalm 190

Psalm 68 – The Victorious Procession of God to Zion 197

Psalm 69 – Rescued from Deep Waters 209

Psalm 70 – Help Quickly, O Lord 220

Psalm 71 – Older in Years, Strong in Faith 224

Psalm 72 – The King and the King of Kings 233

Psalm 73 – "My Feet Almost Slipped" 242

Psalm 74 – Asking God to Remember His Fallen Sanctuary 253

Psalm 75 – The Righteous Judge Exalts and Brings Low 262

Psalm 76 – The Greatness of God & Man's Proper Response 267

Psalm 77 – A Troubled Heart Remembers God's Works 273

Psalm 78 – God's Faithfulness to His Rebellious People 281

Psalm 79 – A Prayer from Conquered Exiles 301

Psalm 80 – Israel, the Sheep & Vineyard of the LORD 307

Bibliography - 315

Author's Remarks - 317

Psalm 41 – Prayer for Help in Sickness and Against Whispering Traitors

The title of this psalm is **To the Chief Musician. A Psalm of David**. *Alexander Maclaren well described it: "The central mass of this psalm describes the singer as suffering from two evils: sickness and treacherous friends."*

A. The blessed one and the enemy of the blessed one.

1. (1-3) Blessings belonging to the one who considers the poor.

Blessed *is* he who considers the poor;
The LORD will deliver him in time of trouble.
The LORD will preserve him and keep him alive,
***And* he will be blessed on the earth;**
You will not deliver him to the will of his enemies.
The LORD will strengthen him on his bed of illness;
You will sustain him on his sickbed.

a. **Blessed is he who considers the poor**: The idea behind the word here translated **poor** may include economic poverty, but it is broader. It has the idea of *weak* or *helpless*. David described the blessings that come to the righteous man or woman, and he summarizes the life of that righteous one by his generosity to **the poor**. David didn't think that this was the only thing that marked the godly, but it was a significant thing.

i. "The poor intended, are such as are poor in substance, weak in bodily strength, despised in repute, and desponding in spirit. These are mostly avoided and frequently scorned." (Spurgeon)

ii. "There are plenty around you, who, if not poor in the things of this world, are poor in love and hope and the knowledge of God." (Meyer)

iii. Upon reflection, **he who considers the poor** – that is, the weak, helpless, and poor – is a broad measure of the righteous man or woman.

- **He who considers the poor** trusts God, willing to give from his own resources.

- **He who considers the poor** is kind to those in need.

- **He who considers the poor** helps those who likely will not help him in return.

- **He who considers the poor** has a generous heart.

- **He who considers the poor** gives for their good, not simply to make himself feel good.

iv. **Considers**: "Implies giving careful thought to this person's situation, rather than perfunctory help." (Kidner)

v. Upon reflection, much charity work – by religious, social, and political organizations – fails in this measure: **he who considers the poor**. Money and assistance are given, but in a way that contributes to chronic dependence and deeply ingrained social problems.

b. **The LORD will deliver him in time of trouble**: This begins a list of several blessings that come to the generous person. This was especially true under the Old Covenant (sometimes also called the Mosaic Covenant). An essential aspect of that covenant was blessings for obedience and curses for disobedience (as in Deuteronomy 28).

i. "Probably, therefore, the general promises of Psalms 41:1-3 are silently applied by the psalmist to himself; and he is comforting his own sorrow with the assurance.... He has been merciful, and believes, though things look dark, that he will obtain mercy." (Maclaren)

c. **He will be blessed on the earth**: This is another indication that this promise of blessing for obedience was connected to the Old Covenant, which dealt much more with earthly and physical blessings than with eternal and spiritual matters.

d. **You will sustain him on his sickbed**: Most commentators believe that David's misery and low state in this psalm were due to sickness (Psalm 41:8). Perhaps he was in danger of death (Psalm 41:5). David trusted that God would bless him for his prior goodness to the weak and needy.

2. (4-6) A sinner's plea for mercy against evil-speaking enemies.

I said, "LORD, be merciful to me;
Heal my soul, for I have sinned against You."
My enemies speak evil of me:
"When will he die, and his name perish?"
And if he comes to see *me*, he speaks lies;

His heart gathers iniquity to itself;
***When* he goes out, he tells *it*.**

a. **LORD, be merciful to me**: Without saying it directly, David seemed to appeal to God on the basis of his own good works, especially consideration of the poor (Psalm 41:1). In light of his relative righteousness, and according to the terms of the Old Covenant, David could and did ask God for mercy and blessing.

 i. "No appeal is made to justice; the petitioner but hints at the promised reward, but goes straightforward to lay his plea at the feet of mercy." (Spurgeon)

 ii. "It is a plea for mercy in view of the merciless treatment the psalmist has been receiving from his foes and friends alike." (Boice)

b. **Heal my soul, for I have sinned against You**: David knew that he had done much good, but that did not erase his sins. He understood that his sins were directed **against** God and that they made him like a sick or injured person who needed healing in his **soul**. His body was sick, but more important was his soul-sickness.

 i. We can identify at least three ways that David say he needed healing for his soul.

 • Heal my soul from its great distress.

 • Heal my soul of the effect of sin.

 • Heal my soul of my tendency to sin.

 ii. David made a plain and honest confession of his sins when he said, **I have sinned against You**.

 • A confession without excuse.

 • A confession without qualification.

 • A confession without superficiality.

 iii. "Saul and Judas each said, 'I have sinned;' but David says, 'I have sinned *against thee*.'" (Plainer, cited in Spurgeon)

 iv. "Applying the petition to David and other sinful believers, how strangely evangelical is the argument: heal me, not for I am innocent, but '*I have sinned.*' How contrary is this to all self-righteous pleading!" (Spurgeon)

 v. "There is no note of despair in his prayer. The psalmist is not depressed by the weight of his sin; it is likely that he makes a general confession of unwitting sins that he may have committed." (VanGemeren)

c. **My enemies speak evil of me**: David knew the hurt and difficulty of **evil** and lies spread about him. Like believers of all ages, David had to endure sometimes-outrageous slander and defamation of character.

i. Don't forget that David was a *good king.* "Why should David have had so many enemies if he was actually a good king and a moral person? The reason is jealousy as well as a desire for power in those who were jealous." (Boice)

ii. "It is often a good man's lot to be evil spoken of; to have his *motives,* and even his most *benevolent acts,* misconstrued." (Clarke)

iii. The early history of Christianity tells us the reasons why Christians were persecuted, or at least why people in the Roman Empire thought Christians were worthy of persecution.

- They accused Christians of hostility to the emperors and conspiracy against the state.
- They accused Christians of incest.
- They accused Christians of cannibalism.
- They accused Christians of being atheists.
- They accused Christians of being "haters of humanity."
- They accused Christians of being the reason why problems plagued the empire.

iv. The **enemies** of early Christianity spoke **evil** of the followers of Jesus, *and they spoke lies.*

- Christians were good citizens and prayed for the emperor.
- Christians lived pure moral lives.
- Christians never practiced anything like cannibalism.
- Christians were certainly not atheists.
- Christians loved others, and showed it all the time.
- Christians made the empire better, not worse.

v. Still, these lies were commonly believed and Christians were persecuted because of them. The apologists of the early church did what they could to tell the truth, but it was a losing public relations battle. These lies were popularly believed.

d. **When will he die, and his name perish?** This is what the evil-speaking enemies of David said among themselves. They couldn't wait for David to die, and they did whatever they could to bring his death to pass.

i. **If he comes to see me**: See "is used for visiting the sick in 2 Kings 8:29, and speaks lying condolence, while he greedily collects encouraging symptoms that the disease is hopeless." (Maclaren)

ii. "When they visited the king his courtiers said the right things: 'We were so sorry to hear that you are sick…. We have been praying for you and will continue to pray…. We hope you are going to be better really soon…. Everything is being taken care of…. Is there anything we can do?' These words were sheer hypocrisy. These people were not hoping that David would get well at all. After they left him they said things like, 'Didn't he look awful?... I don't think he's going to make it, do you?'" (Boice)

e. **His heart gathers iniquity to itself**: David thought of the evil heart like a magnet, constantly drawing additional sin and iniquity unto itself.

3. (7-9) Whispers and betrayal.

All who hate me whisper together against me;
Against me they devise my hurt.
"An evil disease," *they say,* **"clings to him.**
And *now* **that he lies down, he will rise up no more."**
Even my own familiar friend in whom I trusted,
Who ate my bread,
Has lifted up *his* **heel against me.**

a. **All who hate me whisper together against me**: David knew of – or at least could sense – the whispered conspiracies set in motion against him, meant to **devise** his **hurt**.

i. **All who hate me whisper together**: "The spy meets his comrades in conclave and sets them all a-whispering. Why could they not speak out? Were they afraid of the sick warrior? Or were their designs so treacherous that they must needs be hatched in secrecy?" (Spurgeon)

ii. "The same weapons are frequently employed against the servants of Christ; but let them not be, on that account, discouraged from following their Master." (Horne)

b. **An evil disease...clings to him**: This may have been true. David described such a time of illness in Psalm 38:3 and 38:6-8. David's enemies were happy at the thought that he might die and **rise up no more**.

i. We can imagine how his enemies – probably pretended friends – said this of David as he suffered on his sickbed.

ii. What they said was strong and condemning towards David. "The word 'vile' [**evil**] is a translation of 'Belial' and could also be rendered as 'a sickness from the devil' or 'an accursed disease.'" (VanGemeren)

c. **Even my own familiar friend in whom I trusted, who ate my bread, has lifted up his heel against me**: David's woe was made more bitter because among his enemies were those who had once been a **familiar friend** to him. He knew what it was like when **trusted** friends – those he had close relationship with (**who ate my bread**) – betrayed him.

i. David was betrayed by his own son Absalom (2 Samuel 15) and by a trusted adviser named Ahithophel (2 Samuel 15:12 and 15:31). "What greater wound can there be than a treacherous friend?" (Trapp)

ii. In the ultimate and most sinister sense, this was fulfilled when Judas betrayed Jesus. Jesus specifically applied these words to Judas and his treachery. In John 13:18 Jesus quoted this phrase, but only the words *He who eats bread with Me has lifted up his heel against Me*. Some think Jesus deliberately left off the words **in whom I trusted** because He *didn't* trust Judas. However, Jesus did make him the treasurer among the disciples (John 12:6 and 13:29).

iii. "The kiss of the traitor wounded our Lord's heart as much as the nail wounded his hand." (Spurgeon)

iv. "So these words were literally fulfilled in David, and yet the Holy Ghost, which dictated them, looked further in them, even to Christ and Judas, in whom they received a further and fuller accomplishment." (Poole)

v. "The idiom 'has lifted up his heel against me' signifies a treacherous act (cf. Genesis 3:15; Psalm 55:12-14)." (VanGemeren)

vi. "Not merely turned his back on me, but left me with a heavy kick such as a vicious horse might give." (Spurgeon)

B. A plea and praise.

1. (10-12) David prays for mercy from God and triumph over his enemies.

But You, O LORD, be merciful to me, and raise me up,
That I may repay them.
By this I know that You are well pleased with me,
Because my enemy does not triumph over me.
As for me, You uphold me in my integrity,
And set me before Your face forever.

a. **O LORD, be merciful to me and raise me up, that I may repay them**: David prayed not only for forgiveness and deliverance, but also for triumph over his enemies. As the LORD's anointed, he felt justified in this, and looked for God's deliverance as evidence that God was **well pleased** with him.

   i. "The plea *that I may repay them* is unusual, in that the psalms mostly pray that God Himself will do this." (Kidner)

b. **You uphold me in my integrity**: David felt that in contrast to his enemies, he was a man of **integrity**. Still, he needed God to **uphold** him in his integrity – recognizing that it was God's work in him.

c. **And set me before Your face forever**: This was the most important thing to David, more important than triumph over his enemies. To be **set...** **before** the **face** of God meant to enjoy His favor and fellowship.

   i. "To stand before an earthly monarch is considered to be a singular honour, but what must it be to be a perpetual courtier in the palace of the King Eternal, Immortal, Invisible?" (Spurgeon)

   ii. We notice that all the benefits of 11-12 are in the present tense. David did not believe that God *would* bring them to him; he believed that *he had them* already.

2. (13) Ending with praise.

Blessed *be* **the LORD God of Israel**
From everlasting to everlasting!
Amen and Amen.

a. **Blessed be the LORD God of Israel**: Many commentators believe that this is an end not only to this psalm, but to first book of Psalms. Here Yahweh is honored as the covenant God of Israel. It was fitting for David to end the song with his eyes on the LORD, not upon himself or his enemies.

   i. The five books of the Psalms are as follows:

   • Book One – Psalms 1 to 41 (41 psalms).
   • Book Two – Psalms 42 to 72 (31 psalms).
   • Book Three – Psalms 73 to 89 (17 psalms).
   • Book Four – Psalms 90 to 105 (16 psalms).
   • Book Five – Psalms 106 to 150 (45 psalms).

   ii. "Each of the five books ends with an outburst of praise, clinched by a double Amen (here and at 72:19; 89:52), an Amen and Hallelujah [Praise the Lord, NKJV] (106:48) or, finally, what is virtually a double Hallelujah (150:6), indeed a whole psalm of doxology." (Kidner)

   iii. Morgan thought that the emphasis on **the LORD God of Israel** in this doxology was fitting for the first book of Psalms. "The prevailing name of God found in this collection is Jehovah. The songs have set forth in varied ways all that this name meant to the men of faith. Thus the Doxology utters the praise of Jehovah, Who is the God of Israel." (Morgan)

b. **From everlasting to everlasting**: The LORD is to be praised as the eternal God, stretching from eternity past to eternity future.

i. "The word *everlasting* in Hebrew means the vanishing point. The idea is that the God of Israel is Jehovah from the past which is beyond human knowledge, to the future which is equally so…. To us the great truth is made more clear in the words of Jesus: 'I am the Alpha and the Omega.'" (Morgan)

Psalm 42 – Honest Prayer from a Discouraged Saint

This psalm is titled **To the Chief Musician. A Contemplation of the sons of Korah**.

We don't know when the psalms were gathered into five books, but the separation dates back to before our oldest manuscripts, compiled in the Masoretic Text. This is the first psalm of Book Two; the psalms of Book Two share some general differences with the psalms of the Book One.

The Hebrew word in reference to God is emphasized differently in the first two books of Psalms. "According to Franz Delitsch, in book one the name Jehovah occurs 272 times and Elohim only 15. But in book two, Elohim occurs 164 times and Jehovah only 30 times." (James Montgomery Boice)

In Book One of Psalms, 37 of the 41 are specifically attributed to David, and the four remaining are unattributed. David is the only known psalmist in Book One.

In Book Two of Psalms, David authored 18 of the 31, more than half. But now, other psalmists appear: Asaph and Solomon have one each, seven (perhaps eight) psalms belong to the sons of Korah, and three have no author listed.

The sons of Korah *were Levites, from the family of Kohath. By David's time it seems they served in the musical aspect of the temple worship (2 Chronicles 20:19).*

Korah led a rebellion of 250 community leaders against Moses during the wilderness days of the Exodus. God judged Korah and his leaders and they all died, but the sons of Korah remained. Perhaps they were so grateful for this mercy that they became notable in Israel for praising God.

A. The deep need of the psalmist.

1. (1-3) A sense of great need, distance from God's house, and discouraging words bring a deep sense of despair.

As the deer pants for the water brooks,
So pants my soul for You, O God.
My soul thirsts for God, for the living God.
When shall I come and appear before God?
My tears have been my food day and night,
While they continually say to me,
"Where *is* your God?"

a. **As the deer pants for the water brooks, so pants my soul for You, O God**: The sons of Korah began this psalm with a powerful image – a **deer** aching with thirst. Perhaps the thirst came from drought or from heated pursuit; either way, the deer *longed for* and *needed* water. In the same way, the psalmist's **soul** *longed for* and *needed* God.

i. "Ease he did not seek, honour he did not covet, but the enjoyment of communion with God was an urgent need of his soul; he viewed it not merely as the sweetest of all luxuries, but as an absolute necessity, like water to a stag." (Spurgeon)

b. **My soul thirsts for God, for the living God**: The psalmist wasn't thirsty for water, but for God. Drinking and thirst are common pictures of man's spiritual need and God's supply. Here, the emphasis is on the *desperation* of the need.

i. One may go many days without food, but **thirsts** shows an even more urgent need. "Which is more than hungering; hunger you can palliate, but thirst is awful, insatiable, clamorous, deadly." (Spurgeon)

ii. **For God**: "Not merely for the temple and the ordinances, but for fellowship with God himself. None but spiritual men can sympathise with this thirst." (Spurgeon)

iii. "Sorrow is always a sense of lack. The sorrow of bereavement is the sense of the loss of a loved one. The sorrow of sickness is the lack of health. The ultimate sorrow is the sense of the lack of God. This was the supreme sorrow of the singer." (Morgan)

iv. He is the **living God** in at least three senses:

• He alone has life in Himself and of Himself.

• He alone gives life.

• He is distinct from the dead, imagined gods of the heathen.

c. **When shall I come and appear before God**: For the sons of Korah – connected to the tabernacle and the temple and their rituals – there was an appointed place to **appear before God**. This was a longing to connect again with God and His people at the tabernacle or temple.

i. **Appear before God**: "In the place of his special presence and public worship. See Exodus 23:15, 25:30. What is called before the Lord, 1 Chronicles 13:10, is before or with the ark, 2 Samuel 6:7." (Poole)

ii. "It is not that he does not believe that God is everywhere, or that God is not with him. He is praying to God in the psalms, after all. But his being away from home has gotten him down, and his depressed state has caused him to feel that God is absent." (Boice)

iii. "A wicked man can never say in good earnest, '*When shall I come and appear before God?*' because he shall do so too soon, and before he would, as the devils that said Christ came 'to torment them before their time.' Ask a thief and a malefactor whether he would willingly appear before the judge." (Horton, cited in Spurgeon)

d. **My tears have been my food day and night**: These tears can perhaps be understood in at least two ways. First, they demonstrated the grief that made the psalmist long for relief in God. Second, they showed the psalmist's grief over the perceived distance from God. Either or both of these could be the case; yet the need was plainly deep and great.

i. "The next best thing to living in the light of the Lord's love is to be unhappy till we have it, and to pant hourly after it." (Spurgeon)

ii. "Possibly his tears and grief took away his appetite, and so were to him instead of food." (Poole)

e. **While they continually say to me, "Where is your God"**: Making the problem worse was being in the company of those who wanted to discourage the psalmist. They wanted to make him feel that at his moment of need, God was nowhere to be found.

i. "The first real atheism came with Greek philosophy. So the taunt did not mean that God did not exist, but that God had abandoned the psalmist." (Boice)

ii. "Other of God's suffering saints have met with the like measure. At Orleans, in France, as the bloody Papists murdered the Protestants, they cried out, Where is now your God? What is become of all your prayers and psalms now? Let your God that you called upon save you now if he can." (Trapp)

iii. **Where is your God**: "David might rather have said to them, Where are your eyes? where is your sight? for God is not only in heaven, but in me." (Sibbes, cited in Spurgeon)

2. (4) Painful memories bring further discouragement.

When I remember these *things*,
I pour out my soul within me.
For I used to go with the multitude;
I went with them to the house of God,
With the voice of joy and praise,
With a multitude that kept a pilgrim feast.

a. **I used to go with the multitude; I went with them to the house of God**: The remembering of happier times made the psalmist sadder. He thought of the times of joyful worship at the **house of God** and felt so distant from those better days.

i. **Pour out my soul**: "My soul is dissolved, becomes weak as water, when I reflect on what I have had, and on what I have lost." (Clarke)

ii. **I pour out my soul within me**: "*In me*, i.e. within my own breast, between God and my own soul; not openly, lest mine enemies should turn it into a matter of rejoicing and insulting over me." (Poole)

b. **With a multitude that kept a pilgrim feast**: He especially remembered the high times of the holidays that marked the Jewish calendar. He thought of the **multitude** and excitement (**voice of joy and praise**) that marked the feasts of Passover, Pentecost, and Tabernacles.

3. (5) Wise speaking to his own soul.

Why are you cast down, O my soul?
And *why* are you disquieted within me?
Hope in God, for I shall yet praise Him
***For* the help of His countenance.**

a. **Why are you cast down, O my soul**: The psalmist paused from the painful memory to challenge his own soul. He did not surrender to his feelings of spiritual depression and discouragement. Instead, he *challenged* them and brought them before God. He said to those **cast down** and **disquieted** feelings, "**Hope in God**. He will come through again, because He has before."

i. This is a long way from the surrender that often traps the discouraged or spiritually depressed person. He didn't say, "My soul is cast down and that's how it is. There is nothing I can do about it." The challenge made to his own soul – demanding that it explain a *reason* why it should be so cast down – is a wonderful example. There were some valid reasons for discouragement; there were many more reasons for hope.

ii. It also wasn't as if he had not already given many reasons for his discouragement. Many things bothered him.

- Distance from home and the house of God (42:2, 42:6).
- Taunting unbelievers (42:3, 42:10).
- Memories of better days (42:4).
- The present absence of past spiritual thrills (42:4).
- Overwhelming trials of life (42:7).
- God's seemingly slow response (42:9).

Still, it was as if the psalmist said, "Those are not good enough reasons to be **cast down** when I think of the greatness of God and the **help** of His favor and presence."

iii. "The result is not deadening his sense of sorrow but rather setting it in right relationship to God." (Morgan)

iv. "You have to take yourself in hand, you have to address yourself, preach to yourself, question yourself. You must say to your soul: 'Why art thou cast down – what business have you to be disquieted?'" (Lloyd-Jones, cited in Boice)

v. "David chideth David out of the dumps." (Trapp)

b. **Hope in God, for I shall yet praise Him**: In his discouragement, the psalmist spoke to himself – perhaps even preached to himself. He didn't feel filled with praise at the moment. Yet he was confident that as he did what he could to direct his **hope in God**, that praise would come forth. "I don't feel like praising Him now, but He is worthy of my **hope** – and **I shall yet praise Him.**"

i. "Hope is like the sun, which, as we journey towards it, casts the shadow of our burden behind us." (Smiles, cited in Spurgeon)

c. **The help of His countenance**: The psalmist knew to look for help in God's **countenance** – that is, the approving face of God. He found a better place by challenging his sense of gloom and seeking after God's face, **His countenance.**

i. **For the help of His countenance**: "Hebrew, *for the salvations of his face*." (Poole) "Note well that the main hope and chief desire of David rest in the smile of God. His face is what he seeks and hopes to see, and this will recover his low spirits." (Spurgeon)

ii. "When the sun arises, we cannot be without light; when God turns his countenance towards us, we cannot be without 'salvation.'" (Horne)

iii. In seeking **the help of His countenance**, the psalmist understood that the answers were not within himself, but in the living God. He didn't look within; he looked up.

B. Bringing the need to God.

1. (6) An honest prayer from a distant place.

O my God, my soul is cast down within me;
Therefore I will remember You from the land of the Jordan,
And from the heights of Hermon,
From the Hill Mizar.

a. **O my God, my soul is cast down within me**: In an almost detached sense, the psalmist reported his **cast down** soul to God. This was wise, because a common tendency in such times is to *stay away* from God or act as if we could *hide* the problem from him. The psalmist did neither.

b. **Therefore I will remember You from the land of the Jordan**: This explains why he was so far from the house of God and could not appear at the tabernacle or temple. He was far north of Jerusalem, in **the heights of Hermon**.

i. "We know the chief thing that was bothering him. He was far from Jerusalem and its temple worship on Mount Zion, and therefore felt himself to be cut off from God." (Boice)

ii. **The Hill Mizar**: "'Mizar' is probably the name of a hill otherwise unknown, and specifies the singer's locality more minutely, though not helpfully to us." (Maclaren)

2. (7-8) A prayer from the depths of discouragement.

Deep calls unto deep at the noise of Your waterfalls;
All Your waves and billows have gone over me.
The LORD will command His lovingkindness in the daytime,
And in the night His song *shall be* with me—
A prayer to the God of my life.

a. **Deep calls unto deep at the noise of Your waterfalls**: Perhaps the psalmist saw or thought of a waterfall in this high country. He saw how the water plunged down into a deep pool at the base of the waterfall and thought, "I feel that deeply buried under my misery." It was as if **all Your waves and billows have gone over me** and he was buried under.

i. The psalmist knew, "I'm in deep trouble on the outside and I'm in deep trouble on the inside." These two depths seemed to collide in him, sending him deeper still. It is a powerful and poetic description of despair.

- I hear the constant **noise** of the waterfalls; it never stops.
- I fell from a previous height.
- I plunged down quickly, and was taken down deep.
- I feel buried under all of this.
- I feel like I'm drowning.

ii. Even in this, there are points of light, giving hope.

- I am deep; but You are also – so Your depths call unto me in my depths.
- The waterfalls are Yours; if I am plunged under, then You are with me.
- The waves and billows are Yours; You have measured all this.

iii. "The whole compass of creation affordeth not, perhaps, a more just and striking image of nature and number of those calamities which sin hath brought upon the children of Adam." (Horne)

iv. **Deep calls unto deep**: "One wave of sorrow rolls on me, impelled by another. There is something *dismal* in the sound of the original [Hebrew]." (Clarke)

v. F.B. Meyer thought of this as the depths of God answering to the depths of human need. "Whatever depths there are in God, they appeal to corresponding depths in us. And whatever the depths of our sorrow, desire, or necessity, there are correspondences in God from which full supplies may be obtained." (Meyer)

- "The deep of divine redemption calls to the deep of human need." (Meyer)
- "The deep of Christ's wealth calls to the deep of the saint's poverty." (Meyer)
- "The deep of the Holy Spirit's intercession calls to the deep of the Church's prayer." (Meyer)

b. **The LORD will command His lovingkindness in the daytime**: The covenant name of God – the LORD, Yahweh – is somewhat rarely used in Book Two of Psalms. Here it is used with special strength, with great confidence that God will **command His lovingkindness** to be extended to the despairing one.

i. "His expression is remarkable; he does not say simply that the Lord will bestow, but, '*command his lovingkindness.*' As the gift bestowed is grace – free favour to the unworthy; so the manner of bestowing it is sovereign. It is given by decree; it is a royal donative. And if *he* commands the blessing, who shall hinder its reception?" (March, cited in Spurgeon)

c. **His lovingkindness in the daytime, and in the night His song shall be with me**: The psalmist came to a place of greater confidence, secure in God's goodness to him in the **daytime** or at **night**. In the more frightening **night**, he would have the gracious comfort of **His song** to be **with** him.

d. **A prayer to the God of my life**: This is another statement of confidence. The song from God will be a prayer, but not unto the God of his death, but to the **God of my life**.

3. (9-10) More honest telling of the psalmist's discouragement.

I will say to God my Rock,
"Why have You forgotten me?
Why do I go mourning because of the oppression of the enemy?"
As **with a breaking of my bones,**
My enemies reproach me,
While they say to me all day long,
"Where *is* your God?"

a. **I will say to God my Rock, "Why have You forgotten me"**: There is a pleasant contradiction in this line. The psalmist had the confidence to call God his **Rock** – his place of security, stability, and strength. At the same time he could honestly bring his feelings to God and ask, **"Why have You forgotten me?"**

i. The more experienced saint knows there is no contradiction. It was *because* he regarded God as his **Rock** that he could pour out his soul before Him so honestly.

b. **Why do I go mourning because of the oppression of the enemy**: The psalmist senses God sustaining him, but his battle is not over. There is the constant **oppression of the enemy**. The taunt, **"Where is your God?"** continued from them.

4. (11) A return to a confident challenge of self and focus upon God.

Why are you cast down, O my soul?
And why are you disquieted within me?
Hope in God;
For I shall yet praise Him,
The help of my countenance and my God.

a. **Why are you cast down, O my soul?** As the *oppression of the enemy* continued, so the psalmist would continue to speak to himself and challenge his own sense of discouragement.

> i. "It is an important dialogue between the two aspects of the believer, who is at once a man of convictions and a creature of change." (Kidner)

> ii. "The higher self repeats its half-rebuke, half-encouragement." (Maclaren)

b. **Hope in God**: The pleasant words of Psalm 42:5 are repeated as both important and helpful. The psalmist – and everyone buried under discouragement – needed to keep **hope in God** and keep confidence that he **shall yet praise Him**.

Psalm 43 – From Depression to a Procession of Praise

"This psalm is either a part of the previous one or is closely connected with it." (G. Campbell Morgan) In fact, in a number of ancient Hebrew manuscripts, Psalm 42 and Psalm 43 are joined together as one. They are probably separate psalms, linked by a common problem: spiritual depression.

"We believe the fact is that the style of the poetry was pleasant to the writer, and therefore in after life he wrote this supplemental hymn after the same manner. As an appendix it needed no title." (Charles Spurgeon)

A. The psalmist cries out to God.

1. (1) God, where are You when the wicked surround me?

Vindicate me, O God,
And plead my cause against an ungodly nation;
Oh, deliver me from the deceitful and unjust man!

a. **Vindicate me, O God**: The psalmist repeated a familiar theme in psalms – a cry for *vindication*. He felt unjustly accused and took his sense of injustice to the right place – to the throne of God, and he left his vindication up to God.

b. **Deliver me from the deceitful and unjust man**: The psalmist knew the difficulty of dealing with **deceitful** and **unjust** people, because they not only do wrong, but they also know how to cover it up with deceit. In such a tough situation, the psalmist did the right thing – he cried out to God.

i. *"Deceitful and unjust*; who covereth his wicked designs with fair and false pretences; which sort of men are hateful to thee, and to all good men." (Poole)

2. (2) God, why do You seem so distant from me?

For You *are* the God of my strength;
Why do You cast me off?
Why do I go mourning because of the oppression of the enemy?

a. **For You are the God of my strength**: If the psalmist didn't have a relationship with God, he wouldn't have this problem. Yet he did love the Lord, and his trust was in the **strength** of God and not his own strength – so he wondered where God was at his critical moment of need.

b. **Why do You cast me off? Why do I go mourning**: The repeated asking of *why* is familiar to the tested people of faith. The psalmist wondered why God did not do things according to his thinking, especially when the answer might seem obvious.

3. (3a) God, I need to be led by Your light and truth.

Oh, send out Your light and Your truth!
Let them lead me;

a. **Send out Your light and Your truth**: The psalmist knew that *his* light and *his* truth were not enough – he needed the **light** and **truth** of God. It wasn't within him, so if God didn't **send** it, he would not have it.

i. "*Thy light and thy truth,* i.e. thy favour, or the light of thy countenance, and the truth of thy promises made to me." (Poole)

b. **Let them lead me**: This was a prayer of *submission*. "Lord, I don't want You to send out Your light and truth just so I may *admire* them. I want to submit myself to **Your light** and **Your truth** and have them **lead me**. I need a leader, so **lead me**."

i. This began the psalmist's *procession of praise*. He began in depression, but he will end up praising God. It all began with the **light** and **truth** of God leading the way.

ii. "We seek not light to sin by, nor truth to be exalted by it, but that they may become our practical guides to the nearest communion with God." (Spurgeon)

B. The psalmist describes his response to God's coming answer.

1. (3b) When You answer my prayer, I will come to Your house.

Let them bring me to Your holy hill
And to Your tabernacle.

a. **Let them bring me**: The **them** of this statement refers back to the *light* and *truth* of the same verse. The psalmist wanted God's light and truth to lead him to a specific place – to **Your holy hill and to Your tabernacle**.

i. Here was the second step in the procession of praise. Led by the light and truth of God, the psalmist came to the **tabernacle**, to the tent of meeting with God. Any place God's people gather together to meet Him can become a **tabernacle**.

b. **Your holy hill to Your tabernacle**: The psalmist wanted to go to the *tent of meeting*. He wanted to because:

- He knew the Lord was there is a special way.
- He knew that God's people were there.
- He knew that it was a place where he could focus on God.

2. (4) When You answer my prayer, I will praise You.

Then I will go to the altar of God,
To God my exceeding joy;
And on the harp I will praise You,
O God, my God.

a. **I will go to the altar of God**: Full of faith, the psalmist anticipated God's answer to his prayer and declared that he would sacrifice (**go to the altar**) when the answer came. This wouldn't be a sacrifice of atonement for sin, but for gratitude and celebration of fellowship with God.

i. This was the third stop on the *procession of praise*: **the altar**. "The way to God is ever the way of the altar. The way to the altar is opened by the sending out of light and truth from God." (Morgan) When we follow the light and truth of the LORD, it will lead us to *His* altar – the cross where Jesus was given as a sacrifice for our sins.

ii. When the writer to the Hebrews stated, *We have an altar from which those who serve the tabernacle have no right to eat* (Hebrews 13:10), he likely referred to God's provision at the cross, the ultimate offering on the ultimate **altar of God**. We can **go to the altar of God** by going in faith to the cross of Jesus and thinking deeply upon His work and victory there.

iii. Under the New Covenant we no longer offer animal sacrifices, but we still bring the sacrifice of praise. Hebrews 13:15 tells us how: *Therefore by Him let us continually offer the sacrifice of praise to God, that is, the fruit of our lips, giving thanks to His name.* Our words and songs of praise become a sweet-smelling sacrifice to God.

b. **On the harp I will praise You**: The psalmist would not only praise God with animal sacrifice, but also with music and song. He reached his destination on the *procession of praise* – led by the light and truth of the Lord, he came to the house of God, to the **altar of God**, and then it culminated in **praise**.

3. (5) When You answer my prayer, I will challenge my feelings.

Why are you cast down, O my soul?
And why are you disquieted within me?
Hope in God;
For I shall yet praise Him,
The help of my countenance and my God.

a. **Why are you cast down, O my soul**: The psalmist had hope of God's redemption, but it had not come yet. In the meantime, he would not surrender to his feelings of depression and discouragement. Instead, he *challenged* those feelings and brought them to God. He said to those **cast down** and **disquieted** feelings, "**Hope in God**. He will faithfully answer again, because He has before."

i. We see that at the end of the psalm, none of the circumstances of the psalmist had changed – only his attitude, and what a difference that made. "Not yet has the answer come. The darkness and the mystery are still about him, but the shining way is seen; and again the soul is forbidden to despair and hope is encouraged in God." (Morgan)

ii. **For I shall yet praise Him**: "The refrain returns to the conflict between faith and doubt, to the contrast between the present and the future, and to the hope that 'I will yet praise him.'" (VanGemeren)

b. **The help of my countenance**: The psalmist knew his **countenance** needed **help** – and God was just the one to bring it. The peace and joy that comes from trusting and praising God will **help** our face.

i. The sense of the Hebrew word is more *salvation* than **help**. One might say that God *saves* the countenance of His people. "The poet can praise God as his 'exceeding joy' and – not merely his *help*, which is too weak a word – his 'salvation.' Outwardly nothing has changed: but he has won through." (Kidner)

ii. "Is there a cure for depression? Yes. But it is not in us. It is in God. The cure is to seek God's face, so ours will not be downcast, which is what the psalmist does." (Boice)

iii. "Faith may have a long struggle with fear, but it will have the last word, and that word will be 'the help of my countenance and my God.'" (Maclaren)

Psalm 44 – Accounted as Sheep to the Slaughter

As with Psalm 42, this psalm is titled **To the Chief Musician. A Contemplation Of the sons of Korah**. *It speaks of the nation of Israel in a season of great defeat, calling out to God for rescue. Some have thought it to be a psalm of the exile period or even afterwards in the days of the Maccabees. Yet there is reason enough to keep this psalm in the days of Israel's monarchy.*

Derek Kidner notes that Thomas Cranmer's Anglican Litany (1544) put together the first and last lines of this psalm "as declaration and petition." In Cranmer's Litany the priest said, O god, we have heard with oure eares, and our fathers have declarid unto us the noble workes that thou dyddest in their dayes, and in the olde tyme. *The choir was to respond,* O lorde, arise, help us, and delyver us for thy honour. *Kidner observed, "It was treating the prayer as a Christian inheritance, not merely an Israelite relic."*

A. The great victories of God for Israel, in the past and present.

1. (1-3) God's victory for Israel in the days of Joshua's conquest.

We have heard with our ears, O God,
Our fathers have told us,
The deeds You did in their days,
In days of old:
You drove out the nations with Your hand,
But them You planted;
You afflicted the peoples, and cast them out.
For they did not gain possession of the land by their own sword,
Nor did their own arm save them;
But it was Your right hand, Your arm, and the light of Your
countenance,
Because You favored them.

a. **Our fathers have told us, the deeds You did in their days**: The psalmist received a special legacy from his **fathers**, from their elder generation. Those **fathers** were careful to tell them what God did in generations past.

> i. "They made their mouths as it were books, wherein the noble acts of the Lord might be read to his praise, and to the drawing of their children's hearts unto him." (Trapp)

b. **You drove out the nations with Your hand, but them You planted**: Those of the elder generation told the psalmist of the great work God did when He **drove out** the Canaanites and **planted** Israel in the land promised to the descendants of Abraham, Isaac, and Jacob.

c. **They did not gain possession of the land by their own sword...but it was Your right hand**: In reading the story of the conquest in the days of Joshua, there were times when Israel did *nothing* – God alone did the work (Joshua 24:12-13). There were other times when Israel had to fight, but their fighting would have accomplished nothing without the **right hand** of God on their behalf.

d. **The light of Your countenance, because You favored them**: This was more important than and prior to having the **right hand** or **arm** of the Lord for them. It was more important to have the face and favor of God for them.

> i. We note that these were battles and conquests that happened long before the generation immediately before the time of the psalmist. The **fathers** of Psalm 44:1 spoke not only of what they personally had experienced of God, but they also taught what God did many generations before.

> ii. "Our equivalent of this memory would be reflections on our spiritual heritage, on events like the Protestant Reformation, the Wesleyan Revivals, or the Great Awakenings." (Boice)

2. (4-8) Confident prayer for God's victory for Israel in the psalmist's own day.

You are my King, O God;
Command victories for Jacob.
Through You we will push down our enemies;
Through Your name we will trample those who rise up against us.
For I will not trust in my bow,
Nor shall my sword save me.
But You have saved us from our enemies,
And have put to shame those who hated us.
In God we boast all day long,
And praise Your name forever. Selah

a. **You are my King, O God; command victories for Jacob**: The psalmist received a gift from his **fathers** – telling of God's great work in the past. There was a price for that gift; it made the psalmist dissatisfied with any sense that God wasn't doing the same works in his own day. Therefore he prayed that God **command victories for Jacob** in the present day, as well as in the stories of the past.

b. **Through You we will push down our enemies**: The prayer was prayed with faith. With confidence, the psalmist anticipated the answers to his prayers as if already done.

> i. **We will push down our enemies**: "Literally 'We will toss them in the air with our horn;' a metaphor taken from an ox or bull tossing the dogs into the air which attack him." (Clarke)

> ii. **Push down...trample**: "The vivid image of Psalm 44:5 is taken from the manner of fighting common to wild horned animals, buffaloes and the like, who first prostrate their foe by their fierce charge and then trample him." (Maclaren)

c. **I will not trust in my bow, nor shall my sword save me**: Speaking on behalf of Israel, the psalmist assured God that their faith was in God and His power, not in their own strength or skill.

> i. "In spiritual, as well as temporal warfare, the appointed means are to be used, but not 'trusted in'; man is to fight, but God giveth the victory; and to him must be ascribed the praise, and the power, and the glory." (Horne)

d. **You have saved us from our enemies**: This implies thanks for past victories. The psalmist didn't speak as if God had done nothing like this before in his own generation.

e. **In God we boast all day long, and praise Your name forever**: We may suppose that this **praise** was both for what God had done (in the distant and recent past) and in anticipation for what God would do in answer to the present prayer.

> i. "At this point we would expect the psalm to be a thanksgiving psalm, a praise psalm, or a psalm of confidence." (Boice) The first word of Psalm 44:9 will change the tone completely.

> ii. **Selah**: "A pause comes in fitly here, when we are about to descend from the highest to the lowest key. No longer are we to hear Miriam's timbrel, but rather Rachel's weeping." (Spurgeon)

B. Israel's crisis, disappointment, and ultimate trust.

1. (9-16) Israel's defeat and crisis, and the hand of the Lord in it.

But You have cast *us* off and put us to shame,
And You do not go out with our armies.
You make us turn back from the enemy,
And those who hate us have taken spoil for themselves.
You have given us up like sheep *intended* for food,
And have scattered us among the nations.
You sell Your people for *next to* nothing,
And are not enriched by selling them.
You make us a reproach to our neighbors,
A scorn and a derision to those all around us.
You make us a byword among the nations,
A shaking of the head among the peoples.
My dishonor *is* continually before me,
And the shame of my face has covered me,
Because of the voice of him who reproaches and reviles,
Because of the enemy and the avenger.

a. **You have cast us off and put us to shame**: The psalmist now stated his great present need. They felt that God did not fight for Israel and therefore they were without hope in battle. The key to prevailing over their enemies was to first prevail with God.

i. "*Put us to shame*; made us ashamed of our boasting, and trust in thee, which we have oft professed to the face of our enemies." (Poole)

b. **You have given us up like sheep intended for food**: The psalmist understood that for Israel, as a covenant nation, victory or defeat was in the hand of the LORD. Therefore if they were defeated, **scattered**, sold into slavery, made a **reproach** or **derision**, it was because God's hand was behind it in some way. Notice the repetition of the word **You**.

i. "The distress of God's people deepens with every line of verses 10-12, with rout, spoil, slaughter, scattering and slavery." (Kidner)

ii. **You make us a byword among the nations**: "We are evidently abandoned by thee, and are become so very miserable in consequence, that we are a proverb among the people: 'See the Hebrews! *see their misery and wretchedness! see how low the wrath of God has brought down an offending people!*'" (Clarke)

iii. "The scattering among the nations (Psalm 44:11) and the people's clear conscience about idolatry (Psalm 44:17ff.) seem at first sight to indicate post-exilic times for the composition of this psalm; but there were deportations before the exile (*cf.* Amos 1:6, 9), and such a psalm as the Davidic Psalm 60 (with strong similarities to the present one) is

a reminder that defeat was not unknown in the reigns of loyal kings."
(Kidner)

c. **My dishonor is continually before me, and the shame of my face has
covered me**: The psalmist was brought low, and not only because of the
defeat and disgrace suffered from their enemies. Worse was the sense that
it was because God had abandoned Israel, or perhaps was against them.

> i. **Reproaches and reviles**: "It seems that from mocking the people of
> God, the adversaries advanced to reviling God himself, they proceeded
> from persecution to the sin which is next of kin, namely blasphemy."
> (Spurgeon)

2. (17-19) The psalmist protests that Israel had kept faithful to God.

All this has come upon us;
But we have not forgotten You,
Nor have we dealt falsely with Your covenant.
Our heart has not turned back,
Nor have our steps departed from Your way;
But You have severely broken us in the place of jackals,
And covered us with the shadow of death.

a. **All this has come upon us; but we have not forgotten You**: The
psalmist felt duty bound to tell God that despite the feeling they had been
forsaken, they had not departed from God. They remembered Him and
remained faithful to His **covenant**.

> i. The mention of the **covenant** was of special purpose. Under the Old
> Covenant (sometimes known as the Mosaic or Sinai Covenant) God
> promised to bless an obedient Israel and curse a disobedient Israel (as
> in Deuteronomy 28). The psalmist implied that God must now be
> faithful to His part of the covenant because Israel had been faithful to
> their part.
>
> ii. "The law of Moses had forewarned that disobedience to the covenant
> leads to God's displeasure and ultimately to being defeated, despoiled,
> exiled, and dispersed among the nations (Deuteronomy 28:15-68)."
> (VanGemeren)

b. **Our heart has not turned back, nor have our steps departed from
Your way**: Without claiming sinless perfection, the psalmist insisted that
as a whole, Israel was still committed to God in **heart** and in conduct (**our
steps**).

> i. We might call this an honest, anti-penitential psalm. Several psalms
> are deep with a sense of personal sinfulness and contrition. In Psalm
> 44 we sense the psalmist honestly (and not self-righteously) makes

the case that their present distress was *not* due to unaddressed sin or rebellion.

ii. "The arresting fact is, that here is a song revealing an experience of defeat and humiliation, and consequently of suffering, for which no cause is to be found in the conduct of the sufferers." (Morgan)

iii. "The psalm is exploring the baffling fluctuations that have their counterpart in Christian history: periods of blessing and barrenness, advance and retreat, which may correspond to no apparent changes of men's loyalty or methods." (Kidner)

c. **But You have severely broken us in the place of jackals, and covered us with the shadow of death**: In firm but polite protest, the psalmist insisted that Israel's faithfulness to God had been answered by disaster sent by God.

i. **Broken us**: "Better to be broken by God than from God. Better to be in the place of dragons [**jackals**] than of deceivers." (Spurgeon)

3. (20-22) Israel's obedience answered with defeat.

If we had forgotten the name of our God,
Or stretched out our hands to a foreign god,
Would not God search this out?
For He knows the secrets of the heart.
Yet for Your sake we are killed all day long;
We are accounted as sheep for the slaughter.

a. **If we had forgotten the name of our God**: The psalmist continued to insist that Israel had remained faithful. They had remembered the Lord and had not prayed to idols (**stretched out our hands to a foreign god**). If they had, God would know and there was no use in denying it (**He knows the secrets of the heart**).

i. **Stretched out our hands to a foreign god**: "It was customary among the ancients, while praying, to *stretch out their hands* towards the *heavens*, or the *image* they were worshipping, as if they expected to *receive* the favour they were asking." (Clarke)

b. **Would not God search this out**: This means that as far as the psalmist was concerned, in his day there was no Achan moment as in Joshua 7, where calamity came to the people of God because of hidden sin. They had sincerely sought God for just such an understanding.

i. "The words 'would not God have discovered it' mean 'would not God have discovered it *to us*.' That is, 'Wouldn't God have told us what we have done wrong, if we had done wrong?'" (Boice)

c. Yet for Your sake we are killed all day long; we are accounted as sheep for the slaughter: Despite their claimed faithfulness to God, Israel was afflicted with death and was as helpless before their enemies as **sheep for the slaughter.**

> i. "As if we were only meant to be killed, and made on purpose to be victims; as if it were as easy and as innocent a thing to slay us as to slaughter sheep." (Spurgeon)

> ii. "The routed fugitives are defenceless and unresisting as sheep, and their fate is to be devoured...the usual butchery of a defeated army." (Maclaren)

> iii. **For Your sake** are the important words. It means that they suffered in faithfulness to God, and because of their faithfulness to God. Without developing the thought, this psalm suggests a revolutionary concept to the Old Testament man or woman of God: suffering may not be a punishment, but a battle scar, "the price of loyalty in a world which is at war with God." (Kidner)

> iv. "They suffer for God's sake...In their fidelity to the Lord, they receive greater abuse than if they had conformed to the pagan world." (VanGemeren)

> v. The Apostle Paul quoted Psalm 44:22 in Romans 8:35-36. The sense is that even in such terrible defeat and disgrace, none of this can separate us from the love of Christ or change our destiny as being more than conquerors in Him.

> vi. "Thus we are reminded of the fact that those who are the people of God are called upon to endure suffering for which there is no explanation at the time, and certainly none in their own disloyalty. Such sufferings are part of the high and holy privilege of fellowship with God." (Morgan)

4. (23-26) A plea and a hopeful prayer for help.

Awake! Why do You sleep, O Lord?
Arise! Do not cast *us* off forever.
Why do You hide Your face,
***And* forget our affliction and our oppression?**
For our soul is bowed down to the dust;
Our body clings to the ground.
Arise for our help,
And redeem us for Your mercies' sake.

a. Awake! Why do You sleep, O Lord? Arise! Do not cast us off forever: The psalmist had the depth of relationship with God to speak this freely, and God had the love and grace to not only hear it, but also to record such a prayer in His word. The psalmist openly spoke his feeling that God had forsaken and forgotten a faithful Israel.

i. The psalmist did not actually believe that God was asleep, but it felt to him so. "This is a *freedom of speech* which can only be allowed to inspired men; and in their mouths it is always to be *figuratively* understood." (Clarke)

ii. This feeling or sense was powerfully captured when Jesus slept in the boat on the stormy Sea of Galilee. The disciples feared they would perish as He slept and cried out for Jesus to awake. "Although the picture of the sleeping Lord may seem naïve to us, it was acted out in the New Testament." (Kidner)

b. **For our soul is bowed down to the dust; our body clings to the dust**: In body and soul Israel was at the crisis point and in **the dust** of shame and defeat.

i. "They who are not brought into this state of humiliation by outward sufferings, should bring themselves into it by inward mortification and self-denial, by contrition and abasement, if they would put up such prayers as the Majesty of heaven will deign to accept and answer." (Horne)

c. **Arise for our help, and redeem us for Your mercies' sake**: The psalmist has stated Israel's problem as clearly and strongly as possible. We might expect him to be angry with God or to lose hope. Instead the psalm leaves him with trusting God even in his pain and disappointment. He made his final appeal not on the basis of what Israel deserved, but for the **sake** of God's mercy (lovingkindness).

i. **Arise for our help**: "A short, but sweet and comprehensive prayer, much to the point, clear, simple, urgent, as all prayers should be." (Spurgeon)

ii. "We mentioned our sincerity and constancy in thy worship only as an argument to move thee to pity, and not as a ground of our trust and confidence, or as if we merited deliverance by it; but that we expect and implore only upon the account of thine own free and rich mercy." (Poole)

Psalm 45 – The Anointed King and His Bride

The title of this psalm is **To the Chief Musician. Set to "The Lilies." A Contemplation of the sons of Korah. A Song of Love**. *The phrase* **Set to "The Lilies"** *may refer to general beauty of the composition, to the tune, or even to a six-stringed instrument known as the Shoshannim (the literal translation of the Hebrew).*

In a roundabout way, C.S. Lewis saw this psalm pointing to Christmas: "The birth of Christ is the arrival of the great warrior and the great king. Also of the Lover, the Bridegroom, whose beauty surpasses that of man. But not only the Bridegroom as the lover, the desired; the Bridegroom also who makes fruitful, the Father of children still to be begotten and born." (C.S. Lewis, cited in Willem VanGemeren)

A. The Glory of the King.

1. (1) Ready to write this psalm.

My heart is overflowing with a good theme;
I recite my composition concerning the King;
My tongue *is* the pen of a ready writer.

> a. **My heart is overflowing with a good theme**: The tone of this psalm is a **good theme**. There is a sense of joy and celebration throughout the psalm. Yet these words also hint that the psalmist had a sense of inspiration in writing this, as if the **good theme** *flowed up* within him.

> > i. "The language in this verse is so unusual that some commentators believe the poet is claiming special inspiration." (Boice)

> > ii. "It is a sad thing when the heart is cold with a good matter, and worse when it is warm with a bad matter, but incomparably well when a warm heart and a good matter meet together." (Spurgeon)

> b. **I recite my composition concerning the King**: The idea is either that this psalm is *about* **the King** or it is *to* **the King**. It celebrates a royal wedding, but there is no firm place to connect it to a specific king in the

royal House of David. Many older commentators regard the wedding as Solomon's to the Princess of Egypt, but this is not certain.

i. At the same time, the text of the psalm itself and the way the New Testament quotes this psalm require us to regard its general tone and many of its specific lines to speak of the ultimate **King**, Jesus the Messiah.

ii. "By its language and its title, '*a love song*' the psalm comes as clearly into the category of literal wedding verse…yet speaks undoubtedly of Christ. It is proof enough that the one level of meaning need not exclude the other. But Ephesians 5:32 [and following] puts the matter beyond doubt." (Kidner)

iii. "We are to assume, then, that the poet is writing of a specific Jewish king, whose identity is unknown, but that he is also looking ahead and upward to that ideal promised King whose perfect and eternal reign was foreshadowed by the Jewish monarchy." (Boice)

iv. Maclaren noted that in the original it is **concerning** *a* **King**, without the specific article *the*. "The absence of the definite article suggesting that the office is more prominent than the person."

2. (2-5) The beauty, majesty, and might of the bridegroom King.

You are fairer than the sons of men;
Grace is poured upon Your lips;
Therefore God has blessed You forever.
Gird Your sword upon *Your* thigh, O Mighty One,
With Your glory and Your majesty.
And in Your majesty ride prosperously because of truth, humility, *and* righteousness;
And Your right hand shall teach You awesome things.
Your arrows *are* sharp in the heart of the King's enemies;
The peoples fall under You.

a. **You are fairer than the sons of men**: This begins a poetic and powerful description of the King, praising and exalting Him both for who He is and what He does. The psalmist begins by simply noting the *beauty* of the King, saying He is more beautiful (**fairer**) than all others.

i. "This monarch is fairer than the sons of men. The note of superhuman excellence is struck at the outset." (Maclaren)

ii. We believe the emphasis here is on the character of the Messiah, on the beauty of His nature and personality. Isaiah 53:2 says that the Messiah was not remarkable for His physical appearance or beauty.

Fulfilled in Jesus Christ, we can say there was never a more beautiful human being than Jesus of Nazareth.

iii. "His soul was like a rich pearl in a rough shell; like the tabernacle, goat's hair without, but gold within." (Trapp)

b. **Grace is poured upon Your lips**: The beauty of the King extends to His words, which are filled with **grace**. His grace-blessed **lips** speak grace-filled words.

i. This was marvelously true of Jesus Christ. In His early years it was said, *So all bore witness to Him, and marveled at the gracious words which proceeded out of His mouth.* (Luke 4:22) Even the opponents of Jesus said, *No man ever spoke like this Man!* (John 7:46)

ii. "His word instructed the ignorant, resolved the doubtful, comforted the mourners, reclaimed the wicked, silenced his adversaries, healed diseases, controlled the elements, and raised the dead." (Horne)

c. **Therefore God has blessed You forever**: In the beauty of His character and the graciousness of His words, the King enjoys the blessing of God, and enjoys it **forever**.

i. The phrase, "**Therefore God**" also suggests that there is an aspect or dimension to deity that is not encompassed in the King spoken of in this psalm. There is an aspect or dimension of **God** that deals with Him and blesses Him.

d. **Gird Your sword upon Your thigh, O Mighty One**: The King is beautiful in character and speaks grace-filled words, but is nothing like a soft or effeminate man. This King is a man of war, a **Mighty One** armed with a sword.

i. The phrasing of this psalm is likely the source of some of the phrasing of John's description of Jesus returning in triumph in Revelation 19:11-16.

ii. **O Mighty One**: "A title well-deserved, and not given from empty courtesy like the serenities, excellencies, and highnesses of our fellow mortals – titles, which are but sops for vain glory. Jesus is the truest of heroes. Hero worship in his case alone is commendable. He is mighty to save, mighty in love." (Spurgeon)

e. **In Your majesty ride prosperously because of truth, humility, and righteousness**: The King is full of **majesty** and blessing, but not primarily out of conquest and force. It flows from His **truth, humility, and righteousness**.

i. "The 'splendor and majesty' speak of his past victories and the confident expectation of additional victories every time he marches at the head of his troops." (VanGemeren)

ii. "For thou neither didst obtain nor wilt manage thy kingdom by deceit or violence and unrighteousness, as the princes of the earth frequently do, but with truth and faithfulness, with meekness and gentleness towards thy people, and to all that shall submit to thee." (Poole)

iii. Spurgeon envisioned King Jesus riding a chariot pulled by three horses: "These words may be rendered, '*ride forth upon truth and meekness and righteousness*' – three noble chargers to draw the war-chariot of the gospel." (Spurgeon)

f. **Your right hand shall teach You awesome things**: In the thinking of ancient Israel, the **right hand** spoke of a person's strength and skill, because most people are right-handed. This means that the exercise of the strength and skill of the King teaches Him, and teaches Him **awesome things**.

i. Applying this to Jesus Christ may seem strange. We may wonder what **awesome things** Jesus learned through His own **right hand**. Hebrews 5:8 says of Jesus that *He learned obedience by the things which He suffered*. Jesus learned the practice of obedience in the fiery test of His own suffering. This was an exercise of His strength and skill, and one of the **awesome things** He learned.

g. **Your arrows are sharp in the heart of the King's enemies**: The weapons of the King are many. He not only has a **sword**, but also sharp **arrows**, ready and sent out against His **enemies**. His might brings the world into submission (**the peoples fall under You**).

i. Jesus shoots His arrows at **the heart**, and they are **sharp** – ready and able to pierce. "Peter's converts were pricked at heart; and Stephen's hearers were pricked at heart, Acts 2:37; 7:54." (Trapp)

ii. "These arrows are spoken of in the plural because, while there are arrows of conviction, arrows of justice, arrows of terror, there are also arrows of mercy, arrows of consolation. While there are arrows that kill sin, there are also arrows that kill despair, which also is a sin; and as there are arrows that smite and slay our carnal hopes, so there are other arrows that effectually destroy our sinful fears; and all these arrows are sharp in the heart of the King's enemies, there is not a blunt one in the whole quiver." (Spurgeon)

3. (6-7) God praises Messiah the King as God.

Your throne, O God, *is* **forever and ever;**
A scepter of righteousness *is* **the scepter of Your kingdom.**
You love righteousness and hate wickedness;
Therefore God, Your God, has anointed You
With the oil of gladness more than Your companions.

a. **Your throne, O God, is forever and ever**: The King is praised and exalted as **God**. The description of Psalm 45:2-5 might apply to a remarkable man who was nevertheless merely a man. As the description continued, it clearly refers to this King Himself as God, seated upon an eternal **throne**.

i. The writer of the letter to the Hebrews explained how these words specifically apply to Jesus (Hebrews 1:8-9). He noted not only that these words say that Jesus is the eternally enthroned God, but also *that God the Father regards Him so*. The writer of the Hebrews explained that prophetically, the sons of Korah gave us the words that God the Father spoke to God the Son.

ii. "Even the ancient Jewish translators regarded these words as referring to the Messiah." (Boice)

iii. "The faithfulness of the pre-Christian LXX [Septuagint] in translating these verses unaltered is very striking." (Kidner)

iv. "From the earliest times it has been considered as definitely Messianic; and that by Jewish, as well as Christian expositors." (Morgan)

b. **A scepter of righteousness is the scepter of Your kingdom**: This King's reign is not founded on mere aggression and conquest; it isn't merely a matter of might making right. His **kingdom** is founded with **righteousness**, so much so that the symbol of His authority (**a scepter**) is **righteousness** itself.

c. **You love righteousness and hate wickedness**: The righteousness of His kingdom comes from the character of the King. It is the natural result of His **love** of righteousness and His **hate** towards wickedness. He doesn't have to work hard to make His kingdom righteous; it is in His nature and character.

d. **Therefore God, Your God, has anointed You with the oil of gladness**: Because of His great righteousness, Messiah the King receives a blessing from God. He is blessed with **the oil of gladness** – He is glad and satisfied, and that more than any other (**more than Your companions**). He is an anointed King.

i. It is true that Jesus was a Man of Sorrows, well acquainted with grief (Isaiah 53:3). Yet His work of righteousness – in all its fullness and dimensions – was rewarded as the most glad and satisfying work ever performed. Despite the sorrow and grief in His work, the accomplishment of Jesus' work left Him **anointed...with the oil of gladness**, and that more than any other person.

ii. "True, He was 'a man of sorrows,' but beneath His sorrow had abiding and central joy.... He, the saddest, was likewise the gladdest of men, and 'anointed with the oil of joy above His fellows.'" (Maclaren)

e. **Therefore God, Your God, has anointed You**: The Person of the anointed King is described in a fascinating way. In Psalm 45:6 He Himself is addressed as **God**; now in Psalm 45:7 the King is described as *relating to* God, from Whom He has received an anointing.

i. This is a strange statement – this King *is* God, and yet *receives from* God. Passages like this are the foundation for the idea of the Trinity – that there is One God who exists in Three Persons. This is the way to make sense of what seems to be contradictory statements in the Bible.

- That there is one God (Deuteronomy 6:4, Galatians 3:20).

- That Three Persons are said to be God, and they relate to One another (here and many other passages).

ii. Psalm 45 shows a striking interaction between the Persons of the Trinity. "**God, Your God**" speaks of the Father and His position of authority over the Second Person of the Trinity. "**You**" refers to the Son. "**Anointed**" has in mind the ministry and presence of the Holy Spirit, the Third Person of the Trinity.

iii. "The words of these two verses together are incomprehensible unless they are understood to refer to the incarnation of Jesus Christ. Only he can be called God and at the same time the Father as his God." (Boice)

4. (8-9) The complete greatness of the anointed King.

All Your garments are scented with myrrh and aloes *and* cassia,
Out of the ivory palaces, by which they have made You glad.
Kings' daughters *are* among Your honorable women;
At Your right hand stands the queen in gold from Ophir.

a. **All Your garments are scented with myrrh and aloes and cassia**: This is another reference to the beauty and pleasantness of the anointed King. In some way it could be said that *He smells good*, giving a more complete picture of His beauty and pleasantness.

i. We might imagine a very good-looking man of remarkable character, righteousness, and courage – who nevertheless smells bad and is therefore unpleasant to be around. Jesus isn't like that.

b. **Out of the ivory palaces, by which they have made You glad**: The psalmist thought of not just a palace but multiple **palaces**, so majestic that they were inlaid and decorated with **ivory**. We can think of majestic palaces worthy of Solomon in his splendor, pointing towards the white and pure dwelling place of God in heaven.

> i. "*Ivory palaces* were so named for the inlays of ivory in their paneling and ornamentation." (Kidner)

> ii. Looking to God's future work, **out of the ivory palaces** tells us that *the anointed King comes from heaven*. He is not only of earth, but came forth from **palaces** found only in heaven.

c. **King's daughters are among Your honorable women**: The anointed King is great not only for who He is, but also for those He associates with. The highest royalty (**king's daughters...the queen**) are the maids of honor at His wedding.

> i. Prophetically speaking this reminds us that one measure of the greatness and majesty of Jesus is the greatness of the men and women through the centuries who have been His most devoted followers. These were and are, men and women *of whom the world was not worthy* (Hebrews 11:38).

d. **At Your right hand stands the queen**: The wedding is about to begin, with the bride (**the queen**) standing in the place of honor next to the King.

> i. "The bride was seated to the right of the king and was adorned with the valuable gold of Ophir, a proverbial fine gold (cf. 1 Kings 9:28; 10:11)." (VanGemeren)

> ii. "As Christ is at the Father's right hand, so the Church is at Christ's right hand; where, as his wife, she shineth with her Husband's beams." (Trapp)

B. The bride of Messiah the King.

1. (10-12) Speaking to the bride of Messiah the King.

Listen, O daughter,
Consider and incline your ear;
Forget your own people also, and your father's house;
So the King will greatly desire your beauty;
Because He *is* your Lord, worship Him.
And the daughter of Tyre *will come* with a gift;
The rich among the people will seek your favor.

a. **Listen, O daughter**: Now the psalmist turned to the bride and spoke to her. He had encouragement and guidance for her.

b. **Forget your own people also, and your father's house**: Using the concept of Genesis 2:24, this was an invitation to this particular royal daughter to leave her people and her father's house to be joined to the anointed King in marriage.

i. If we knew nothing else of this King, we might think that this described a literal invitation of marriage to an actual woman to literally become His wife. Knowing that Jesus of Nazareth is Messiah the King and that He was never married during His earthly life, we understand this connects with a familiar metaphor: the people of God as a wife of God, and the Church of Jesus as His bride.

c. **So the King will greatly desire your beauty**: One reason the King invited the royal daughter to marriage was He saw her as beautiful, and so desired her. Since the King's beauty was that of character (Psalm 45:2), we can be sure that the bride's beauty included character.

i. Extending the analogy, Jesus – Messiah and King – sees the beauty of His people collectively, the Church – and He desires them in committed relationship, in the sharing of all things, in a future linked together.

ii. "Her beauty, so greatly desired and delighted in by Messiah, is spiritual; it is the beauty of holiness; and her clothing is 'the righteousness of saints' 1 Peter 3:3; Revelation 19:8." (Horne)

d. **Because He is your Lord, worship Him**: This has the sense of something greater than the normal respect due unto a husband, even a royal husband. This bride, this royal daughter, sees that her husband is also her **Lord** and worthy of **worship**.

e. **The daughter of Tyre will come with a gift; the rich among the people will seek your favor**: Being joined to the anointed King in marriage means many benefits for this royal daughter. She receives **gifts** from the nations, and is set in such a high place that even the **rich** seek her **favor**. Normally others seek the favor of the rich; the anointed King has set her in an even higher place.

i. "The bride's submission to her partner as both husband and king goes hand in hand with the dignity she also derives from him. His friends and subjects are now hers; she is gainer, not the loser, by her homage." (Kidner)

2. (13-15) The glory of the companion of the anointed King.

The royal daughter *is* all glorious within *the palace*;
Her clothing *is* woven with gold.
She shall be brought to the King in robes of many colors;

The virgins, her companions who follow her, shall be brought to You.
With gladness and rejoicing they shall be brought;
They shall enter the King's palace.

a. **The royal daughter is all glorious**: Because she is joined to the anointed King in a relationship of committed love, great benefits come to the royal daughter. She is **all glorious**, and not because of herself but because of her connection with the King.

i. We can't help but read this with application to how Jesus sees *His* bride, and how she is in objective truth: **all glorious**. We see the Church and notice many flaws; Jesus looks at His blood-bought people and says, "**all glorious.**"

ii. "Perhaps nowhere in Old Testament writings do we find a nearer approach to the disclosure of the secret of the Church than in this Psalm." (Morgan)

iii. **Within the palace**: "Within her secret chambers her glory is great. Though unseen of men her Lord sees her, and commends her. 'It doth not yet appear what we shall be.'" (Spurgeon)

b. **Her clothing is woven with gold**: She is clothed with valuable and beautiful clothing. She has several **robes of many colors**, which she wears in the presence of the King.

i. **Woven with gold**: "The different graces of the faithful, all wrought in them by the same Spirit, compose that divine 'embroidery' which adorns the wedding garment of the church, who is therein presented to the King, attended by the bridesmaids, after the nuptial manner." (Horne)

c. **The virgins, her companions who follow her, shall be brought to You**: The royal daughter, wife to the anointed King, is accompanied by bridesmaids and together they come before the King for the wedding service.

i. "This escorting of the bride, *led to the king* in her finest attire while he awaits her in full state, is no superfluous formality: it is the acted equivalent of Paul's phrase 'to present you as a pure bride to her one husband' (2 Corinthians 11:2)." (Kidner)

ii. "In one sense they are a part of the church, but for the sake of the imagery they are represented as maids of honour; and, though the figure may seem incongruous, they are represented as brought to the King with the same loving familiarity as the bride, because the true servants of the church are of the church, and partake in all her happiness." (Spurgeon)

3. (16-17) The legacy of the companion of Messiah the King.

Instead of Your fathers shall be Your sons,
Whom You shall make princes in all the earth.
I will make Your name to be remembered in all generations;
Therefore the people shall praise You forever and ever.

a. **Instead of Your fathers shall be Your sons, whom You shall make princes in all the earth**: A blessing is pronounced on the marriage of the anointed King. The **fathers** have passed away, but will be replaced by **sons** that come from the marriage. The King's legacy passes from generation unto generation. This ongoing work means that the **name** of the King will be **remembered in all generations**.

i. "It is the king who is addressed now; the *you* and *your* are masculine." (Kidner)

ii. The metaphors are a bit mixed, but the idea is clear. The union between the Messiah and His bride brings forth children who themselves are **princes in all the earth**. Many sons are brought to glory (Hebrews 2:10).

ii. "O church of God, think not thyself abandoned then, because thou seest not Peter, nor seest Paul – seest not those through whom thou wast born. Out of thine own offspring has a body of 'fathers' been raised up to thee." (Augustine, cited in Spurgeon)

b. **Therefore the people shall praise You**: The result of it all is that the anointed King is exalted and praised **forever and ever**. His choosing of a bride, granting great privileges to her, and giving a blessing that endures through generations all bring praise to Him.

i. "It is [because of] the glory of the Lord that we become ready to renounce all our own people and possessions that we may be wholly to His praise, and so the instruments through whom the royal race is propagated and the glory of the King made known, among the generations and the peoples." (Morgan)

ii. "Are we doing as the psalmist did? Do we praise him who has purchased us to himself to be his bride? Are we working to see that the nations come to honor him as well?" (Boice)

Psalm 46 – Confident in God's Protection and Power

The title of this psalm is **To the Chief Musician. A Psalm of the sons of Korah. A Song for Alamoth**. *"An ode upon* Alamoth, *or concerning the virgins: possibly meaning a choir of singing girls." (Adam Clarke) Spurgeon wondered if* **Alamoth** *referred to a high-pitched stringed instrument as suggested by 1 Chronicles 15:20.*

"Comment on this great song of confidence seems almost unnecessary so powerfully has it taken hold on the heart of humanity, and so perfectly does it set forth the experience of trusting souls in all ages and tumultuous times." (G. Campbell Morgan)

"Luther, when in greatest distress, was wont to call for this psalm, saying, Let us sing the forty-sixth psalm in concert; and then let the devil do his worst." (John Trapp)

A. God present among His people.

1. (1-3) The help of God greater than any crisis.

God *is* our refuge and strength,
A very present help in trouble.
Therefore we will not fear,
Even though the earth be removed,
And though the mountains be carried into the midst of the sea;
***Though* its waters roar *and* be troubled,**
***Though* the mountains shake with its swelling. Selah**

> a. **God is our refuge and strength**: Many of the other psalms begin with a description of the psalmist's crisis. In Psalm 46, the poet begins with God's provision. He looked to God for help in difficult times and found it. He could say these things by experience:

> - That God Himself was a place of **refuge**, as the cities of refuge protected the fugitive in Israel.

46

- That God Himself was **strength** for His people, being strong for them and in them.

- That God alone was his **refuge and strength**, not God *and* something or someone else.

- That God Himself was their **help** – not from a distance, but a **very present help**.

  i. **A very present help**: "The secret of the confidence is the consciousness of the nearness of God." (Morgan)

  ii. This has nothing to do with the safety or strength inherent in the creature. "We may be as timid by nature as the coneys, but God is our refuge; we are as weak by nature as bruised reeds, but God is our strength." (Spurgeon)

  iii. "All creatures, when in distress, run to their refuges, Proverbs 30:26 [*The rock badgers are a feeble folk, yet they make their homes in the crags*]." (Trapp)

b. **Therefore we will not fear**: The psalmist applied the logic of faith. If God is a real **refuge**, **strength**, and **help** to His people, then there is no logical reason to **fear** – even in the biggest crisis (**though the earth be removed**).

  i. "Its robust, defiant tone suggests that it was composed at a time of crisis, which makes the confession of faith doubly impressive." (Kidner)

c. **The earth be moved...the mountains carried...the waters roar... the mountains shake**: The psalmist considered the most frightening, humbling natural phenomenon imaginable. He then made the reasoned estimation that God was greater than them all, and **fear** before these in some way robbed God of some of His honor.

d. **Selah**: The greatness of thought in this psalm was and is worthy of pause and careful thought.

  i. "It were well if all of us could say, '*Selah*,' under tempestuous trials, but alas! too often we speak in our haste, lay our trembling hands bewildered among the strings, strike the lyre with a rude crash, and mar the melody of our life-song." (Spurgeon)

2. (4-6) The peaceful provision of God.

There *is* a river whose streams shall make glad the city of God,
The holy *place* of the tabernacle of the Most High.
God *is* in the midst of her, she shall not be moved;
God shall help her, just at the break of dawn.

The nations raged, the kingdoms were moved;
He uttered His voice, the earth melted.

a. **There is a river whose streams shall make glad the city of God**: The psalmist pictured the abundant, constant provision of a **river** for Jerusalem. The image is significant because Jerusalem does not in fact have such a river, only a few small streams. Yet the prophets anticipated the day when a mighty river would flow from the temple itself (Ezekiel 47:12, Revelation 22:1). The future reality is already in the mind of the psalmist.

i. "We might almost translate, 'Lo! a river!' Jerusalem was unique among historical cities in that it had no great river. It had one tiny thread of water." (Maclaren)

ii. "With God the waters are no longer menacing seas but a life-giving *river*." (Kidner)

iii. The **river** flows and makes all the **city of God** happy.

- The **city of God** is **glad** because life-giving water is always present in that dry, semi-arid land.

- The **city of God** is **glad** because the river has many **streams**, a picture perhaps connected to the rivers that watered the Garden of Eden (Genesis 2:10-14).

- The **city of God** is **glad** because a **river** is sometimes a picture of *peace* (Isaiah 48:18, 66:12). Jerusalem is in perfect peace.

- The **city of God** is **glad** because the city is secure, having one of the best defenses against an enemy besieging the city – guaranteed water.

b. **The city of God**: The connection is clearly with Jerusalem, the location of **the holy place of the tabernacle of the Most High**. At the same time, the title "**The City of God**" lifts the concept to God's ideal, perfect city – the *New Jerusalem* (Revelation 3:12 and 21:2).

c. **God is in the midst of her, she shall not be moved**: All the blessing and provision of **the city of God** comes because of God's presence. Because of His presence she is more firmly set than the earth which may be moved (Psalm 46:2). The city is so established because **God shall help her**.

i. "The promise *she shall not be moved* gains special force from the repetition of the same word, *moved*, used of the mountains and of the kingdoms." (Kidner)

ii. **Just at the break of dawn**: "As by the day-break the shadows and darkness are dissipated; so by the bright rising of Jehovah, the darkness of adversity shall be scattered." (Clarke)

d. **The nations raged...He uttered His voice, the earth melted**: As in Psalm 2, God pays no regard to the rage of the nations. At His mere **voice** the earth melts away.

3. (7) The confident chorus.

The LORD of hosts *is* with us;
The God of Jacob *is* our refuge. Selah

a. **The LORD of hosts is with us**: The idea behind the title *Yahweh Saboath* is that He is the commander of armies, both the army of His people and the armies of heaven. The title emphasizes His glory and might, connecting it with the idea that *this* glorious God is **with** His people.

i. **LORD of hosts**: "Under whose command are all the hosts of heaven and earth, angels and men, and all other creatures." (Poole) "In fact, the conception underlying the name is that of the universe as an ordered whole, a disciplined army, a cosmos obedient to His voice." (Maclaren)

b. **The God of Jacob is our refuge**: The title **God of Jacob** not only emphasizes the aspect of covenant, but also grace – in that Jacob was a rather shabby character, not known for his great holiness. *This* gracious and merciful God is an open **refuge** for His people.

i. **Is our refuge**: "The word *refuge*, here and in verse 11, is distinct from that of verse 1, and implies inaccessible height: hence NEB [New English Bible] 'our high stronghold.'" (Kidner)

ii. In these two phrases we see God in two aspects. He is the King of the multitude, the community, of all **hosts**. He is also the God of the individual, with personal relationship even to a **Jacob**.

iii. **God of Jacob**: "When we say 'The God of Jacob,' we reach back into the past and lay hold of the Helper of the men of old as ours." (Maclaren)

B. The LORD exalted among the nations.

1. (8-9) Beholding the works of the LORD.

Come, behold the works of the LORD,
Who has made desolations in the earth.
He makes wars cease to the end of the earth;
He breaks the bow and cuts the spear in two;
He burns the chariot in the fire.

a. **Come, behold the works of the LORD**: If the dominant idea in the first section of the psalm was God as a refuge and help, here the emphasis shifts to a consideration of the glory of God.

i. "The recitation of the mighty acts of God plants deep in the memory of God's people the evidences of his care, protection, and providential rule." (VanGemeren)

b. **Who has made desolations in the earth**: God is mighty to make **desolations** or to enforce peace, making **wars to cease**. The idea may be that God's people are invited to look over the field of battle after God has completely routed His enemies, and their instruments of war are scattered, broken, and burning.

i. "Since God's people have reason to be glad in distress because of God's presence, how much greater will be their joy when the causes of distress are no more!" (VanGemeren)

2. (10) A word from God Himself.

Be still, and know that I *am* God;
I will be exalted among the nations,
I will be exalted in the earth!

a. **Be still, and know that I am God**: The idea is not that the faithful reader should stop activity and stand in one place. The sense is more that argument and opposition should stop and **be still**. This is done in recognition of God's glory and greatness, as mentioned in the previous verse.

i. "In this verse there is a change of person, and Jehovah himself is introduced, as commanding the world to cease its opposition, to own his power, and to acknowledge his sovereignty over all the kingdoms of the nations." (Horne)

ii. The idea is something like this: "As you know the glory and greatness of God, stop your mouth from arguing with Him or opposing Him. Simply surrender."

iii. "*Be still*...is not in the first place comfort for the harassed but a rebuke to a restless and turbulent world: 'Quiet!' – in fact, 'Leave off!'" (Kidner)

iv. "In this setting, 'be still and know that I am God' is not advice to us to lead a contemplative life, however important that may be.... It means rather, 'Lay down your arms. Surrender, and acknowledge that I am the one and only victorious God.'" (Boice)

v. **Know that I am God**: "Our submission is to be such as becomes rational creatures. God doth not require us to submit contrary to reason, but to submit as seeing the reason and ground of submission. Hence, the bare consideration *that God is God* may well be sufficient

to still all objections and oppositions against the divine sovereign."
(Edwards, cited in Spurgeon)

b. **I will be exalted among the nations**: The appropriately silenced man
or woman of God can glory in God's exaltation. God's triumph will extend
far beyond Israel to all **the earth**.

3. (11) The confident chorus.

The LORD of hosts *is* with us;
The God of Jacob *is* our refuge. Selah

a. **The LORD of hosts is with us**: We can have the confidence that the same
God exalted in all the earth is **with us**. We need no more.

i. **Is with us**: "On the day he died John Wesley had already nearly lost
his voice and could be understood only with difficulty. But at the last
with all his strength he could summon, Wesley suddenly called out,
'The best of all is, God is with us.' Then, raising his hand slightly and
waving it in triumph, he exclaimed again with thrilling effect, 'The
best of all is, God is with us.'" (Boice)

b. **The God of Jacob is our refuge**: We leave the psalm with confidence
and serenity. This is worthy of reflection, closing with **Selah**.

Psalm 47 – Praising the King of All the Earth

The title tells us both the authors and the audience of the psalm: **To the Chief Musician. A Psalm of the sons of Korah.** *Some believe that* **the Chief Musician** *is the* LORD *God Himself, and others suppose him to be a leader of choirs or musicians in David's time, such as Heman the singer or Asaph (1 Chronicles 6:33, 16:5-7, and 25:6). Korah was a descendant of Levi (Exodus 6:16-24), and therefore the* **sons of Korah** *were Levites. Most assume that the specific* **sons of Korah** *addressed here and in the titles of ten other psalms were Levitical singers in the tabernacle/temple ceremonies, and perhaps they were performers of the psalm rather than the authors of it.*

This is a wonderful psalm celebrating a great victory of a great King. Perhaps it was occasioned by the victory of a king such as Jehoshaphat (as in 2 Chronicles 20:15-23), but there is no doubt that it prophetically has in mind the ascension of the Messiah to His throne and celebrates His reign over the whole earth. "In later Jewish usage Psalm 47 was utilized as part of the New Year's service." (Willem VanGemeren)

A. The King of all the earth blesses His chosen people.

1. (1) The command to praise.

Oh, clap your hands, all you peoples!
Shout to God with the voice of triumph!

> a. **Oh, clap your hands**: The clapping of hands *draws attention* to something, usually as an outward expression of inward joy. The Bible uses it both in a negative and positive sense.

>> i. There is both clapping for praise (Psalm 47:1, Psalm 98:8, Isaiah 55:12) and clapping in derision (Job 27:23, Lamentations 2:15, Nahum 3:19).

ii. This is a word for all nations, and "If they cannot all speak the same tongue, the symbolic language of the hands they can all use." (Spurgeon)

b. **All you peoples**: This is a command to more than Israel or followers of God; it is a command to **all...peoples**. It is ultimately the fulfillment of God's promise to Abraham to bless all the peoples of the earth through his Descendant, the Messiah (Genesis 12:2-3).

i. "Psalm 47 follows quite naturally after Psalm 46. Psalm 46 is focused on the security of God's people, noting how God had delivered them from one of their great enemies. It challenged the nations to observe that deliverance and stand in awe before God. Now, in Psalm 47 God says to those same people: 'Rejoice and be happy; the King of Israel is also the King of all the Earth.'" (Boice)

c. **Shout to God**: The note is strong and happy. The psalmist did not have in mind sleepy singing or whispered prayers.

i. Most people are not against shouting or enthusiastic outbursts; they simply believe there is a right and wrong place for such shouting. Sadly, many who think a loud exclamation is fine at a football game think it is a scandal in the church.

2. (2) The reason for praise.

For the LORD Most High is awesome;
He is a great King over all the earth.

a. **The LORD Most High is awesome**: The psalmist presented this without proof, as a *self-evident fact*. He considered it obvious to everyone, as much as water is wet and fire is hot.

b. **He is a great King over all the earth**: Both the *office* and the *realm* are important. He is a **great King**, in that He is the King of Kings and the highest monarch. His realm extends **over all the earth**, and He is sovereign in all places.

i. The pagan gods of the ancient world (Baal, Molech, Ashtoreth, and so forth) were imagined to be *territorial* gods. Their authority was limited to a nation or a region. The psalmist proclaimed that the LORD God is not like one of these imagined gods.

3. (3-4) God's special care for His chosen.

He will subdue the peoples under us,
And the nations under our feet.
He will choose our inheritance for us,
The excellence of Jacob whom He loves. Selah

a. **He will subdue the peoples under us**: Here the psalmist spoke as one of God's chosen nation, Israel. He looked forward to the time when the righteous reign of the great King would be exercised over all the earth, and Israel would assume its destined place of leadership among the nations.

i. Without doubt, the psalmist knew that this great King would be the Messiah; yet he looked *ahead* to the hope of the Messiah. We look back at the fulfillment of the promise to send the Messiah, fulfilled in Jesus Christ. He is the great King who will rule the earth and subdue the nations, granting believing Israel superpower status in the coming age.

b. **He will choose our inheritance for us**: The psalmist was confident in the wisdom and goodness of the great King. He was happy to let the great King **choose our inheritance**.

i. It is a glorious fact that our great King Jesus has chosen the inheritance of His people. Ephesians 1:3-6 is just one passage that describes some of His choosing for us:

- He chose us in Him before the foundation of the world.
- He chose us to be holy and blameless before Him in love.
- He chose us to be adopted as sons into His family.

ii. It is a wise prayer, to ask our great King Jesus to **choose our inheritance for us**. We often get into trouble by wanting to choose our own inheritance.

- We sometimes want to choose our own *blessings*. One has health, another has wealth, a third has great talents; each wishes he had what the other has. Yet it is far better to let God choose our blessings.

- We sometimes want to choose our own *calling*. One sees the calling of another and thinks that the calling of the other is better, or he wants to imitate the calling of another instead of running his own race.

- We sometimes want to choose our own *crosses*. We think that our own problems are so much worse than others, and we think that we could bear any number of crosses – *except* the one He chose for us.

iii. Charles Spurgeon thought that this was a psalm of David and not the sons of Korah – that David *wrote* it, but they *sang* it. He wrote, "Our ear has grown accustomed to the ring of David's compositions, and we are morally certain that we hear it in this Psalm." This may or may not be true, but certainly David knew that his King chose his inheritance at each stage of his life, and he showed contentment with the inheritance God chose for him:

- As an anonymous shepherd boy.
- As a warrior against Goliath.
- As a fugitive running from Saul.
- As a king over Israel.
- As a disciplined sinner.

c. **The excellence of Jacob whom He loves**: This explains *why* we can be at peace with the inheritance He chooses for us. We know that for Jesus' sake and because we are in Him, God is for us and not against us. He **loves** us as His chosen; because He chose us we are happy to let Him **choose our inheritance for us**.

i. "The Holy Land is called 'the excellency of Jacob,' or 'the pride of Jacob,' on account of its beauty, and the excellence and variety of its productions (see Deuteronomy 8:7-9; 2 Kings 18:32)." (Rawlinson)

ii. **The excellence of Jacob**: "*The pride of Jacob* is a brief way of saying 'Jacob's glorious land.'" (Kidner)

iii. **Whom He loves** provokes a question: *Why* does God so love Jacob? Why does God so love the church? Why does God so love the world? The answer is that the reasons for His love are in *Him*, and not in the ones whom He loves.

B. A call to praise the King of all the earth.

1. (5) The fact of praise.

God has gone up with a shout,
The Lord with the sound of a trumpet.

a. **God has gone up with a shout**: The *going up* here refers to ascending to a royal throne. The idea is that the great King has taken His throne and therefore receives a **shout** of praise.

i. The idea is that God comes down from heaven to help and save His people, and when He goes back up to heaven, He deserves praise and acclamation from His people.

ii. Jesus ascended the royal throne in heaven after He finished His work for us on the cross and proved it by the empty tomb. He can only go **up with a shout** because He came down in humility to fight for His people and to save them.

b. **The Lord with the sound of a trumpet**: In the world of ancient Israel, the **trumpet** made the strongest and clearest sound; it was the sound of victory. To honor God clearly and strongly for His victory on our behalf, the **sound of a trumpet** is heard.

2. (6-7) The call to praise and the reason for it.

Sing praises to God, sing praises!
Sing praises to our King, sing praises!
For God is the King of all the earth;
Sing praises with understanding.

a. **Sing praises**: In this context, this is almost a *command*. It is a fitting command in light of the glory of **the King of all the earth**. God might have given speech to humanity without the gift of song; there are some tone-deaf people in the world. What is the case of some might have been the case of all; but God gave the gift of song and music to men, and the highest use of this gift is to praise the God who gave it.

i. "Let a thousand people speak at once; all thought and feeling are drowned in hubbub. But let them sing together in perfect time and tune; both thought and feeling are raised to a pitch of energy else inconceivable." (Rawlinson)

ii. **Sing praises**: "A single word in Hebrew, with therefore a swifter, livelier impact." (Kidner)

iii. "This word is four times repeated in this short verse, and shows at once the earnestness and happiness of the people. They are the words of exultation and triumph. Feel your obligation to God; express it in thanksgiving." (Clarke)

b. **The King of all the earth**: The idea from the second verse is repeated for emphasis. God's glorious authority extends far beyond the land or people of Israel. He is the global God, the **King of all the earth**.

c. **Sing praises with understanding**: Praise is appropriately offered with singing and should also be made **with understanding**. God wants our worship to be intelligent and not mindless. It is not necessary to be smart to worship God, but we should worship Him with all our being, including our mind (Mark 12:30).

i. "We must not be guided by the *time*, but the *words* of the Psalm; we must mind the matter more than the music, and consider what we sing, as well as how we sing; the tune may affect the fancy, but it is the matter affects the heart, and that God principally eyes." (Spurgeon)

ii. **Sing praises with understanding**: According to Kidner, Paul had the Septuagint translation of this phrase in mind when he wrote in 1 Corinthians 14:15, *I will also sing with the understanding.*

iii. All in all, this psalm shows us how we are to praise God:

- Praise Him *cheerfully* when you *clap your hands* as an expression of your inward joy.

- Praise Him *universally* together with *all you peoples* who should praise the Lord.

- Praise Him *vocally* as you *shout unto God with the voice of triumph*.

- Praise Him *frequently*, as the idea of **sing praises** is repeated often. You cannot praise Him too much.

- Praise Him *intelligently*, as you are to **sing praises with understanding** and to know and proclaim the reasons for our praise.

C. The King of all the earth and the nations.

1. (8) The reign of the King.

God reigns over the nations;
God sits on His holy throne.

a. **God reigns over the nations**: The LORD is not *King of all the earth* in only a passive or ceremonial sense. He **reigns over the nations** and moves history towards His desired destination.

b. **God sits on His holy throne**: When John had his heavenly experience as recorded in Revelation 4 and 5, he described everything in heaven in relation to this occupied throne. The center of heaven – indeed, the center of all creation – is this occupied throne in heaven.

i. God **sits** upon the throne; it is not empty. He is not an empty or ceremonial ruler.

ii. It is **His** throne; it belongs to Him and to none other.

iii. It is a **holy** throne, where the holiness of God has been perfectly satisfied by the work of Jesus on the cross. Therefore, it is both a **holy throne** and a throne of grace (Hebrews 4:16).

2. (9) The King is exalted above the nations.

The princes of the people have gathered together,
The people of the God of Abraham.
For the shields of the earth *belong* to God;
He is greatly exalted.

a. **The princes of the people have gathered**: In the mind of the psalmist, the leaders of God's people gather to both receive and exalt the King of all the earth.

i. "The promise concerning the blessing of the tribes of the nations in the seed of the patriarch is being fulfilled; for the nobles draw the peoples who are protected by them after themselves." (Keil and Delitzsch)

ii. "The princes of the earth belong especially to God, since 'by him kings reign, and princes decree justice' (Proverbs 8:15)." (Rawlinson)

b. **The shields of the earth belong to God**: "The Septuagint translates this *hoi krataioi*, the strong ones of the earth.... The words refer to something by which the inhabitants of the earth are defended; God's providence, guardian angels, etc." (Clarke)

i. "It is the abundant fulfillment of the promise of Genesis 12:3; it anticipates what Paul expounds of the inclusion of the Gentiles as Abraham's sons (Romans 4:11; Galatians 3:7-9)." (Kidner)

Psalm 48 – The City of the Great King

The title of this psalm is **A Song. A Psalm of the sons of Korah.** *Matthew Poole on* **A Song**: *"This Hebrew word* schir *may be here taken not simply for a* song, *but for a* joyful song, *as it is in Genesis 31:27; Exodus 15:1; Psalm 33:3."*

A. The city of the Great King.

1. (1-3) The Great King and His city.

Great *is* the LORD, and greatly to be praised
In the city of our God,
***In* His holy mountain.**
Beautiful in elevation,
The joy of the whole earth,
***Is* Mount Zion *on* the sides of the north,**
The city of the great King.
God *is* in her palaces;
He is known as her refuge.

a. **Great is the LORD, and greatly to be praised**: The psalmist began simply describing the greatness of God and His worthiness to be praised. He connected this praise with a place: Jerusalem, described as **the city of our God, in His holy mountain**.

i. **Great is the LORD**: He is great indeed.

- He is greater: *For God is greater than man* (Job 33:12).
- He is greatest of all: *For the LORD is the great God, and the great King above all gods* (Psalm 95:3).
- He is greatness itself: *His greatness is unsearchable* (Psalm 145:3).

ii. "How great Jehovah is essentially none can conceive; but we can all see that he is great in the deliverance of his people, great in their esteem who are delivered, and great in the hearts of those enemies whom he scatters by their own fears. Instead of the mad cry of Ephesus, 'Great is Diana,' we hear the reasonable, demonstrable, self-evident testimony, 'Great is Jehovah.'" (Spurgeon)

b. **In His holy mountain**: The idea of Jerusalem as a **holy mountain** is a thought-provoking contrast to another holy mountain – Mount Sinai. Sinai was so holy that a fence kept God's people from it, lest they die (Exodus 19:12-13). The New Testament develops this comparison and contrast between Mount Sinai and **Mount Zion** (Jerusalem) in Galatians 4:24-26 and Hebrews 12:18-24.

> i. This reminds us that though the psalmist certainly had the literal, historic city of Jerusalem in mind, he was also carried away by the inspiration of the Holy Spirit to also see the idealized city of Jerusalem, the city of God, the New Jerusalem (Revelation 3:12 and 21:2). The two aspects do not cancel each other out; they compliment each other.

c. **Is Mount Zion on the sides of the north**: Commentators are divided on the meaning of this phrase. Many or most think it describes Jerusalem's situation mainly on the northern slope of Mount Zion, though this is contested. It's possible that by **sides of the north** the psalmist intended us to connect *literal* Jerusalem with God's heavenly city.

> i. Isaiah 14:13 uses the phrase *the farthest sides of the north* to refer to heaven, the place where God is enthroned. "By an effective turn of phrase it portrays the literal Zion in terms of the heavenly one – the community whose king is God – by identifying it with *the far north*." (Kidner)

d. **Beautiful in elevation, the joy of the whole earth, is Mount Zion**: Jerusalem is idealized as elevated and the cause of joy for all peoples. Certainly, the redemption there won rescues people from every tribe and tongue (Revelation 5:9).

e. **The city of the great King**: Ultimately, this is what makes Jerusalem wonderful. There are cities with better natural resources and more natural beauty. Yet there is only one **city of the great King**, the King of kings. He is present (**God is in her palaces**) and her defense (**her refuge**).

> i. "The godly had a special feeling about Jerusalem that is beautifully and sensitively expressed in this psalm. They looked on the city, mountain, and temple as symbols of God's presence with his people." (VanGemeren)

2. (4-7) The troubled kings of the earth.

For behold, the kings assembled,
They passed by together.
They saw *it, and* so they marveled;
They were troubled, they hastened away.
Fear took hold of them there,
And pain, as of a woman in birth pangs,
As when You break the ships of Tarshish
With an east wind.

a. **Behold, the kings assembled**: With God the refuge of Jerusalem (Psalm 48:3), the **kings** of the earth came to it – yet they could not attack. Instead they **marveled** and **they were troubled**.

i. **They passed by together** may be too weak. The NIV [New International Version] translates, *they advanced together*. "The united effort of the nations gave them confidence, best expressed by A.A. Anderson: 'they stormed furiously.'" (VanGemeren)

ii. **They saw…they marveled…they were troubled, they hastened away**: "In Hebrew the words are similar to the well-known report of Julius Caesar about his victories in Gaul: *Veni, vidi, vici* ('I came, I saw, I conquered'). Only here the kings did not conquer; they fled from the city in terror. The verbs literally say: 'They saw [Jerusalem is implied]; they were dumbfounded; they were overwhelmed; they fled in panic.' The fast pace of the language captures the confusion and fearful flight." (Boice)

iii. "As has been often noticed, they recall Caesar's *Veni, vidi, vici*; but these kings came, saw, were conquered. No cause for the rout is named. No weapons were drawn in the city." (Maclaren)

b. **Fear took hold of them there**: When they saw and understood the great King guarding His holy city, they were afraid to either attack the city or offend the King. They hurt like a **woman** in labor and they were scattered like **ships** in a storm.

i. "Even thus shall the haters of the church vanish from the field, Papists, Ritualists, Arians, Sceptics, they shall each have their day, and shall pass on to the limbo of forgetfulness." (Spurgeon)

3. (8) The established city of the LORD.

As we have heard,
So we have seen
In the city of the LORD of hosts,
In the city of our God:
God will establish it forever. Selah

a. **As we have heard, so we have seen**: This is a simple yet beautiful statement of God fulfilling His promises and working in the present day, not only in the past. We should be aware of the great things He has done in the past ages (**we have heard**) and pray with faith for great works to be done in our own time (**so we have seen**).

i. "Perhaps you were told of such special acts of God by your parents. As you learn to trust him, you should begin to experience such personal blessings yourself, and you should be able to say, 'As I have heard, so I have seen.'" (Boice)

b. **In the city of the LORD of hosts, in the city of our God**: The repetition is for emphasis. *This city belongs to God. It is His city.* **God will establish it forever**.

B. Responding to the Great King.

1. (9-11) Meditating on His mercies.

We have thought, O God, on Your lovingkindness,

In the midst of Your temple.

According to Your name, O God,

So *is* Your praise to the ends of the earth;

Your right hand is full of righteousness.

Let Mount Zion rejoice,

Let the daughters of Judah be glad,
Because of Your judgments.

a. **We have thought, O God, on Your lovingkindness**: The thought turns from a focus on the strength and majesty of God to a consideration of His covenant love (*hesed*, **lovingkindness**).

i. In his sermon *A Worthy Theme for Thought*, Charles Spurgeon thought of three different people in the church and how they should each think and speak more of the **lovingkindness** of the LORD.

• "Now, my dear sister, you have talked about that rheumatism of yours to at least fifty people who have been to see you; suppose you tell your next visitor about the lovingkindness of the Lord to you."

• "Yes, my dear brother, we all know that trade is bad, for you have told us so, every day, for I do not know how many years. And you have always been losing money, though you had no capital when you started; yet, somehow or other, you have managed to have something left even now. Well, we know that old story;

could you not change your note just a little, and talk about the lovingkindness of the Lord?"

- "Yes, my friend, I know that many professing Christian people are not all that they profess to be; I have heard you say so ever so many times. You say also, 'There is no love in the church.' Well, so far as we can see, you are not overstocked with it. You say, 'There is no zeal among the members,' but have you any to give away to those who need it? Now, henceforward, instead of always harping on the faults and failing of God's people – which, certainly, are numerous enough, but have not become any fewer since you talked so much about them – would it not be better to think and talk of the lovingkindness of the Lord?"

b. **In the midst of Your temple**: Being at the temple led the psalmist to consider the lovingkindness of God. In many ways the **temple** itself testified to the covenant love of God to His people.

- God's covenant love was shown in providing a place to meet with Him.
- God's covenant love was shown in providing even the nations a place to meet with Him.
- God's covenant love was shown in providing an atoning sacrifice of a substitute.
- God's covenant love was shown in providing a sacrifice to give thanks.
- God's covenant love was shown in providing a place to receive prayer as sweet-smelling incense unto Him.
- God's covenant love was shown in providing a place for Him to be enthroned among His people.

c. **According to Your name, O God, so is Your praise to the ends of the earth**: God's name is filled with majesty and greatness; so is His **praise**. His praiseworthy character is shown in His **righteousness** and **judgments**.

i. **Let the daughters of Judah be glad**: "*The daughters of Judah* are its cities and villages: *cf.*, *e.g.*, Judges 1:27, Hebrew." (Kidner)

2. (12-14) The city represents God's faithfulness.

Walk about Zion,
And go all around her.
Count her towers;
Mark well her bulwarks;
Consider her palaces;

That you may tell *it* **to the generation following.**
For this *is* **God,**
Our God forever and ever;
He will be our guide
Even to death.

a. **Count her towers; mark well her bulwarks**: The psalmist asks us to take a tour of Jerusalem, noting its defenses, strengths, and **palaces** reflecting royal dignity.

b. **For this is God, our God forever and ever**: In these last two verses the city itself fades from view and we see God alone. All these marks of Jerusalem's glory and strength come from **God**, and this should be told **to the generation following**. The same God that builds and beautifies Jerusalem is **our God forever and ever** and **will be our guide even to death**.

i. We can say "**forever and ever**" about God in a way that we cannot say it about anything else. "The landlord cannot say of his fields, these are mine, forever and ever. The king cannot say of his crown, this is mine forever and ever. These possessions shall soon change masters; these possessors shall soon mingle with the dust, and even the graves they shall occupy may not long be theirs." (Burder, cited in Spurgeon)

ii. **Even unto death**: "And after, too; for this is not to be taken [as] exclusive. He will never leave us, nor forsake us." (Trapp)

Psalm 49 – What Money Can't Buy

As are many of the songs in Book Two of the Psalter, this psalm is titled **To the Chief Musician. A Psalm of the sons of Korah**.

"The teaching of the song is simple, and sublime, present, and perpetual." (G. Campbell Morgan) "This psalm touches the high-water mark of Old Testament faith in a future life." (Alexander Maclaren)

A. The limits of material wealth.

1. (1-4) Introduction to this psalm of wisdom.

Hear this, all peoples;
Give ear, all inhabitants of the world,
Both low and high,
Rich and poor together.
My mouth shall speak wisdom,
And the meditation of my heart *shall give* **understanding.**
I will incline my ear to a proverb;
I will disclose my dark saying on the harp.

a. **Hear this, all peoples**: The psalmist spoke to everyone, especially including **rich and poor together**. He hoped to guide those who were troubled about the wealth of the wicked.

i. There are four kinds of riches. There are riches in what you *have*, riches in what you *do*, riches in what you *know*, and riches in what you *are* – riches of *character*. The psalmist spoke of those who are only rich in the first way – the least important kind of wealth.

ii. "It is evident that he was conscious of the greatness of the thing he sang, in that he commenced by calling all people, of all classes, to listen." (Morgan)

iii. "Like most of the Wisdom writings, this psalm speaks to men in the common humanity, not only to Israelites in their special bond of covenant with God." (Kidner)

b. **My mouth shall speak wisdom**: Other psalms praise and pray to God; this psalm teaches **wisdom** and imparts **understanding**. The psalm will focus on the folly of trusting in wealth or envying others just for their wealth. It sets the present prosperity of those who don't know God in an eternal perspective.

i. VanGemeren wrote this regarding the somewhat long introduction to the heart of this psalm: "He keeps them in suspense by impressing on them the importance of the discussion."

c. **My dark saying**: The better translation is *riddle*. The psalmist wasn't interested in hidden, mystical knowledge but in things that were simply difficult to understand and perceive. He hoped that doing it **on the harp** might help the message to be better remembered.

i. "NEB [New English Bible] paraphrases it well: 'and tell on the harp how I read the riddle.'" (Kidner)

ii. "The doctrine of life eternal, and the judgment to come, here more clearly delivered than anywhere else almost in the Old Testament, is a mystery." (Trapp)

2. (5-9) What money can't buy.

Why should I fear in the days of evil,
***When* the iniquity at my heels surrounds me?**
Those who trust in their wealth
And boast in the multitude of their riches,
None *of them* can by any means redeem *his* brother,
Nor give to God a ransom for him—
For the redemption of their souls *is* costly,
And it shall cease forever—
That he should continue to live eternally,
***And* not see the Pit.**

a. **Why should I fear in the days of evil, when the iniquity at my heels surrounds me**: The psalmist made a contrast between himself and those he will mention in the following lines. *He*, in contrast to *them*, has no reason to **fear** in the **days of evil**.

i. "Days of evil to others cannot be so to me, for the presence of God transmutes the evil to good." (Meyer)

b. **Those who trust in their wealth and boast in the multitude of their riches**: When this psalm speaks of the rich, this is what it means. It isn't merely the possession of material things that makes one rich in the sense that Psalm 49 means it. It is to **trust** in that wealth and to **boast** in their riches.

i. This is simply idolatry. Though the Bible presents several godly rich men to us (such as Abraham and King David, who by modern measures would probably be billionaires), they were men who still trusted in the LORD and made their boast in Him. They did not **trust in their wealth** or **boast** in their **riches**.

- One can know if he puts his **trust** in heir wealth if he finds too much peace and security by his accounts and holdings, and if he despairs when such things decline. He can ask the question, *What loss in life would most trouble me – material or spiritual?*

- One can know if he **boasts** in his riches if he finds deepest satisfaction in gaining and measuring his wealth and if he looks for ways to display his riches. He can ask the question, *What am I appropriately proud of – material things or spiritual things?*

- In general, God's answer to these things for the rich is to practice radical generosity – a way for them to declare their trust in the LORD and to guard against a boast in their riches.

ii. Boice pointed out that in some ways this psalm is a commentary on the story of the rich fool in Luke 12:15-21. Jesus applied the principle from that story: *So is he who lays up treasure for himself, and is not rich toward God.* Psalm 49 has in mind just that kind of man.

c. **None of them can by any means redeem his brother, nor give to God a ransom for him**: The psalmist revealed the great limitation of the idolatry of trusting and boasting in material wealth – this idol is of no help in the spiritual world. Money itself can't rescue a soul because **the redemption of their souls is costly** – that is, beyond the ability of material things to purchase.

i. The **redemption of their souls** is a spiritual work, accomplished only by God's atoning sacrifice. This sacrifice began in the Garden of Eden (Genesis 3:21), was practiced among the patriarchs (Genesis 22:13-14), and instituted in a sacrificial system (Leviticus 1-7). The concept of a substitutionary, atoning sacrifice was fulfilled and perfected by the work of Jesus at the cross (Isaiah 53:10-11, Hebrews 10:12 and many others). This spiritual work is what provides for the **redemption of their souls**.

ii. "And therefore all the money that hath been given for masses, dirges, trentals, etc., hath been cast away; seeing Christ is the only Redeemer, and in the other world money beareth no mastery." (Trapp)

iii. Voltaire was a French atheist and enemy of Christianity, and his popularity made him very wealthy. "Yet when Voltaire came to die, it is reported that he cried to his doctor in pained desperation, 'I will give you half of all I possess if you will give me six months more of life.'" (Boice) Voltaire died in despair.

iv. **Redeem...ransom**: "The *ransom* picture is doubly appropriate, since being held to ransom is as much the hazard of the very rich as redemption is the need of the very poor." (Kidner)

d. **That he should continue to live eternally, and not see the Pit**: Those who have the **redemption of their souls** will **live eternally** and not **see the Pit**. Here we see the concept of *sheol* (**the Pit**) as more than just the grave, but the ultimate and empty destiny of those who reject God.

i. **The Pit**: "The Chaldee understandeth it of hell; to which the wicked man's death is as a trap-door." (Trapp)

B. True wealth and the world to come.

1. (10-12) Unreliable wealth, limited honor.

For he sees wise men die;
Likewise the fool and the senseless person perish,
And leave their wealth to others.
Their inner thought *is that* their houses *will last* forever,
Their dwelling places to all generations;
They call *their* lands after their own names.
Nevertheless man, *though* in honor, does not remain;
He is like the beasts *that* perish.

a. **The fool and the senseless person perish, and leave their wealth to others**: Much in the pattern of the writer of Ecclesiastes (6:1-2), the psalmist noted that we can't take our material wealth with us into the world beyond.

i. "Money is the monarch of this world, but not of the next." (Trapp)

ii. We can't take our material wealth with us to the world beyond, but there is a real sense in which we *can send it on ahead*. Jesus spoke of using our present material resources to store up treasure in heaven (Mark 10:21). Our material wealth can do us good in the world to come, but that happens through kingdom-minded generosity more than accumulation.

b. **Their inner thought is that their houses will last forever**: Hungering for some kind of immortality, they that trust in riches believe their estates will **last forever**, beyond their own life **to all generations**. They memorialize themselves by calling **their lands after their own names**.

 i. "This is the ambition still of many, that take little care to know that their names are written in heaven; but strive to propagate them, as they are able, upon earth, Nimrod by his tower, Absalom by his pillar, Alexander by his Alexandria.... But the name of the wicked shall rot, Proverbs 10:7." (Trapp)

 ii. "Common enough is this practice. His grounds are made to bear the groundling's name; he might as well write it on the water. Men have even called countries by their own names, but what are they better for the idle compliment, even if men perpetuate their nomenclature?" (Spurgeon)

c. **Nevertheless man, though in honor, does not remain**: Though a man may have some measure of **honor** through estates or descendants or memorials, *he still dies* – just like an animal dies.

 i. Therefore, the truly wise man or woman does not trust in riches or boast in wealth. He prepares for eternity by trusting God and making their boast in the LORD.

 ii. **He is like the beasts that perish**: "It is the ability to think and reason that sets human beings apart from the remainder of creation. Yet how animal-like we are when we fail to consider the shortness of our days and prepare for how we will spend eternity!" (Boice)

2. (13) Two paths to perish.

This is the way of those who *are* foolish,
And of their posterity who approve their sayings. Selah

a. **This is the way of those who are foolish**: The psalmist noted that the **way** that values the material over the spiritual and that does not prepare for the world to come is **foolish** and will be revealed as so.

b. **And of their posterity who approve their sayings**: There is a second **foolish** way: to be a descendant of the one who trusted and boasted in riches and to **approve** of his world view. This also is **foolish** and will be revealed as so.

 i. **Of their posterity**: "Grace is not hereditary, but sordid worldliness goes from generation to generation. The race of fools never dies out." (Spurgeon)

ii. **Who approve of their sayings**: "Those who agree with their words, often benefiting from their power and prestige, will also die and be no more." (VanGemeren)

3. (14-15) The dominion of the upright.

Like sheep they are laid in the grave;
Death shall feed on them;
The upright shall have dominion over them in the morning;
And their beauty shall be consumed in the grave, far from their dwelling.
But God will redeem my soul from the power of the grave,
For He shall receive me. Selah

a. **Like sheep they are laid in the grave; death shall feed on them**: The psalmist painted a ghastly picture. A man is buried like an animal (Psalm 49:12) and death consumes his material body. Of their once-beautiful bodies, **their beauty shall be consumed in the grave**.

i. The idea is that the **upright** – those who did not trust or boast in riches – have a **beauty** beyond the material and therefore beyond the grave. Those whose beauty was mainly measured in mirrors and bank accounts will find that **their beauty shall be consumed in the grave**. *There is a better beauty to live for.*

ii. **Like sheep they are laid in the grave**: "Those fatlings of the world, these brainless yonkers, that will not be warned by other men's harms, but walk on in the same dark and dangerous ways." (Trapp)

iii. "Why *like sheep*? I answer, not for the innocency of their lives, but for their impotency in death; as if it had been said, when once death took them in hand to lay them in the grave, they could make no more resistance than a sheep can against a lion or a wolf." (Caryl, cited in Spurgeon)

b. **The upright shall have dominion over them in the morning**: When that **morning** finally comes, those who did not trust or boast in wealth (**the upright**) will be justified. They will **have dominion** over those who lived and died with a focus on the material and with no urgency to prepare for the world to come.

i. "Yet there is a mastery over Sheol and death. It is found in uprightness." (Morgan)

c. **But God will redeem my soul from the power of the grave, for He shall receive me**: The psalmist was confident that he was among the **upright**, and not among those who foolishly trusted and boasted in riches.

i. The one who trusted and boasted in riches had no power to ransom or redeem a soul (Psalm 49:7-8). The psalmist understood that **God** and God alone had the power to **redeem my soul from the power of the grave**.

ii. God gave a similar staggering announcement in Hosea 13:14:

I will ransom them from the power of the grave;
I will redeem them from death.
O Death, I will be your plagues!
O Grave, I will be your destruction!

iii. **The power of the grave** is staggering. Every graveyard tells of the power that death has over humanity. Yet God is greater than the power of the grave, and in Jesus Christ we can even taunt the grave saying, *O Death, where is your sting? O Hades, where is your victory?* (1 Corinthians 15:55).

iv. As a wisdom psalm, this shares many characteristics as the Book of Ecclesiastes. Yet the words **But God** begin a significant difference. "The great *But God...*(Psalm 49:15) is one of the mountain-tops of Old Testament hope...it brings out into the open the assurance of victory over death which Ecclesiastes leaves concealed." (Kidner)

v. **God will redeem my soul**: "We must remember that *redeem* is a commercial term, meaning 'to buy,' 'buy out,' or 'buy [a slave so that he or she need never again return to the marketplace].' Spiritually, it refers to God's work in buying us out of sin's marketplace and setting us free. Who can do this? No one but God." (Boice)

d. **For He shall receive me**: The assurance and confidence of the psalmist is worthy of note and should be taken as an example for us. He was confident that God would **receive** the one who trusted in Him and made his boast in the Lord.

i. "The *he* and *me* confirm that this is not salvation at arm's length, but face to face." (Kidner)

ii. "The word *receive* is more positive than it may sound to us; it is Enoch's word: 'God took him' (Genesis 5:24)." (Kidner)

4. (16-20) Practical application of this wisdom.

Do not be afraid when one becomes rich,
When the glory of his house is increased;
For when he dies he shall carry nothing away;
His glory shall not descend after him.
Though while he lives he blesses himself

(For *men* will praise you when you do well for yourself),
He shall go to the generation of his fathers;
They shall never see light.
A man *who is* in honor, yet does not understand,
Is like the beasts *that* perish.

a. **Do not be afraid when one becomes rich**: This might seem like a strange way to phrase the matter. Most of us are not consciously **afraid** at the prosperity of another or when **the glory of his house is increased**. Yet the fears may come in subtle ways:

- Afraid because I think they prosper at my expense.

- Afraid because perhaps material things matter more than spiritual things do.

- Afraid because maybe God does not govern the universe as I believe He does.

- Afraid because maybe there is no reward for the righteous or punishment for the wicked in the world beyond; there is no moral government to the universe.

- Afraid because the jerks of the world won't get what is coming to them.

b. **When he dies he shall carry nothing away**: The psalmist assures us that our reasons for fear are unfounded. The fool who trusted and boasted in riches can take **nothing** with him to the world beyond. **His glory shall not descend after him**; all the glory he will ever deserve he has had in this life.

i. For the upright, the opposite is true; their glory shall ascend after them, and they will in some sense be brought to glory (Hebrews 2:10) and even obtain God's glory in the world to come (2 Thessalonians 2:14).

ii. For those who trust and boast in riches, this world is the best they will ever have it. For the upright who look to God for their redemption, this world is the worst they will ever have it.

iii. **His glory shall not descend after him**: "His worship, his honour, his lordship, and his grace, will alike find their titles ridiculous in the tomb. Hell knows no aristocracy. Your dainty and delicate sinners shall find that eternal burnings have no respect for their affectations and refinements." (Spurgeon)

c. **While he lives he blesses himself...for men will praise you**: Yes, the men and women who trust and boast in riches are often pleased with themselves and others are pleased with them. Yet that is short-lived. Each will die, and **go to the generations of his fathers**.

> i. **For men will praise you**: "The generality of men worship success, however it may be gained. The colour of the winning horse is no matter; it is the winner, and that is enough." (Spurgeon)

d. **They shall never see light**: The psalmist only had a dim understanding of punishment in the world to come, but he knew it to be in some sense a place of darkness. This is reserved for those who are **in honor** yet do **not understand**.

e. **A man who is in honor, yet does not understand, is like the beasts that perish**: The psalm ends by repeating the warning first given in Psalm 49:12. It is the grave warning to those who may have **honor** in this world but no understanding. Their honor in this world will not preserve them in the next.

> i. "The banker rots as fast as the shoe-black, and the peer becomes as putrid as the pauper." (Spurgeon)

> ii. "Oh that wicked rich men would think of this, before the cold grave hold their bodies, and hot hell hold their souls." (Trapp)

Psalm 50 – Judgment Begins Among the People of God

*The title of this psalm (**A Psalm of Asaph**) tells us that it is the first of Asaph's psalms in the order of the psalter. **Asaph** was the great singer and musician of David and Solomon's era (1 Chronicles 15:17-19, 16:5-7, 16:7, 25:6). 1 Chronicles 25:1 and 2 Chronicles 29:30 add that Asaph was a prophet in his musical compositions.*

A. The Mighty One and His judgment.

1. (1-3) The Mighty One comes to judge the earth.

The Mighty One, God the LORD,
Has spoken and called the earth
From the rising of the sun to its going down.
Out of Zion, the perfection of beauty,
God will shine forth.
Our God shall come, and shall not keep silent;
A fire shall devour before Him,
And it shall be very tempestuous all around Him.

a. **The Mighty One, God the LORD**: Asaph the psalmist began by referring to God in terms of utmost majesty, using several of the words or names in Scripture to refer to the God who is really there.

- **The Mighty One**: "El stands for the might of God simply and absolutely." (Morgan)

- **God**: "Elohim, the plural form, intensifies that idea; and in use always connotes the wisdom of God as well as His might." (Morgan)

- **The LORD**: "Jehovah [*Yahweh*] is the title by which He is ever revealed in His grace." (Morgan)

i. "The first three words of the Hebrew text emphasize that it is God who has spoken: El (= God), Elohim (= God), Yahweh (= Lᴏʀᴅ)." (VanGemeren)

ii. "The psalm begins with a majestic heaping together of the Divine names, as if a herald were proclaiming the style and titles of a mighty king at the opening of a solemn assize.... Each name has its own force of meaning. *El* speaks of God as mighty; *Elohim*, as the object of religious fear; *Jehovah*, as the self-existent and covenant God." (Maclaren)

b. **Has spoken and called the earth**: The idea is that God has come to Jerusalem to judge the world, and the entire **earth – from the rising of the sun to its going down** – is gathered for that purpose.

c. **Our God shall come, and shall not keep silent; a fire shall devour before Him**: Using reminders of God coming to Mount Sinai (Exodus 19:16-19), Asaph built anticipation for the righteous judgment of God about to be performed. This time God comes to Zion, not Sinai.

i. "In this powerful psalm the imagined scene is a theophany, God appearing in fire and tempest at Mount Zion to summon the entire world to His judgment seat. But if all eyes are on Him, His eyes are on Israel." (Kidner)

ii. "Fire is the emblem of justice in action, and the tempest is a token of his overwhelming power." (Spurgeon)

2. (4-6) The scope of judgment narrows to the people of God.

He shall call to the heavens from above,
And to the earth, that He may judge His people:
"Gather My saints together to Me,
Those who have made a covenant with Me by sacrifice."
Let the heavens declare His righteousness,
For God Himself *is* Judge. Selah

a. **That He may judge His people**: As God assembled **heavens** and **earth** for His judgment, He did not begin among the nations. God began His judgment among **His people** – His **saints**, those **who have made a covenant with Me by sacrifice**.

i. "Suddenly – for it emerges with the last word of verse 4 – the tables are turned. Israel has appealed to God, only to find that she is herself the one on trial." (Kidner)

ii. In the psalm this feels like a surprise, but it shouldn't be. Many centuries later the Apostle Peter described the principle: *For the time has come for judgment to begin at the house of God; and if it begins with*

us first, what will be the end of those who do not obey the gospel of God?
(1 Peter 4:17)

b. **Gather My saints together to Me**: God gathers His saints for judgment *before the witnessing world*. When God deals thus with His people, He often does it before a watching world. We would prefer that He deal with the sins of His people privately, but if they will not listen to His correction, the day will come when He deals with their sin with the earth as an audience.

c. **Those who have made a covenant with Me by sacrifice**: It can be argued that Psalm 50 only has in direct view God's judgment of Israel because it is the nation joined to Him in covenant as described here (Exodus 19:5-6; 24:5-8). Yet by extension (and the principle of 1 Peter 4:17), this has all the people of God in view. Both aspects are true.

i. "'*Made*,' or *ratifying a covenant*; literally, *cutting*, striking, perhaps in allusion to the practice of slaying and dividing victims as a religious rite, accompanying solemn compacts." (Alexander, cited in Spurgeon)

ii. Believers will not face a judgment regarding their eternal destiny; they have trusted in Jesus and His work for them and are saved. However, they will face what Paul called *the judgment seat of Christ* (Romans 14:10 and 2 Corinthians 5:10), where their works and motives *as believers* will be judged – presumably, for the sake of reward and measure of authority in the age to come.

d. **Let the heavens declare His righteousness, for God Himself is Judge**: God most certainly will judge the earth, including all the wicked, and He will do so in **righteousness**. Yet He absolutely has the right to begin His judgment among His own.

B. The judgment of God against His people.

1. (7-15) Rebuking their ritualism.

"Hear, O My people, and I will speak,
O Israel, and I will testify against you;
I *am* God, your God!
I will not rebuke you for your sacrifices
Or your burnt offerings,
***Which are* continually before Me.**
I will not take a bull from your house,
***Nor* goats out of your folds.**
For every beast of the forest *is* Mine,
***And* the cattle on a thousand hills.**
I know all the birds of the mountains,
And the wild beasts of the field *are* Mine.

If I were hungry, I would not tell you;
For the world *is* Mine, and all its fullness.
Will I eat the flesh of bulls,
Or drink the blood of goats?
Offer to God thanksgiving,
And pay your vows to the Most High.
Call upon Me in the day of trouble;
I will deliver you, and you shall glorify Me."

a. **Hear, O My people, and I will speak**: The point from the previous lines is repeated and emphasized. God speaks here to His people, beginning His judgment among them.

i. **I am God, your God**: "And should, therefore, have been better obeyed." (Trapp)

ii. "The law began with, 'I am the Lord thy God, which brought thee up out of the land of Egypt,' and now the session of their judgment opens with the same reminder of their singular position, privilege, and responsibility. It is not only that Jehovah is God, but *thy* God, O Israel." (Spurgeon)

b. **I will not rebuke you for your sacrifices or your burnt offerings**: God did not **rebuke** His people for offering sacrifices. He commanded them to do that. Yet, He was not interested in receiving *more* animal offerings (**I will not take a bull from your house, nor goats from your folds**) *apart from* their trusting obedience. This was a rebuke of ritualism, of empty repetition of religious ceremonies.

i. God spoke to their ritualism first, because it was under ritualism that they excused the sin described later in the psalm and thought themselves approved before God. "Why, at the first signs of His displeasure (50:7), do their thoughts fly to points of ritual, not of relationship?" (Kidner)

ii. The practice of sacrifice under the Old Covenant might easily become a mere ritual and empty formality. The one bringing the sacrifice might forget the principle of transferring sin to an innocent victim and how the lifeblood had to be poured out in death as a substitute. "The sacrifices under the Jewish law were of God's appointment; but now that the people began to put their trust in them, God despised them." (Clarke)

iii. "What he intended for their instruction, they made their confidence." (Spurgeon)

iv. Believers under the New Covenant no longer offer animal sacrifices, but they are still tempted to practice their Christian duties in a spirit of ritualism. This must be actively avoided; God is not pleased by our ritualism.

v. "This was afterwards the sin of the Pharisees, is still of the Papists, and of too many carnal gospellers, who think they have served God, for they have been at church, done their devoir, for they have said their prayers, etc." (Trapp)

vi. **I will not take a bull from your house**: Understanding the modern slang or street use of the word *bull*, we may smile at the unintended truth in the Revised Standard Version's translation, *I will accept no bull from your house*.

c. **For every beast of the forest is Mine, and the cattle on a thousand hills**: With a little thought, it's easy to see how ritualism does not please God. He has no *need* for the meat of sacrificed animals; **if I were hungry, I would not tell you; for the world is Mine and all its fullness**. When we sacrifice to God, we don't give Him something He doesn't have; in this sense our sacrifice is for *our sake* and not His. Ritualism defeats its work for our sake.

i. "All sacrifices are God's before they are offered, and do not become any more His by being offered. He neither needs nor can partake of material sustenance. But men's hearts are not His without their glad surrender." (Maclaren)

ii. "Do men fancy that the Lord needs banners, and music, and incense, and fine linen? If he did, the stars would emblazon his standard, the winds and the waves become his orchestra, ten thousand times ten thousand flowers would breathe forth perfume, the snow should be his alb, the rainbow his girdle, the clouds of light his mantle. O fools and slow of heart, ye worship ye know not what!" (Spurgeon)

iii. "'*If I were hungry,*' etc. Pagan sacrifices were considered as feasts of the gods." (Cresswell, cited in Spurgeon)

iv. **The cattle on a thousand hills**: There's a story – which may or may not be true, but is a good illustration – that shortly after Dallas Seminary was founded in the 1920s, it almost closed because of bankruptcy. The founders met for prayer and one of them was Harry Ironside. When it was his turn to pray, he said, "Lord we know that the cattle on a thousand hills are Thine. Please sell some of them and send us the money." As the story goes, just then a Texas rancher came into the business office with a check from two carloads of cattle he had just sold. The secretary came into the office where the founders prayed, told them what happened and presented the check – it was for just the amount they needed to keep the seminary going. Dr. Lewis Sperry Chafer, the founder and president of the school, turned to Dr. Ironside and said, "Harry, God sold the cattle."

d. **Offer to God thanksgiving, and pay your vows to the Most High. Call upon Me in the day of trouble**: God described what He wanted more than rituals of sacrifice. He wanted a thankful heart, a life of obedience, and a living trust in Him. This God rewards; to this He says, **I will deliver you and you shall glorify Me**.

i. "The glorious God cares nothing for pomp and show; but when you call upon him in the day of trouble, and ask him to deliver you, there is meaning in your groan of anguish.... God prefers the prayer of a broken heart to the finest service that ever was performed by priests and choirs." (Spurgeon)

ii. Spurgeon preached a sermon on Psalm 50:15 and titled it, *Robinson Crusoe's Text*. Spurgeon recounted how in DeFoe's book that after the shipwreck and on the island, Crusoe was about to die from illness. "He is ready to perish. He had been accustomed to sin, and had all the vices of a sailor; but his hard case brought him to think. He opens a Bible which he finds in his chest, and he lights upon this passage, '*Call upon me in the day of trouble: I will deliver thee, and thou shalt glorify me.*' That night he prayed for the first time in his life, and ever after there was in him a hope in God, which marked the birth of the heavenly life." (Spurgeon)

2. (16-21) Rebuking their disobedience to His commands.

But to the wicked God says:
"What *right* have you to declare My statutes,
Or take My covenant in your mouth,
Seeing you hate instruction
And cast My words behind you?
When you saw a thief, you consented with him,
And have been a partaker with adulterers.
You give your mouth to evil,
And your tongue frames deceit.
You sit *and* speak against your brother;
You slander your own mother's son.
These *things* you have done, and I kept silent;
You thought that I was altogether like you;

But I will rebuke you,
And set *them* in order before your eyes.

a. **But to the wicked God says**: We might think that now God has turned away from judging His people for their ritualism and has turned towards the nations, to judge them for their wickedness. This isn't the case, as the following references to declaring God's **statutes** and taking His **covenant** show. He speaks to **the wicked** among the people of God.

i. "Formalism is a sin against God. Hypocrisy is its outcome, a sin against man, and so still against God." (Morgan)

ii. "The real problem with ritual is that, if forms are all there is to our religion, they give us feelings of being right with God when actually we may be guilty of the most terrible sins." (Boice)

b. **What right have you to declare My statutes**: God questioned their right to speak forth His word when their lives were stuck in fundamental disobedience. Their words (**declare My statutes...My covenant in your mouth**) spoke of God, but their lives dishonored Him.

i. **To declare My statutes**: "This verse may well refer to the public law-reading commanded in Deuteronomy 31:10ff." (Kidner)

ii. **What right have you to declare My statutes**: "Origen, after his foul fall, opening the book and lighting upon this text, was not able to preach, but broke out into abundance of tears." (Trapp)

c. **Seeing you hate instruction and cast My words behind you**: Their lives showed a hatred and disregard for the word of God, no matter what their words said. How they lived spoke louder to God than what they said.

d. **When you saw a thief...partaker with adulterers...tongue frames deceit**: They had specifically broken many of God's commandments, including the eighth, seventh, and ninth commandments. This was another way they displeased God, in addition to the ritualism mentioned in the previous lines.

i. "The particular charges are representative of the whole Decalogue." (VanGemeren)

ii. **You consented with him**: "It is true that the people who have broken the seventh, eighth, and ninth commandments have broken the whole covenant. But it is also true that those who associate with covenant breakers fall under the same condemnation! Sin lies both in the act and in the consent." (VanGemeren)

e. **You thought that I was altogether like you**: In some ways this was their greatest sin, losing sight of the holiness of God. The main idea behind the concept of the *holy* is separation. In thinking that God **was altogether like you**, they considered Him more like a super-man instead of who He actually is: a holy God, enthroned in the heavens. They had become too casual and easy in their relationship with God.

i. One way that they forgot God's holiness was in mistaking His patience and longsuffering for not caring about sin (**these things you have done, and I kept silent**). We often make the same mistake and confuse the generous space God gives for confession and repentance to mean that He doesn't really care about our sin.

ii. **I kept silent**: "God's silence is an emphatic way of expressing His patient tolerance of evil unpunished. Such 'longsuffering' is meant to lead to repentance, and indicates God's unwillingness to smite. But, as experience shows, it is often abused." (Maclaren)

iii. "A wonderful thing is that silence of God, that longsuffering with sinners and another wonderful thing is the impudent interpretation which the sinner gives to that silence." (Spurgeon)

f. **But I will rebuke you, and set them in order before your eyes**: They had misjudged God's graciousness and forgotten His holiness. In His love, God would not allow that to continue among His people. He would **set them in order before your eyes**.

3. (22-23) Conclusion: The urgency to get right with God.

"Now consider this, you who forget God,
Lest I tear *you* in pieces,
And *there be* none to deliver:
Whoever offers praise glorifies Me;
And to him who orders *his* conduct *aright*
I will show the salvation of God."

a. **Consider this, you who forget God**: Graciously, God offered those who **forget** Him an opportunity to **consider** and change their thinking and their ways before He comes to them in the judgment described in the first few verses of this psalm.

b. **Whoever offers praise glorifies Me**: This speaks to the aspect of forsaking ritualism and coming to God not in empty ceremonies but in surrendered heart.

i. **Whoever offers praise**: "The phrase 'he who sacrifices a thanksgiving,' while it leaves room for a literal sacrifice, is suggestive of an offering of pure praise." (Kidner)

c. **Who orders his conduct aright**: This speaks to the aspect of forsaking the hypocrisy and wickedness and coming to God in confession and repentance.

d. **I will show the salvation of God**: Performing these two things – forsaking ritualism and shunning wicked hypocrisy – even those do not *earn* the saint salvation. It simply puts them in a place to receive what God reveals and gives: **the salvation of God**.

Psalm 51 – Restoration of a Broken and Contrite King

This psalm is titled **To the Chief Musician. A Psalm of David when Nathan the Prophet went to him, after he had gone in to Bathsheba.** *The events are plainly and painfully described in 2 Samuel chapters 11 and 12.*

James Montgomery Boice noted that this psalm has been long beloved by believers: "It was recited in full by Sir Thomas More and Lady Jane Grey when they were on the scaffold in the bloody days of Henry VIII and Queen Mary. William Carey, the great pioneer missionary to India, asked that it might be the text of his funeral sermon."

"This great song, pulsating with the agony of a sin-stricken soul, helps us to understand the stupendous wonder of the everlasting mercy of our God." (G. Campbell Morgan)

A. Sin confessed, and forgiveness requested.

1. (1-2) The direct plea for mercy.

Have mercy upon me, O God,
According to Your lovingkindness;
According to the multitude of Your tender mercies,
Blot out my transgressions.
Wash me thoroughly from my iniquity,
And cleanse me from my sin.

> a. **Have mercy upon me, O God, according to Your lovingkindness**: The title of this psalm gives the tragic context for David's plea. He had sinned in murder, in adultery, in covering his sin, and in hardness against repentance. It took the bold confrontation of Nathan the Prophet to shake him from this (2 Samuel 12); yet once shaken, David came in great honesty and brokenness before God.

> > i. **Have mercy upon me, O God** is the prayer of a man who knows he has sinned and has stopped all self-justification. David said to Nathan,

I have sinned against the Lord (2 Samuel 12:13) – a good and direct confession, without excuse and with clarity.

ii. David asked for **mercy**, and that **according to** the measure of God's **lovingkindness**. This is God's *hesed*, His loyal love, His covenant mercy. It was a well-phrased request with the eloquence of true brokenness.

b. **According to the multitude of Your tender mercies**: In slightly different words, David repeated the thought of the previous appeal. He had before experienced the **multitude** of God's **tender mercies**; he asks for this outpouring again.

i. **Multitude of Your tender mercies**: "Men are greatly terrified at the multitude of their sins, but here is a comfort – our God hath multitude of mercies. If our sins be in number as the hairs of our head, God's mercies are as the stars of heaven." (Symson, cited in Spurgeon)

ii. David used several words to speak of the kindness he desired from God. "*Mercy* denotes God's loving assistance to the pitiful. *Unfailing love* [**lovingkindness**] points to the continuing operation of this mercy. *Compassion* [**tender mercies**] teaches that God feels for our infirmities." (Boice)

c. **Blot out my transgressions**: David felt a register of his many sins condemned him, and he wanted the account of them to be erased. The blotting out may refer to David's own conscience, or to God's accounting of sin – or perhaps to both.

i. **Blot out my transgressions**: "The plea, *blot out*, means 'wipe away,' like the writing from a book (*cf.* Exodus 32:32; Numbers 5:23)." (Kidner)

ii. **Blot out my transgressions**: "Out of thy debt-book; cross out the black lines of my sins with the red lines of Christ's blood; cancel the bond, though written in black and bloody characters." (Trapp)

d. **Wash me thoroughly from my iniquity**: The word of God through Nathan the Prophet worked like a mirror to show David how dirty and stained he was. He had lived in that condition for some time (perhaps a year) without an acute knowledge of his **iniquity** and **sin**. Now the sense of the stain drove him to beg to be cleansed.

i. "*Wash me thoroughly*, Hebrew *multiply to wash me*; by which phrase he implies the greatness of his guilt, and the insufficiency of all legal washings, and the absolute necessity of some other and better thing to wash him." (Poole)

ii. **Wash me thoroughly**: "The word employed is significant, in that it probably means washing by kneading or beating, not by simple rinsing." (Maclaren)

iii. **Wash me thoroughly**: "To be cleansed not only from outward defilements, but from his swinish nature; for though a swine be washed never so clean, if she retain her nature, she will be ready to wallow in the next guzzle." (Trapp)

iv. David used several words to speak of his offense against God.

- **Transgressions** has the idea of crossing a boundary.

- **Iniquity** has the idea of twistedness or perversion.

- **Sin** has the idea of falling short or missing the mark.

2. (3-4) The open confession of sin.

For I acknowledge my transgressions,
And my sin *is* always before me.
Against You, You only, have I sinned,
And done *this* evil in Your sight–
That You may be found just when You speak,
***And* blameless when You judge.**

a. **I acknowledge my transgressions**: David realized it was not only one, but multiple **transgressions**. He did this without excuse, blame-shifting, or rationalization.

i. "The author is fully aware of his condition before God. He confesses 'I know' with an emphasis on 'I.' He knows himself intimately and sees how rebellious he has been." (VanGemeren)

b. **My sin is always before me**: In the many months between the time David committed these sins and this confession, he had not escaped the sense of sin – it was **always before** him. He did his best to ignore it and deny it, but as a genuine child of God he could not escape it. He was in unconfessed sin, but *miserable* in it, as a child of God should be.

i. David didn't say, "My punishment is ever before me," or "My consequences are ever before me." What bothered him was his **sin**. Many grieve over the consequences of sin, but few over sin itself.

ii. **Is ever before me**: "To my great grief and regret, my conscience twitteth me with it, and the devil layeth it in my dish." (Trapp)

iii. We remember that David suffered this agony *as a king*. "The riches, the power, and the glory of a kingdom, can neither prevent nor remove the torment of sin, which puts the monarch and the beggar upon a level." (Horne)

iv. **My sin**: "We note, too, how the psalmist realises his personal responsibility. He reiterates 'my' – 'my transgressions, my iniquity, my sin.' He does not throw blame on circumstances, or talk about temperament or maxims of society or bodily organisation. All these had some share in impelling him to sin; but after all allowance made for them, the deed is the doer's, and he must bear its burden." (Maclaren)

c. **Against You, You only, have I sinned**: In an objective sense this was not true. David had sinned against Bathsheba, Uriah, their families, his family, his kingdom, and in a sense even against his own body (1 Corinthians 6:18). Yet all of that faded into the background as he considered the greatness of his sin against God. He rightly felt as if, **against You, You only, have I sinned**.

d. **And done this evil in Your sight**: David realized that God was there and God was looking when he did his **evil**. He was not absent from the bedroom of adultery or the place where the command to kill Uriah was given.

i. "David felt that his sin was committed in all its filthiness while Jehovah himself looked on. None but a child of God cares for the eye of God." (Spurgeon)

e. **That You may be found just when You speak, and blameless when You judge**: David's confession of sin was not only to relieve himself of the great burden of his sin and guilt. More so, it was to bring glory to God. In confessing his sin, David hoped to confirm God's justice and holy character, proving that His commands were good and just *even when David broke those commands*.

3. (5-6) The depth of David's need.

Behold, I was brought forth in iniquity,
And in sin my mother conceived me.
Behold, You desire truth in the inward parts,
And in the hidden *part* You will make me to know wisdom.

a. **I was brought forth in iniquity, and in sin my mother conceived me**: David wasn't born out of a sinful relationship; that isn't his idea. Neither is his idea to *excuse* his sin by saying, "Look how bad I started out – what else could be expected?" The purpose was to show the *depths* of his sin, that it went beyond specific sinful actions all the way to a stubborn sin nature, one he was born with.

i. "The act of sin is traced back to its reason in the pollution of the nature." (Morgan)

ii. From this and similar passages we gain the Biblical idea of *original sin* – the idea that all humans are born sinners, receiving a sinful nature as sons of Adam and daughters of Eve. "This verse is both by Jewish and Christian, by ancient and later, interpreters, generally and most truly understood of original sin." (Poole)

iii. "It is a wicked wresting of Scripture to deny that original sin and natural depravity are here taught. Surely men who cavil at this doctrine have need to be taught of the Holy Spirit what be the first principles of the faith." (Spurgeon)

b. **You desire truth in the inward parts**: Though the sin nature was deep within David, God wanted to work deeply in him. God wanted a transformation in David all the way to **the inward parts**, to **the hidden part** that would know wisdom. David did not cry out for a superficial reform, but something much deeper.

i. "Oh! Delude not yourselves with the thought that you have holy desires unless you truly have them. Do not think your desires are true towards God unless they are really so: he desireth truth in our desires." (Spurgeon)

B. Prayers for restoration.

1. (7-9) Restoration through the blood of sacrifice.

Purge me with hyssop, and I shall be clean;
Wash me, and I shall be whiter than snow.
Make me hear joy and gladness,
***That* the bones You have broken may rejoice.**
Hide Your face from my sins,
And blot out all my iniquities.

a. **Purge me with hyssop, and I shall be clean**: David looked for *God* to do a work of spiritual and moral cleansing, and to do it in connection with the atoning sacrifice of a substitute. **Hyssop** was used to apply the blood of the Passover lamb (Exodus 12:22). **Hyssop** was also used to sprinkle the priest's purifying water (Numbers 19:18).

i. In the Levitical law it was the priests who used the **hyssop** to sprinkle the purifying water. "Here the psalmist petitions the Lord to be his priest by taking the hyssop and by declaring him cleansed from all sin." (VanGemeren)

ii. David didn't think for a moment that he could cleanse himself. He needed God to cleanse him, and to do it through the blood of the perfect sacrifice anticipated by animal sacrifices.

iii. **Purge**: "It is based on the word for sin (*chattath*) and literally means 'de-sin' me. David wanted to have his sin completely purged away." (Boice)

b. **Wash me, and I shall be whiter than snow**: David knew that God's cleansing was *effective*. His sin was a deep stain but purity could be restored. We sense that David spoke with the voice of faith; it can be difficult for the convicted sinner to believe in such complete cleansing. It takes faith to believe God despite the doubt and difficulty.

i. "God could make him as if he had never sinned at all. Such is the power of the cleansing work of God upon the heart that he can restore innocence to us, and make us as if we had never been stained with transgression at all." (Spurgeon)

c. **Make me hear joy and gladness, that the bones You have broken may rejoice**: David felt the *brokenness* fitting for the sinner under the conviction of the Holy Spirit; it was so severe he felt as if his **bones** were broken. Confident that this was the work of the Holy Spirit, David could pray that it would lead to **joy and gladness**, that out of his brokenness David would **rejoice**.

i. It is a terrible thing to be so directly confronted with the blackness of our sin, yet God means even this to be a prelude to **joy and gladness**. The restoration of **joy** is His goal.

ii. "He is requesting a great thing; he seeks joy for a sinful heart, music for crushed bones. Preposterous prayer anywhere but at the throne of God!" (Spurgeon)

d. **Hide Your face from my sins, and blot out all my iniquities**: Repeatedly, David asked for forgiveness and restoration. In the repetition we see that this was not a light thing for David. It was not easily expressed or easily received by faith. There was a sense in which he had to contend both with God and himself to bring him to the place he should be.

2. (10-11) Restoration of heart.

Create in me a clean heart, O God,
And renew a steadfast spirit within me.
Do not cast me away from Your presence,
And do not take Your Holy Spirit from me.

a. **Create in me a clean heart, O God**: David felt that it wasn't enough if God simply cleaned up the heart he had. The plea **create** indicated he needed a *new heart* from God, a **clean heart**. In this David anticipated one of the great promises to all who believe under the New Covenant: *I will give you a new heart and put a new spirit within you; I will take the heart of stone out of your flesh and give you a heart of flesh* (Ezekiel 36:26).

> i. "The word that begins this section is the Hebrew verb *bara*, which is used in Genesis 1 for the creation of the heavens and the earth by God. Strictly used, this word describes what only God can do: create *ex nihilo*, out of nothing." (Boice)

> ii. "With the word *Create* he asks for nothing less than a miracle. It is a term for what God alone can do." (Kidner)

b. **And renew a steadfast spirit within me**: Along with a new and clean heart, David needed a **steadfast spirit** to continue in the way of godliness. This expressed a humble reliance upon the LORD.

> i. **Renew a steadfast spirit**: "Or, a firm spirit, firm for God, able to resist the devil, steadfast in the faith, and to abide constant in the way that is called holy." (Trapp)

> ii. "'A steadfast spirit' is needful in order to keep a cleansed heart clean; and, on the other hand, when, by cleanness of heart, a man is freed from the perturbations of rebellious desires and the weakening influences of sin, his spirit will be steadfast." (Maclaren)

c. **Do not cast me away from Your presence, and do not take Your Holy Spirit from me**: This was a further way David expressed his ongoing reliance upon God. For him, the whole point of cleansing and restoration was to renew his relationship with God. David didn't want a God who cleansed him yet remained distant.

> i. **Do not cast me away from Your presence**: "Cain's punishment, which possibly David might have here in mind, as being guilty of murder." (Trapp)

> ii. **Do not take Your Holy Spirit from me**: "The likely background to this fear of being a castaway was the example of Saul, from whom the Spirit of the Lord had departed (1 Samuel 16:14)." (Kidner)

> iii. "The soul that is truly penitent, dreads nothing but the thought of being rejected from the 'presence,' and deserted by the 'Spirit' of God. This is the most deplorable and irremediable effect of sin; but it is one that in general, perhaps, is the least considered and regarded of all others." (Horne)

iv. It has been noted that several of these requests don't fit for the believer under the New Covenant (Jeremiah 31:31-34, Ezekiel 36:25-27). In the New Covenant the believer already has a new heart and is promised the abiding presence of the Holy Spirit. This point is technically true, yet doesn't take away from the deep sense of a need for restoration and return to the first things that may mark an erring child of God even under the New Covenant.

3. (12-13) Restoration to the joy of salvation.

Restore to me the joy of Your salvation,
And uphold me *by Your* **generous Spirit.**
***Then* I will teach transgressors Your ways,**
And sinners shall be converted to You.

a. **Restore to me the joy of Your salvation**: In his many months of unconfessed sin, David felt the misery of spiritual defeat. He wanted once again the **joy** appropriate to **salvation**, to those whom the LORD rescues.

b. **Uphold me by Your generous Spirit**: This expresses again David's confidence in God for his future. He did not dream of upholding himself. Such self-confidence is what typically leads even good men into sin.

c. **Then I will teach transgressors Your ways, and sinners shall be converted to You**: In the dark days before this confession of sin, David was not able to **teach** those who were far from God and saw none **converted** to Him. We don't know if David never made the attempt because of a sense of guilt, or if he attempted and saw no blessing on his work. One way or another, getting this right with God was key to effectiveness in his spiritual work.

i. **Sinners shall be converted**: VanGemeren notes that David used the same word here translated **converted** that was previously translated **restore** (Psalm 51:12). "The psalmist who prayed 'restore to me' also prays that he may be instrumental in restoring sinners to the 'ways' of the Lord." (VanGemeren)

4. (14-17) Restoration of praise.

Deliver me from the guilt of bloodshed, O God,
The God of my salvation,
***And* my tongue shall sing aloud of Your righteousness.**
O Lord, open my lips,
And my mouth shall show forth Your praise.
For You do not desire sacrifice, or else I would give *it;*
You do not delight in burnt offering.
The sacrifices of God *are* **a broken spirit,**

A broken and a contrite heart–
These, O God, You will not despise.

a. **Deliver me from the guilt of bloodshed**: David was deeply aware of his sin of murder against Uriah (2 Samuel 11). Though he makes no specific reference to his adultery in this psalm, he felt that he must make specific mention of this great sin. Such a request presented to **the God of my salvation** would surely be answered.

i. "The unhappy criminal entreats, in this verse, for the divine help and deliverance, as if he not only heard the voice of innocent blood crying from the ground, but as if he saw the murdered Uriah coming upon him for vengeance, like an armed man." (Horne)

b. **And my tongue shall sing aloud of Your righteousness**: David knew that with his guilt dealt with before God, he would again be able to **sing aloud**; that **my mouth shall show forth Your praise**. We believe that the months of unconfessed sin were silent from a spirit of true praise.

c. **You do not desire sacrifice, or else I would give it**: David expressed the principle brought forth in the previous psalm (Psalm 50). He understood that though animal sacrifice had its place, what God really desired was in the heart of man.

i. **Or else I would give it**: "He would have been glad enough to present tens of thousands of victims if these would have met the case. Indeed, anything which the Lord prescribed he would cheerfully have rendered." (Spurgeon)

d. **The sacrifices of God are a broken spirit, a broken and contrite heart**: David had a great love for the House of the LORD and had sponsored great sacrifices unto God (2 Samuel 6:13, 6:17-18). Yet he understood that one could sacrifice an animal or many animals to God without a **broken and contrite heart**. Perhaps David had offered many sacrifices at God's altar in his months of unconfessed sin. He recognized the emptiness of all that, and the value of his present **broken spirit** and **broken and contrite heart**.

i. **A broken spirit**: "If you and I have a broken spirit, all idea of our own importance is gone. What is the use of a broken heart? Why, much the same as the use of a broken pot, or a broken jug, or a broken bottle!" (Spurgeon)

ii. **A broken and contrite heart**: "This is opposed to that *hard* or *stony heart*, of which we read so oft, which signifies a heart insensible of the burden of sin, stubborn and rebellious against God, imminent and incorrigible." (Poole)

iii. "The clean heart must continue contrite, if it is not to cease to be clean." (Maclaren)

e. **These, O God, You will not despise**: It's easy to imagine that many in David's day would despise his **broken and contrite heart**. What he did – taking whatever woman he wanted and killing anyone who got in his way – these were expected conduct for the kings of the world. Perhaps his neighboring kings were mystified as to why any of this bothered David. To him, it did not matter what others thought; God did **not despise** his **broken and contrite heart**, and that was enough.

i. **You will not despise**: "This is great comfort to those that droop under a sense of sin and fear of wrath, being at next door to despair." (Trapp)

5. (18-19) Restoration of good to the kingdom.

Do good in Your good pleasure to Zion;
Build the walls of Jerusalem.
Then You shall be pleased with the sacrifices of righteousness,
With burnt offering and whole burnt offering;
Then they shall offer bulls on Your altar.

a. **Do good in Your good pleasure to Zion; build the walls of Jerusalem**: David realized that in his sin he did not only fail as a man, a husband, and a father. He also failed as a king over God's people. He humbly asked God to restore His favor to the kingdom.

i. We don't know if there was an obvious demonstration of God's displeasure against the kingdom of Israel in the period of David's unconfessed sin. Whether there was or was not, David understood that there was an aspect of restoration in terms of the kingdom that needed to be addressed.

b. **Then You shall be pleased with the sacrifices of righteousness**: Under the Old Covenant, David knew that God was not yet done with animal sacrifices. They would still **offer bulls on Your altar**. With the heart issues addressed, those sacrifices could be full of meaning and benefit.

i. It's also possible that David had in mind the sacrifices that were regularly offered on behalf of Israel, and that they could be restored to meaning and benefit on behalf of the nation.

Psalm 52 – Praying About the Man Who Loved Evil

This psalm is titled **To the Chief Musician. A Contemplation of David when Doeg the Edomite went and told Saul, and said to him, "David has gone to the house of Ahimelech."** *The terrible events that prompted this chapter are recorded in 1 Samuel 21 and 22. Doeg informed Saul regarding David's presence at the tabernacle of God and regarding the help he received from the priest there. In an evil and paranoid response, Saul had Doeg kill the priests and others at the tabernacle (1 Samuel 22:18-19).*

Though the condemnation of Doeg in this psalm is strong, we sense it should be stronger in light of the mass-murder he committed. Yet this is David's **Contemplation** *upon the incident, a careful examination of the root and end of Doeg's evil.*

A. The sin and its punishment.

1. (1-4) The man who loved evil and lying.

Why do you boast in evil, O mighty man?
The goodness of God *endures* continually.
Your tongue devises destruction,
Like a sharp razor, working deceitfully.
You love evil more than good,
Lying rather than speaking righteousness. Selah
You love all devouring words,
***You* deceitful tongue.**

> a. **Why do you boast in evil, O mighty man**: David thought of Doeg the Edomite and the evil report he brought to King Saul. He thought not only of the report itself, but also in the **boast** and joy Doeg took in delivering the message.
>
> > i. **Boast**: Sometimes boasting is a cover for deep insecurity. That wasn't the case with Doeg. He really thought quite highly of himself. "The

thought conveyed in this Hebrew word is not necessarily that of a person strutting around making extravagant claims to others about his or her abilities. Rather it is that of a smug self-sufficiency that does not parade itself openly simply because it is so convinced of its superiority." (Boice)

ii. Doeg murdered 85 priests who were not trained for battle – hardly the work of a true **mighty man**. Like several other commentators, Poole thought this was used in an ironic sense: "*O mighty man!* he speaks ironically. O valiant captain! O glorious action! to kill a few weak and unarmed persons in the king's presence, and under the protection of his guards! Surely thy name will be famous to all ages for such heroical courage." (Poole)

iii. "A mighty man indeed to kill men who never touched a sword! He ought to have been ashamed of his cowardice." (Spurgeon)

iv. "Miles Coverdale rendered this phrase, 'O mighty man,' as 'Thou Tyrant,' and thus gave an accurate interpretation of the kind of man this Edomite, Doeg, really was." (Morgan)

b. **The goodness of God endures continually**: David earnestly believed that Doeg's way would fail. God's **goodness** would outlast his evil. It's true that Doeg was a **mighty man**, but that was nothing compared to **God** and His never-ending **goodness**.

i. When David wrote **the goodness of God**, he used the word *El* to refer to deity instead of the more common *Elohim*. Some commentators believe the use of *El* emphasizes the strength and might of God. "Not without emphasis does he say the goodness *of the strong God,* a contrast to Doeg the *hero,* and the ruinous foundation of his fortune." (Venema, cited in Spurgeon)

c. **Your tongue devises destruction**: Since this psalm concerns the evil report of Doeg, David mentions the **destruction** that came from what Doeg said. There was an evil heart, mind, and life directing that **tongue** to work **like a sharp razor, working deceitfully** but it was all evident by what Doeg *said*.

i. The **destruction** brought by Doeg's evil report was real and terrible. 1 Samuel 22:18-19 tells us that he murdered 85 priests, and others in the city of Nob.

ii. "The prominence given to sins of speech is peculiar. We should have expected high-handed violence rather than these. But the psalmist is tracking the deeds to their source." (Maclaren)

iii. "*Like a sharp razor, working deceitfully*; wherewith a man pretending only to shave off the hair, doth suddenly and unexpectedly cut the throat." (Poole)

iv. "One is reminded of James' description of the tongue and its fearful power, as the psalmist describes the mischief of evil speech, growing out of an evil nature." (Morgan)

d. **You love evil more than good, lying rather than speaking righteousness**: David here addressed Doeg's wicked heart and mind. The destruction of these razor-sharp words were not an accident or out of character. Some people love evil, and some people love to lie. Doeg fulfilled both aspects. He loved the destruction his **devouring words** brought.

i. "Thy heart is naught, and thence it is that thy tongue is so mischievous, as stinking breath cometh from corrupt inwards." (Trapp)

ii. There is reason to believe there was a gap in time between David visiting the tabernacle at Nob and Doeg's report to King Saul. "It was not a case of the Edomite's merely blurting out what he knew at the first opportunity. On the contrary, he knew he had a piece of valuable information and kept it to himself until it would best serve his interests to divulge it." (Boice)

iii. David had done some wrong at the tabernacle of God at the city of Nob; he did lie to the priest Ahimelech. David did own up to his aspect of the responsibility in the matter (1 Samuel 22:22). Yet in this psalm he wisely and properly did not blame himself for the massacre of the priests there. This was the work of a man who loved **evil**. *There remain such men in the world.*

2. (5) The response from heaven.

God shall likewise destroy you forever;
He shall take you away, and pluck you out of *your* dwelling place,
And uproot you from the land of the living. Selah

a. **God shall likewise destroy you forever**: Because *the goodness of God endures continually* (Psalm 52:1), Doeg and his kind would be destroyed **forever**. He will not always allow this kind of destructive lie to rule the day.

i. "Instead of the assertive, the optative reading is preferable: 'Truly, may God bring you down.... May he snatch you.... May he uproot you....' The verbs are jussives, expressive of a desire." (VanGemeren)

ii. For emphasis and for the sake of good poetry, David used four vivid images of judgment against wicked mean like Doeg.

• The wicked will be demolished (**destroy you**).

- The wicked will be snatched up like a coal from a fire (**take you away**).

- The wicked will have their abode taken away (**pluck you out of your dwelling place**).

- The wicked will be uprooted like a tree (**uproot you**).

iii. **He shall take you away**: "He is laid hold of, as a coal in the fire, with tongs (for so the word means), and dragged, as in that iron grip, out of the midst of his dwelling." (Maclaren)

iv. "As thou hast destroyed the Lord's priests, and their whole city, razing and harassing it; so God will demolish and destroy thee utterly as a house pulled down to the ground, so that one stone is not left upon another." (Trapp)

b. **He shall take you away**: David prophesied the judgment of God against Doeg. Not only would he be cast out of his house (**your dwelling place**) but also from **the land of the living**. Doeg was destined for death.

i. **Uproot you**: "The bad fruit which it has borne shall bring God's curse upon the tree; it shall not merely wither, or die, but it shall be plucked up from the roots, intimating that such a sinner shall die a violent death." (Clarke)

ii. "*Out of the land of the living*; out of this world, as the phrase is taken, Isaiah 53:8, Ezekiel 32:32, and elsewhere; which was very terrible to him, who had all his portion in this world." (Poole)

B. The reaction of the righteous.

1. (6-7) The general response.

The righteous also shall see and fear,
And shall laugh at him, *saying,*
"Here is the man *who* **did not make God his strength,**
But trusted in the abundance of his riches,
And **strengthened himself in his wickedness."**

a. **The righteous also shall see and fear, and shall laugh at him**: When the coming judgment against Doeg happens, the people of God will notice it and it will cause them to honor and reverence God. It will also make them **laugh** in satisfaction at the destruction of such an evil man.

i. It is **the righteous** who learn from Doeg's judgment. We might have wished it were the wicked. "But this is the tragedy of life, that its teachings are prized most by those who have already learned them, and that those who need them most consider them least." (Maclaren)

ii. "*Fear;* both reverence God's just judgment upon thee, and be afraid of provoking God to send like judgment upon them." (Poole)

iii. **Shall laugh at him**: "If not with righteous joy, yet with solemn contempt.... This is a goodly theme for that deep-seated laughter which is more akin to solemnity than merriment." (Spurgeon)

iv. **Shall laugh at him**: "It is easy for those who have never lived under grinding, godless tyranny to reprobate the exultation of the oppressed at the sweeping away of their oppressors; but if the critics had seen their brethren set up as torches to light Nero's gardens, perhaps they would have known some thrill of righteous joy when they heard that he was dead." (Maclaren)

b. **Here is the man who did not make God his strength**: Previously David told us about Doeg's sins of destructive and deceitful words and of loving evil and lying. Here he exposed an associated sin – a failure to trust God and the trust of great **riches** instead.

i. We often are drawn to evil and lying because we fail to trust that God can and will work through goodness and truth. We lie to ourselves, saying that we *must* cut these corners, work this evil, or promote this lie because it's the only way to get things done.

ii. In writing **trusted in the abundance of his riches**, David may point to something only implied in the 1 Samuel 21-22 account: that Doeg did this for the sake of **riches**, either immediate or eventual. For the sake of money he murdered more than 85 people. 1 Samuel 22 indicates that Doeg did this to gain the favor of Saul, and the favor of a king could be a path to significant **riches**.

iii. **Trusted in the abundance of his riches**: "Oh! 'tis hard to abound in riches and not to trust in them. Hence that caution (Psalm 62:10): *If riches increase, set not your heart upon them.*" (Caryl, cited in Spurgeon)

iv. "Wealth and wickedness are dreadful companions; when combined they make a monster. When the devil is master of money bags, he is a devil indeed." (Spurgeon)

2. (8-9) David's response.

But I *am* like a green olive tree in the house of God;
I trust in the mercy of God forever and ever.
I will praise You forever,
Because You have done *it;*
And in the presence of Your saints
I will wait on Your name, for *it is* good.

a. **I am like a green olive tree in the house of God; I trust in the mercy of God**: David's run-in with Doeg happened at the tabernacle (1 Samuel 21:1-7). Perhaps there he saw a healthy **green olive tree** that was even more blessed because of where it was planted (**in the house of God**). This blessedness came to David because he could honestly say, **I trust in the mercy of God** and he would continue to do so **forever and ever**.

i. "The *olive* is one of the longest-living trees; here the point is doubly reinforced, for he pictures an olive 'in full sap' and one that grows in a sacred courtyard." (Kidner)

ii. Psalm 92:13 may indicate that there were trees at or near the house of God. This may have been particularly true for some of the places where the tabernacle was set up.

iii. "He was in the house of God, they were in the world; he was as a fruitful olive-tree, they were as barren, unprofitable wood; he was to be daily more and more strengthened, established, settled, and increased; they were to be cast down, broken, swept away, and extirpated; and all this because he had trusted in the mercy of God, they in the abundance of their riches." (Horne)

b. **I will praise You forever, because You have done it**: Doeg's evil had not yet gone away but David could praise God in the confidence of faith that can say, **You have done it**. The evil of man had not made him lose confidence in God and in the truth that God's **name** is **good** – His character and entire being.

i. **I will wait on Your name**: "Men must not too much fluster us; our strength is to sit still. Let the mighty ones boast, we will wait on the Lord; and if their haste brings them present honour, our patience will have its turn by-and-by, and bring us the honour which excelleth." (Spurgeon)

Psalm 53 – The Faithful God Delivers His People from Fools

This psalm has the title **To the Chief Musician. Set to "Mahalath." A Contemplation of David**. *The title describes for us the author, audience, and tune or instrument of the song (Psalm 88 is the one other psalm set to "Mahalath"). This psalm is essentially a repetition of Psalm 14, with a few small modifications, probably intended to give faith and courage to Israel in the midst of a national challenge, such as the threat of invasion or a siege.*

A. The sad condition of the man who rejects God.

1. (1) David's analysis of the God-rejecting man.

The fool has said in his heart,
"*There is* no God."
They are corrupt, and have done abominable iniquity,
***There is* none who does good.**

> a. **The fool has said in his heart, "There is no God"**: David looked at those who denied the existence of God and came to the conclusion that they are *fools*. The idea behind this ancient Hebrew word translated **fool** is more *moral* than *intellectual*. David did not have in mind those not smart enough to figure God out (no one is that smart); he had in mind those who simply reject God.

> > i. From the italics in the New King James Version, we can see that what the fool actually says is, "**No God**." "That is, 'No God for me.' So his is a practical as well as theoretical atheism. Not only does he not believe in God, he also acts on his conviction." (Boice)

> > ii. David says this because of the plain evidence that there is a God, evidence in both *creation* and *human conscience* that Paul described in Romans 1. The fact that some men insist on denying the existence of God does not erase God from the universe; it instead speaks to their

own standing as *fools*. As Paul wrote in Romans 1:22, *Professing to be wise, they became fools.*

iii. "The Hebrew word for *fool* in this psalm is *nabal*, a word which implies an aggressive perversity, epitomized in the Nabal of 1 Samuel 25:25." (Kidner)

iv. The God-denying man is a **fool** because:

- He denies what is plainly evident.
- He believes in tremendous effect with no cause.
- He denies a moral authority in the universe.
- He believes only what can be proven by the scientific method.
- He takes a dramatic, losing chance on his supposition that there is no God.
- He refuses to be persuaded by the many powerful arguments for the existence of God.

v. There are many powerful arguments for the existence of God; among them are these:

- *The Cosmological Argument*: The existence of the universe means there must be a creator God.
- *The Teleological Argument*: The existence of design in the universe means there must be a designer God.
- *The Anthropological Argument*: The unique nature and character of humanity means there must be a relational God.
- *The Moral Argument*: The existence of morality means there must be a governing God.

vi. "Which is cause, and which is effect? Does atheism result from folly, or folly from atheism? It would be perfectly correct to say that each is cause and each is effect." (Morgan)

b. **The fool has said in his heart**: David not only found *what* the fool said to be significant; *where* he said it is also important (**in his heart**). The God-denying man David has in mind is not merely troubled by intellectual objections to the existence of God; **in his heart** he wishes God away, typically for fundamentally moral reasons.

i. John 3:20 explains it this way: *For everyone practicing evil hates the light and does not come to the light, lest his deeds should be exposed.*

ii. This means that the man David had in mind is not an atheist for primarily intellectual reasons. "Honest intellectual agnosticism does not necessarily produce immorality; dishonest emotional atheism always does." (Morgan)

iii. It means that when we speak with those who deny God, we should not only – or even primarily – speak to their head, but also to their **heart**. "Let the preacher aim at the heart, and preach the all-conquering love of Jesus, and he will by God's grace win more doubters to the faith of the gospel than any hundred of the best reasoners who only direct their arguments to the head." (Spurgeon)

iv. The phrasing of **said in his heart** also reminds us that it is possible for one to *say in his mind* that there is a God, yet deny it in his **heart** and life. One may believe in God in theory, yet be a *practical atheist* in the way he lives.

v. 1 Samuel 27:1 tells us what David **said in his heart** on one occasion: *Now I shall perish someday by the hand of Saul. There is nothing better for me than that I should speedily escape to the land of the Philistines; and Saul will despair of me, to seek me anymore in any part of Israel. So I shall escape out of his hand.* Was this not David, in some sense, also denying God and speaking as a **fool**?

vi. "It is in his heart he says this; this is the secret desire of every unconverted bosom. If the breast of God were within the reach of men, it would be stabbed a million times in one moment. When God was manifest in the flesh, he was altogether lovely; he did no sin; he went about continually doing good: and yet they took him and hung him on a tree; they mocked him and spat upon him. And this is the way men would do with God again." (Macheyne, cited in Spurgeon)

c. **They are corrupt, and have done abominable iniquity**: David here considers the *result* of denying God. It leads men into *corruption* and **abominable iniquity**. This isn't to say that every atheist lives a dissolute life and every God-believer lives a good life; yet there is a marked difference in moral behavior between those who take God seriously and those who do not.

d. **There is none who does good**: As David considered the sin of the God-denier, he looked out over the landscape of humanity and concluded that **there is none who does good**. He did not mean that there is no human good in this world, but that fallen man is so fallen that he does not by instinct do **good**, and even the **good** he may do is tinged with evil.

- We are born with both the will and the capacity to do evil; no one has to teach a child to do bad.

- The path of least resistance usually leads us to bad, not good.

- It is often easier to encourage others to do bad, instead of good.

- Many of our good deeds are tinged with selfish, bad motives.

    i. "This is no exaggeration, since every sin implies the effrontery of supposedly knowing better than God, and the corruption of loving evil more than good." (Kidner)

    ii. "There is too much dainty dealing nowadays with atheism; it is not a harmless error, it is an offensive, putrid sin, and righteous men should look upon it in that light." (Spurgeon)

2. (2-3) Heaven's analysis of fallen humanity.

God looks down from heaven upon the children of men,
To see if there are *any* who understand, who seek God.
Every one of them has turned aside,
They have together become corrupt;
***There is* none who does good,**
No, not one.

a. **God looks down from heaven upon the children of men**: While man may wish to forget about God, God never forgets about man. He is always observing man, looking **down from heaven upon the children of men**.

    i. In man's rejection of God, there is often the wish that God would *just leave us alone*. This is an unwise wish, because all human life depends upon God (Acts 17:28; Matthew 5:45). This is an *impossible* wish, because God has rights of a creator over His creation.

    ii. "The words remind us of God descending from heaven to observe the folly of those building the tower of Babel (Genesis 11:5) or looking down upon the wickedness of the race prior to his judgment by the flood." (Kidner)

    iii. One of the differences between this psalm and Psalm 14 is that the word *Elohim* replaces *Yahweh* repeatedly; it is difficult to discern the exact reason why.

    iv. Both the similarities and the differences of the two psalms are instructive. "Some slight alterations show how a great song may be adapted to meet the need of some special application of its truth." (Morgan)

b. **To see if there are any who understand, who seek God**: When God does look down from heaven, one thing He looks for is if there is any *understanding* or *seeking* among humanity.

    i. God looks for this not primarily as an *intellectual* judgment; He doesn't wonder if there are any smart enough to figure Him out. He looks for this more as a *moral* and *spiritual* judgment; He looks for men who **understand** His heart and plan, and who **seek** Him for righteousness sake.

ii. If someone does actually **seek God**, it is evidence that God is doing a work in that person. One may be religious and conduct rituals yet not really seek God at all. Men often seek an idol of their own making, not the true God who lives and reigns in heaven.

iii. "You have gone through this form of worship, but you have not sought after God. I am sick of this empty religiousness. We see it everywhere; it is not communion with God, it is not getting to God; indeed, God is not in it at all." (Spurgeon, from a sermon on Romans 3)

c. **Every one of them has turned aside, they have together become corrupt**: When God looks, this is what He finds. He finds that man has **turned** away from God, and has therefore **become corrupt**.

i. Poole on **turned aside**: "Or, *are grown sour*, as this word signifies.... And so this is a metaphor from corrupted drinks, as the next [**become corrupt**] is taken from rotten meat."

ii. "The Hebrews have the same word for sin and a dead carcase; and again the same word for sin and stench." (Trapp)

d. **There is none who does good, no, not one**: When God finds **none who does good**, it is because there *are* none. It isn't as if there were some and God couldn't see them. David here observes and remembers that man is truly, profoundly, deeply *fallen*.

i. David's use of "**there is none who does good**" suddenly broadens the scope beyond the atheist to include *us*. "'After all, we are not atheists!' we might say. But now, as we are let in on God's perspective, we see that we are too included. In other words, the outspoken atheist of verse 1 is only one example of mankind in general." (Kidner)

ii. "What a picture of our race is this! Save only where grace reigns, there is none that doeth good; humanity, fallen and debased, is a desert without an oasis, a night without a star, a dunghill without a jewel, a hell without a bottom." (Spurgeon)

B. God's defense of His righteous people.

1. (4-5) God defends His people when attacked.

Have the workers of iniquity no knowledge,
Who eat up my people *as* they eat bread,
And do not call upon God?

There they are in great fear
***Where* no fear was,**
For God has scattered the bones of him who encamps against you;
You have put *them* to shame,
Because God has despised them.

a. **Have all the workers of iniquity no knowledge**: David first considered the profound fallenness of man; now he deals with the fate of God's people in such a fallen world. God's people might seem like the weak fools, but David understood that it is **the workers of iniquity** who have **no knowledge**.

i. "The question has almost a tone of surprise, as if even Omniscience found a matter of wonder in men's mysterious love of evil." (Maclaren)

b. **Who eat up my people as they eat bread**: It *looks* like the **workers of iniquity** are strong and have the upper hand. David wondered if the people of God are abandoned to the fools and the corrupt of this world, to those who **do not call upon God**.

i. "*As they eat bread*, i.e. with as little regret or remorse, and with as much greediness, and delight, and constancy too, as they use to eat their meat." (Poole)

ii. **And do not call upon God**: "Practical atheism is, of course, prayerless." (Maclaren)

c. **There they are in great fear where no fear was**: Here this psalm briefly but significantly departs from the words of Psalm 14. The idea seems to be that David took Psalm 14, slightly modified it to meet the present crisis, and used it to encourage Israel.

i. It seems that it was during a time of attack or siege from an enemy (**him who encamps against you**). David trusted that God would put the enemy **in great fear**, even though their strategic position gave them no real reason to fear (**where no fear was**).

ii. David prayed for something that God had promised an obedient Israel. God promised to send such fear (Leviticus 26:36).

iii. David prayed for something that God had done on other occasions. There were many times when God sent fear into the hearts of Israel's enemies. Examples include Joshua against the Canaanites (Joshua 10:10), Gideon against the Midianites (Judges 7), Jonathan and his armor-bearer against the Philistines (1 Samuel 14), and Hezekiah against the Assyrians (2 Kings 18-19).

iv. "God they feared not, of men they were greatly feared, and yet here they feared a fear where no fear was." (Trapp)

v. "The fear of God is either an impelling motive, leading in the ways of life; or it becomes a compelling terror, issuing in destruction." (Morgan)

d. **You have put them to shame, because God has despised them**: Here God answers the fool who despises Him with despising the fool in return. However, it seems that it was not only the fool's denial of God that provoked the Almighty; it was more pointedly the fool's attack against the people of God. We might say that *attacking the people of God is just as foolish as denying God's existence.*

2. (6) Longing for God's salvation.

Oh, that the salvation of Israel *would come* out of Zion!
When God brings back the captivity of His people,
Let Jacob rejoice *and* Israel be glad.

a. **Oh, that the salvation of Israel would come out of Zion**: David *knew* that God was a refuge for His people and that the workers of iniquity would never win. Yet that was hard to see at the present time, so David expressed his great longing that God would bring the victory and deliverance He had promised to His people.

b. **When God brings back the captivity of His people**: This was not the Babylonian captivity, many generations after David's time. Here **captivity** is used in a general sense, speaking of any time or situation where God's people are oppressed and bound.

i. "We take that phrase 'turns the captivity' in the sense in which it admittedly bears in Job 42:10 and Ezekiel 16:53, namely that of deliverance from misfortune." (Maclaren)

c. **Let Jacob rejoice and Israel be glad**: David anticipated the coming deliverance, and called the people of God to be joyful in consideration of it.

Psalm 54 – Help When Abandoned and Betrayed

This psalm is titled **To the Chief Musician. With stringed instruments. A Contemplation of David when the Ziphites went and said to Saul, "Is David not hiding with us?"** *There were actually two times when the Ziphites betrayed David unto King Saul, first in 1 Samuel 23 and the second in 1 Samuel 26. David escaped both times, but the circumstances of this psalm seem to best fit the circumstances of 1 Samuel 23, when David learned of the Ziphite betrayal but before the deliverance of God was displayed (1 Samuel 23:26-29).*

This is one of the few psalms with a specific musical direction: **With stringed instruments**. *It is also called* **A Contemplation**. *The Hebrew word for* **Contemplation** (maskil) *might be better understood as* instruction *(James Montgomery Boice).*

A. David's danger.

1. (1-2) Looking to the name and strength of God.

Save me, O God, by Your name,
And vindicate me by Your strength.
Hear my prayer, O God;
Give ear to the words of my mouth.

    a. **Save me, O God, by Your name, and vindicate me by Your strength**: In his distress, David relied on both the **name** and the **strength** of God. **Name** speaks of the nature and character of God; **strength** speaks of His great power. David knew that God's **strength** could respond to his need by what he knew of God's **name**.

        i. **By Your name**: "Nothing less than the whole fulness of the manifested God is enough for the necessities of one poor man." (Maclaren)

        ii. David's rescue would be his vindication. His enemies would have greater evidence that David was in the right and they were in the wrong when God answered this prayer and preserved this man after His heart.

iii. God gave David a remarkable vindication after each time the Ziphites betrayed David. Shortly after both times the Ziphites betrayed David, he had the opportunity to kill King Saul. Both times he spared Saul's life (1 Samuel 24 and 26), and both times Saul admitted his great wrong.

b. **Hear my prayer, O God**: It was common for David and others in their prayers to merely ask for God to **hear** or **give ear** to their cry. It was assumed that if the good and merciful God heard, He would act.

2. (3) The description of the need.

For strangers have risen up against me,
And oppressors have sought after my life;
They have not set God before them. Selah

a. **For strangers have risen up against me**: David's troubles came from the Ziphites, as noted in the title of this psalm and in 1 Samuel 23:14-24. The Ziphites were Israelis; they were even of the same tribe as David (Judah). Yet their betrayal of David was so contrary to both David and God's cause that David could rightly refer to them as **strangers**, as **oppressors** who **sought** David's **life**.

i. "The Ziphites, though David's countrymen, acted the part of 'strangers' or 'aliens,' in seeking to deliver him up to his unjust and cruel enemy." (Horne)

ii. Today some who are outwardly counted among the people of God will act as **strangers** as they betray the Son of David to gain the favor of those allied with the king of this world, the Prince of the Power of the Air.

b. **They have not set God before them**: Their problems were not only in relation to David, but also in relation to God. Their rejection of David was just another way that they rejected God. We don't know if David specifically had Saul in mind, but it certainly fit the jealous king.

i. "David felt that atheism lay at the bottom of the enmity which pursued him. Good men are hated for God's sake, and this is a good plea for them to urge in prayer." (Spurgeon)

ii. "This was a bad period for David. It was a time when seemingly he had nowhere to turn. He was unsafe even in the wilderness, and there was hardly anyone he could trust." (Boice)

B. Proclamation and prayer.

1. (4-5a) The proclamation.

Behold, God *is* my helper;
The Lord *is* with those who uphold my life.
He will repay my enemies for their evil.

a. **Behold, God is my helper**: Though a hunted man, David could confidently expect God's help. His present adversity had not led him to question the goodness of God, but to appeal to it.

i. "David was bringing himself and then his enemies to God's attention; he now brings God before his own attention." (Kidner)

ii. Maclaren had in mind that David said, **Behold, God is my helper** to his *enemies*. "The suppliant rises from his knees, and points the enemies round him to his one Helper." (Maclaren)

iii. "Little care we for the defiance of the foe while we have the defence of God." (Spurgeon)

b. **The Lord is with those who uphold my life**: The sense of this remarkable statement is that *Adonai* is among those who help me by upholding my life.

i. "In 4b the ancient versions, followed by most modern ones, seem to have found the Hebrew text too startling, where it numbers God 'among' *the upholders of my life*. But this is not belittling Him; it is seeing His hand behind the human help." (Kidner)

ii. **He will repay my enemies for their evil**: "They worked for evil, and they shall have their wages." (Spurgeon)

2. (5b-6) The prayer.

Cut them off in Your truth.
I will freely sacrifice to You;
I will praise Your name, O Lord, for *it is* good.

a. **Cut them off in Your truth**: David came to prayer again. He asked God to kill or cast out his enemies, and to do it **in Your truth**. David could pray such bold prayers against his enemies because he believed more than his self-interest was at risk; so was God's **truth**.

i. **Cut them off**: "He desires that God would destroy them with a *death-dealing blow*, which is the force the word contains; its primitive sense is *to be silent, to keep silence*, whence it is transferred to a stroke penetrating deeply and striking fatally, such as is called a *silent* blow, opposed to a *sounding* one, which is wont to rebound and not pierce deeply." (Venema, cited in Spurgeon)

ii. "Thou hast *promised* to save me; these have purposed to destroy me. Thy *truth* is engaged in my defence; they will destroy me if permitted to *live*; to save *thy truth*, and to accomplish its *promises, thou must cut them off.*" (Clarke)

iii. Some are uncomfortable with prayers that ask for the doom of enemies. It's true that Jesus told us to pray in a more generous way for our enemies (Matthew 5:43-44). Yet there is nothing wrong with the basic principle of wanting to see good triumph and for God to do His work against those who do evil.

iv. David lived out another aspect of this prayer. He prayed, **Cut them off in Your truth** but refused to take vengeance in his own hands. Immediately after the second betrayal of the Ziphites (1 Samuel 26:1) David had the opportunity to kill King Saul in his sleep and he refused to do it. David would not **cut** him **off**; he waited upon God to do it.

b. **I will freely sacrifice to You**: This described what is sometimes called a *freewill sacrifice* – one that is given to God without specific reference to a previous vow made. It was a **sacrifice** that didn't *need* to be made; it was done **freely** out of gratitude.

i. "*Freely sacrifice*; not by constraint, as many do, because they are obliged to it, and cannot neglect it without shame and inconvenience to themselves; but with a willing and cheerful mind, which thou lovest in and above all sacrifices." (Poole)

c. **I will praise Your name, O LORD, for it is good**: David said this in anticipation of God's rescue, but not in a demand for the rescue. He was able to **praise** God while the problem remained and before the prayer was answered.

i. "Christians should follow his example: they should consider how great things God hath done for them, and should never suffer the voice of praise and thanksgiving to cease in the church of the redeemed." (Horne)

3. (7) The confident conclusion.

For He has delivered me out of all trouble;
And my eye has seen *its desire* upon my enemies.

a. **For He has delivered me out of all trouble**: David confidently brought his request to God, knowing that many times before God had **delivered** him. God's past faithfulness became the ground for future faith.

i. "This is the language of faith; this is the triumph of trust." (Trapp)

ii. It is likely that David said this in faith, in *anticipation* of deliverance. When it came, it was remarkable. After the Ziphites betrayed David in 1 Samuel 23:19 Saul came very close to capturing him. When David was almost in Saul's grasp, the king learned of a Philistine invasion and had to break off his pursuit (1 Samuel 23:27-28).

iii. "David lived a life of dangers and hair-breadth 'scapes, yet was he always safe." (Spurgeon)

b. **My eye has seen its desire upon my enemies**: David knew what it was like to defeat his enemies before (Goliath is one example); he trusted that he would know it again.

i. "As admiring God's justice on his enemies, and love towards his people, he was well pleased with such a providence, and beheld it with comfort." (Trapp)

ii. There is a sense in which David in this psalm prefigured his Great Son. Jesus was the anointed King yet to come into the fullness of His kingdom. He came to rescue and lead God's people, and when He did, some among God's people betrayed Him unto death. We can easily see these lines from the psalm in the mouth of Jesus, praying to His Father:

Save Me, O God, by Your name,
Strangers have risen up against Me.
Behold, God is My helper;
He has delivered Me out of all trouble.

Psalm 55 – Trusting God Against a Treacherous Enemy

The title of this psalm is **To the Chief Musician. With stringed instruments. A Contemplation of David**. *The psalm describes a time of some kind of rebellion or power struggle against David, and a key leader in the struggle was a trusted associate who betrayed David. The city is dangerous because of the rebellion, and David cries out to God. Most commentators fit this psalm to Absalom's rebellion (2 Samuel 15-18) and the trusted associate as Ahithophel. Parts of this psalm seem to fit Absalom's rebellion, but some parts don't. It's hard to imagine David wishing Absalom to hell (Psalm 55:15) when he didn't even want him to die. It may be that the events connected with this psalm are unrecorded in the sacred history of the life of David.*

A. Fear: David describes his trouble.

1. (1-3) Misery in oppression.

Give ear to my prayer, O God,
And do not hide Yourself from my supplication.
Attend to me, and hear me;
I am restless in my complaint, and moan noisily,
Because of the voice of the enemy,
Because of the oppression of the wicked;
For they bring down trouble upon me,
And in wrath they hate me.

a. **Do not hide Yourself from my supplication**: We sense in David's prayer that he felt God was distant, as if He were hiding from David. He asked God to **attend to me, and hear me**. David believed he could face almost anything with the strong sense of God's presence and pleasure.

111

i. "In that dread hour when Jesus bore our sins upon the tree, his Father did hide himself, and this was the most dreadful part of all the Son of David's agony." (Spurgeon)

b. **I am restless in my complaint, and moan noisily**: At the beginning of this psalm, David had little peace. He was **restless**, complaining, and moaning; and his moans were noisy. He needed help from God.

i. "What a comfort that we may be thus familiar with our God! We may not complain *of* him, but we may complain *to* him." (Spurgeon)

c. **They bring down trouble upon me**: David was troubled by **the voice of the enemy** (this psalm seems to emphasize the singular instead of several enemies) and **the oppression of the wicked**. They hated David and caused great **trouble** for him.

i. **They bring down trouble upon me**: "They tumble it on me, as men do stones or anything else upon their besiegers, to endamage them; so did these sin, shame, anything, upon innocent David, to make him odious." (Trapp)

2. (4-8) Fighting fear.

My heart is severely pained within me,
And the terrors of death have fallen upon me.
Fearfulness and trembling have come upon me,
And horror has overwhelmed me.
So I said, "Oh, that I had wings like a dove!
I would fly away and be at rest.
Indeed, I would wander far off,
***And* remain in the wilderness. Selah**
I would hasten my escape
From the windy storm *and* tempest."

a. **My heart is severely pained within me, and the terrors of death have fallen upon me**: The stress of this crisis did cause David mental anguish, increased by the real danger of death. All this made David tremble in fear and feel that **horror has overwhelmed me**.

i. **Severely pained**: "His heart is palpitating like a woman in labor." (VanGemeren)

ii. **The terrors of death**: "I am in hourly expectation of being massacred." (Clarke)

iii. "He can do nothing but groan or moan. His heart 'writhes' in him. Like an avalanche, deadly terrors have fallen on him and crushed him. Fear and trembling have pierced into his inner being, and 'horror' (a rare word, which the LXX [Septuagint] here renders darkness) wraps him round or covers him, as a cloak does." (Maclaren)

iv. Clarke noted what a natural and true description this is of the steps that lead to overwhelming horror. "How natural is this description! He is in *distress* – he *mourns* – *makes a noise* – *sobs* and *sighs* – his *heart is wounded* – he expects nothing but *death* – this produces *fear* – this produces *tremor*, which terminates in that *deep apprehension* of *approaching* and *inevitable ruin* that *overwhelms* him with *horror*. No man ever described a wounded heart like David." (Clarke)

b. **Oh, that I had wings like a dove**: David wished he could just escape this terror-filled situation and **remain in the wilderness**. It is likely that David wrote this under the stress and intrigues of power once he came to the throne. He longed for the simpler days when he repeatedly saw God's faithfulness **in the wilderness**.

i. "An old writer tells us it would have been more honourable for him to have asked for the strength of an ox to bear his trials, than for the wings of a dove to flee from them." (Jay, cited in Spurgeon)

c. **I would hasten my escape, from the windy storm and tempest**: If David had the wings of a bird he would simply **escape** from his present problems. Most people can identify with David's longing.

i. "*Like a dove*; which being fearful, and pursued by birds of prey, flies away, and that very swiftly and far, and into solitary places, where it hides and secures itself in the holes of the rocks, or in some other secret and safe place; all which fitly represents David's present disposition and desire." (Poole)

ii. "It is some comfort to us to know that there are spiritual giants who have had this urge, whether they have succumbed to it like Elijah (1 Kings 19:3ff.) or withstood it like Jeremiah (Jeremiah 9:2; 10:19)." (Kidner)

iii. David wanted to simply **escape** – but he did not. "So the psalmist's wish was but a wish; and he, like the rest of us, had to stand to his post, or be tied to his stake, and let enemies and storms do their worst." (Maclaren)

B. Fury: David asks God to deal with his enemies.

1. (9-11) Destroy them, O Lord.

Destroy, O Lord, *and* divide their tongues,
For I have seen violence and strife in the city.
Day and night they go around it on its walls;

Iniquity and trouble *are* **also in the midst of it.**
Destruction *is* **in its midst;**
Oppression and deceit do not depart from its streets.

a. **Destroy, O Lord, and divide their tongues**: From the repeated reference to the speech of his enemies (verses 3, 9, 11, and 12), we sense this was some kind of whispering attack on David that was serious enough to endanger his life. Here he prayed that God would **divide** those who spoke evil against him.

i. Many see an allusion to the confusion of tongues at Babel (Genesis 11:1-9). "His prayer is perceptive, and a lesson to us: he remembers how God dealt with Babel (55:9a), another arrogant city, by exploiting the inherent divisiveness of evil." (Kidner)

ii. If this psalm is connected to Absalom's rebellion and Ahithophel's treason, the answer to the prayer is recorded in 2 Samuel 17:1-23 when there was a division of opinion among Abasalom's adivsers Ahithophel and Hushai.

b. **I have seen violence and strife in the city**: The attacks against David may have begun with words but did not end with them. People walked the city **day and night** causing trouble for David. The crisis at hand was not merely a problem for David, but for God's people in general.

i. "The city, the holy city had become a den of wickedness: conspirators met in the dark and talked in little knots in the streets even in broad daylight." (Spurgeon)

c. **Destruction is in its midst; oppression and deceit do not depart from its streets**: The instability and intrigue made the whole city unsafe.

2. (12-14) A reflection on the bitterness of a friend's betrayal.

For *it is* **not an enemy** *who* **reproaches me;**
Then I could bear *it.*
Nor *is it* **one** *who* **hates me who has exalted** *himself* **against me;**
Then I could hide from him.
But *it was* **you, a man my equal,**
My companion and my acquaintance.
We took sweet counsel together,
And **walked to the house of God in the throng.**

a. **For it is not an enemy who reproaches me; then I could bear it**: David refers to a specific person who speaks against (**reproaches**) him. This was someone once aligned with David who nevertheless **exalted himself** against David.

i. "None are such real enemies as false friends." (Spurgeon)

b. **But it was you, a man my equal, my companion and my acquaintance**: The unnamed man was a partner and friend to David. They helped each other with advice (**took sweet counsel together**) and went to the **house of God** together.

i. "The psalmist feels that the defection of his false friend is the worst blow of all. He could have braced himself to bear an enemy's reviling; he could have found weapons to repel, or a shelter in which to escape from, open foes; but the baseness which forgets all former sweet companionship in secret, and all association in public and in worship, is more than he can bear up against." (Maclaren)

ii. We don't know exactly when this happened in David's life – if it was before or after his sin with Bathsheba and cover-up murder of Uriah. Yet the connection of David's words here with his sin against Uriah is stunning. "What David was unwittingly describing in this moving passage was also the essence of his own treachery to Uriah, one of his staunchest friends (2 Samuel 23:39)." (Kidner)

3. (15) Asking God to take vengeance.

Let death seize them;
Let them go down alive into hell,
For wickedness *is* in their dwellings *and* among them.

a. **Let death seize them; let them go down alive into hell**: This remarkably strong statement from David shows how dangerous the man was to the peace of God's people and how deeply he had wounded David. It was a strong prayer, but it was a prayer that left vengeance to God, and David refused to take vengeance himself.

i. "The phrase, *let them go down to Sheol alive*, is a clear echo of Numbers 16:30, where Moses had called for proof that in resisting him the rebels of his day were resisting God." (Kidner)

b. **For wickedness is in their dwellings and among them**: David called upon God to bring such a severe judgment because the **wickedness** was so deeply ingrained in them.

i. "It seems significant that David does not specifically mention his former friend in this malediction. In fact, he seems to have distinguished between his enemies, who are cursed here, and his former friend in the previous section, who is not cursed." (Boice)

C. Faith: Finding rest in God.

1. (16-19) Confidence in God despite the attacks of the enemy.

As for me, I will call upon God,
And the LORD shall save me.
Evening and morning and at noon
I will pray, and cry aloud,
And He shall hear my voice.
He has redeemed my soul in peace from the battle *that was* against me,
For there were many against me.
God will hear, and afflict them,
Even He who abides from of old. Selah
Because they do not change,
Therefore they do not fear God.

a. **As for me, I will call upon God, and the LORD shall save me**: David abruptly switched from praying for destruction to declaring calm confidence in God. It's a further indication that he was able to leave his crisis – and his enemies – in the hands of the LORD, who would **save** him.

i. "The Psalmist would not endeavour to meet the plots of his adversaries by counterplots, nor imitate their incessant violence, but in direct opposition to their godless behaviour would continually resort to his God." (Spurgeon)

ii. "If I read the text aright, we here have David talking to himself; and what we are to endeavor to do is, *to talk to ourselves, just as David talked to himself.*" (Spurgeon)

b. **Evening and morning and at noon I will pray**: David's confidence in God was rooted in sincere dependence on God, demonstrated by constant prayer. Together all this gave David the confidence in God to say, **He shall hear my voice**.

i. "The Hebrews began their day in the *evening*, and hence David mentions the *evening first*." (Clarke)

c. **He has redeemed my soul in peace from the battle that was against me**: David felt that his **soul** had been rescued (bought out, **redeemed**) from turmoil and crisis and into **peace**. The battle continued (there were still **many against** him), but his soul was **in peace**.

d. **God will hear, and afflict them, even He who abides from of old**: David was confident that the eternal God would answer His prayer.

e. **Because they do not change, therefore they do not fear God**: The sense of **they do not change** is somewhat obscure. It likely refers either to the idea that they do not change for the better, or they have not had to change because of adversity.

i. "Their not having 'changes' is closely connected with their not fearing God. The word is elsewhere used for changes of raiment, or for the relief of military guards. Calvin and others take the changes intended to be vicissitudes of fortune, and hence draw the true thought that unbroken prosperity tends to forgetfulness of God." (Maclaren)

ii. "Most of those who have few or no afflictions and trials in life, have but little religion. They become sufficient to themselves, and call not upon God." (Clarke)

2. (20-21) The treachery of David's enemy.

He has put forth his hands against those who were at peace with him;
He has broken his covenant.
The words **of his mouth were smoother than butter,**
But war *was* **in his heart;**
His words were softer than oil,
Yet they *were* **drawn swords.**

a. **He has put forth his hands against those who were at peace with him; he has broken his covenant**: David's unnamed enemy was also treacherous, breaking peaceful relationships and breaking agreements with others.

b. **The words of his mouth were smoother than butter, but war was in his heart**: Using repetition and vivid images, David showed how dishonorable his unnamed enemy was. In contrast we see how *honorable* David was in not specifically naming the man.

3. (22-23) Confidently leaving the matter in God's hands.

Cast your burden on the L**ORD****,**
And He shall sustain you;
He shall never permit the righteous to be moved.
But You, O God, shall bring them down to the pit of destruction;
Bloodthirsty and deceitful men shall not live out half their days;
But I will trust in You.

a. **Cast your burden on the L****ORD****, and He shall sustain you**: There are few greater burdens to bear than a one-time friend who becomes a treacherous and dangerous enemy. David knew that even this was a **burden** that God could and should bear.

i. "God imposes burdens, to see what we will do with them. We may carry them to our undoing, or we may cast them on Him for his blessed countenance." (Meyer)

ii. "The word *burden* is too restrictive: it means whatever is given you, your appointed lot (hence in NEB [New English Bible] 'your fortunes'). And the promise is not that God will carry it, but that he will sustain *you*." (Kidner)

iii. **He shall sustain**: "The experience of suffering was not taken away from the servant of God, but he was sustained, and so made strong enough to resist its pressure, and through it to make his service more perfect. This is how God ever sustains us in the bearing of burdens." (Morgan)

iv. "If I cast my burden upon the Lord, what business have I to carry it myself? How can I truthfully say that I have cast it upon him if still I am burdened with it?" (Spurgeon)

b. **He shall never permit the righteous to be moved**: David had hope and confidence because he was persuaded that his fate did not rest in the hands of treacherous men. God was still Lord over all, and God had the final word on whether the righteous would **be moved** or not.

i. Morgan noted the movement in this psalm from *fear* to *fury* and now finally to *faith*. "Fear leads only to desire to flee. Fury only emphasizes the consciousness of the wrong. Faith alone creates courage." (Morgan)

c. **You, O God, shall bring them down to the pit of destruction**: The faithful God would not only help and establish the righteous, He would also **bring down** those **bloodthirsty and deceitful men** who caused so much trouble among God's people.

d. **But I will trust in You**: The psalm appropriately ended with David's focus upon God, not his enemies. He would **trust** in Him and not be disappointed.

i. "The *I* is emphatic, dismissing the preoccupation with the enemy. In effect, there are two parties involved, not three. 'As for me, I will trust in the Lord.'" (Kidner)

Psalm 56 – Faith in the Midst of Fear

The title of this psalm is **To the Chief Musician. Set to "The Silent Dove in Distant Lands." A Michtam of David when the Philistines captured him in Gath.** *It is probable (though not certain) that* **The Silent Dove in Distant Lands** *was the tune to which this psalm was sung; some connect it with the theme, thinking it represents a dove in trouble even as David was in trouble.*

Like Psalm 16 and the next four psalms, Psalm 56 is called **A Michtam of David.** *The title* **Michtam** *is best understood as* golden, *though others think it is related to a word meaning* to cover, *implying necessary secrecy in a time of crisis.*

The time **when the Philistines captured him in Gath** *is recorded in 1 Samuel 21:10-15. It deals with the period between the visit to the tabernacle at Nob and David's arrival at Adullam. David was alone, desperate, afraid – and not thinking too clearly.*

A. Fear and faith in response to constant danger.

1. (1-2) Looking to the Most High for mercy.

Be merciful to me, O God, for man would swallow me up;
Fighting all day he oppresses me.
My enemies would hound *me* all day,
For *there are* many who fight against me, O Most High.

> a. **Be merciful to me, O God**: David was in great and constant danger from many enemies – both the Philistines and Saul's servants. He cried out to God, knowing that divine help could rescue him from any man-made threat. He appealed to the *mercy* of God, not relying on what he may or may not deserve.
>
>> i. "Instead of building up gradually to his complaint, the psalmist pours out his heart immediately." (VanGemeren)
>>
>> ii. **Swallow me up:** "The open mouths of sinners when they rage against us should open our mouths in prayer." (Spurgeon)

119

b. **There are many who fight against me, O Most High**: On earth David was greatly outnumbered, so he looked for help from the God who is enthroned above. David knew the strategic value of high ground in battle; it made sense for him to look for help from the **Most High**.

> i. "To set forth the indignity of the thing, he repeateth the same sentence again in the plural number, noting that there were not a few of them bitterly bent by might and main to mischief him, a poor forlorn, friendless man." (Trapp)

> ii. Adam Clarke understood **O Most High** in a different way: "I do not think that this word expresses any attribute of God, or indeed is at all addressed to him. It signifies, literally, *from on high*, or *from a high* or *elevated place*: 'For the multitudes fight against me from the high or elevated place.'" (Clarke)

2. (3-4) Afraid and not afraid.

Whenever I am afraid,
I will trust in You.
In God (I will praise His word),
In God I have put my trust;
I will not fear.
What can flesh do to me?

a. **Whenever I am afraid, I will trust in You**: The young man who killed the lion and the bear, who killed Goliath, and was a successful young captain in Israel's army, did not deny the presence of fear. There were times when he was **afraid**. Yet he knew what to do with that fear, to boldly proclaim His **trust in** God despite the fear.

> i. "He feared, but that fear did not fill the whole area of his mind, for he adds, '*I will trust in thee.*' It is possible, then, for fear and faith to occupy the mind at the same moment." (Spurgeon)

> ii. Many do not serve God or speak a word in His name to others out of fear, and they wait for a time when they are no longer **afraid** to do so. David would counsel them, "I am sometimes **afraid** – but I **trust in** God and do what is right to do." Don't wait for the fear to stop before you do what is right before the Lord.

> iii. "It is a sure sign of grace when a man can trust in his God, for the natural man, when afraid, falls back on some human trust, or he thinks that he will be able to laugh at the occasion of fear." (Spurgeon)

b. **I will praise His word**: In the midst of the declaration of his trust in God, David calls attention to the praiseworthiness of God's word. His trust in God was directly connected with God's word. His trust wasn't a blind hope or wish cast up to heaven; it was based on God's revealed *character* and revealed *promises*.

> i. We say we trust God, but how do we confidently know anything about God? We know it through His Word, through His self-revelation to us.

> ii. "It might also be the case, however, that David is thinking specifically of the words of God that were brought to him by the prophet Samuel, assuring him that he would be king over Israel (*cf.* 1 Samuel 16:1-13)." (Boice)

c. **In God I have put my trust; I will not fear**: Trusting God has given David the momentum towards even greater faith. He began by trusting God even while **afraid**; with that trust rewarded, he can take a further step: **I will not fear**.

> i. "First, the singer declares that in the hour of fear he will trust. The he declares he will trust and not be afraid." (Morgan)

d. **What can flesh do to me**: Our instinctive reply to this rhetorical question is, *a lot of harm*. We constantly hear of and experience great harm that comes from mankind. Yet in the context of David's trust in the *Most High*, he realizes that with God for him, it doesn't matter what man or men may be against him.

3. (5-7) The continuing danger.

All day they twist my words;
All their thoughts *are* against me for evil.
They gather together,
They hide, they mark my steps,
When they lie in wait for my life.
Shall they escape by iniquity?
In anger cast down the peoples, O God!

a. **All day they twist my words**: The attacks against David were not only violent; they were also devious, with the twisting and distortion of his words and intentions. His many enemies constantly plotted against him **for evil**, hoping to **lie in wait** and kill David with a surprise attack.

> i. "The unremitting pressure is the worst part of the ordeal. It was the first thing David emphasized: *all day long...all day long* (56:1,2); and now he tells of it again (56:5)." (Kidner)

> ii. "The verb 'twist' is derived from a root that signifies a laborious, toilsome, unrewarding act. They plot so as to undo whatever the godly man has spoken and has planned to do right." (VanGemeren)

iii. **Twist my words**: "This is a common mode of warfare among the ungodly. They put our language on the rack; they extort meanings from it which it cannot be made fairly to contain." (Spurgeon)

b. **Shall they escape by iniquity**: David appealed to God's justice. It wasn't right for these wicked enemies to triumph over him. Whether they were the Philistines of Gath or Saul's servants, David asked God to **cast** them **down**.

B. God's sympathetic care for David.

1. (8-9) God noticed David's misery.

You number my wanderings;
Put my tears into Your bottle;
Are they **not in Your book?**
When I cry out *to You,*
Then my enemies will turn back;
This I know, because God *is* **for me.**

a. **You number my wanderings; put my tears into Your bottle**: In this period of David's life, before coming to Adullam Cave (1 Samuel 22), he was completely alone. This made him value the sympathy and care of God all the more, and he found great comfort in the thought that God noted his misery.

i. "The reason for hope in God's justice lies in his divine nature and promise to vindicate his children. For this purpose the psalmist adds a personal note about the extent of his suffering." (VanGemeren)

ii. "*Put my tears into thy bottle;* regard, and remember, and pity them." (Poole)

iii. "His sorrows were so many that there would need a great wine-skin to hold them all." (Spurgeon)

iv. **My tears into Your bottle**: "Here is an allusion to a very ancient custom, which we know long obtained among the *Greeks* and *Romans*, of putting the tears which were shed for the death of any person into small phials, called *lacrymatories* or *urnae lacrymales* and offering them on the tomb of the deceased. Some of these were of *glass*, some of *pottery*, and some of *agate, sardonyx,* etc. A small one in my own collection is of *hard baked clay*." (Clarke)

v. Spurgeon noted this practice and such ancient bottles, but believed that David made no allusion at all to this Roman practice.

b. **This I know, because God is for me**: This was the ground of David's confidence. His **wanderings** and **tears** did not mean that God was against him. Instead he knew that God was **for** him, and would answer his prayer for rescue.

> ii. **God is for me**: "What can we possibly desire more, than this assurance, that, how many, or how formidable soever our enemies may be, yet there is one always ready to appear in our defence, whose power no creature is able to resist? 'This I know,' saith David; and had we the faith of David, we should know it too." (Horne)

> ii. **God is for me**: "Paul was to echo the triumphant end of this verse (or Psalm 118:7a), and cap it with 'who is against us?' (Romans 8:31)." (Kidner)

2. (10-11) Confidence in God declared again.

In God (I will praise *His* word),
In the LORD (I will praise *His* word),
In God I have put my trust;
I will not be afraid.
What can man do to me?

> a. **I will praise His word**: For the second and third times in this psalm, David declared the greatness of God's Word. This was how he knew that God was **for** him. It wasn't just a wish, a dream, or a hope. It was well-grounded, because God said it in **His word**.

> b. **In God I have put my trust; I will not be afraid. What can man do to me**: David repeated this phrase again, preaching confidence to himself. Because God was for him (confirmed by **His word**), David need not fear what man could do to him.

> > i. "When news came to Luther, that both emperor and pope had threatened his ruin, he bravely answered, I care for neither of them, I know whom I have trusted." (Trapp)

3. (12-13) Fulfilling the vow.

Vows *made* to You *are binding* upon me, O God;
I will render praises to You,
For You have delivered my soul from death.
***Have You* not *kept* my feet from falling,**
That I may walk before God
In the light of the living?

> a. **Vows made to You are binding upon me, O God; I will render praises to You**: David referred to the sacrifice he would offer for the deliverance he knew God would bring. He was a long distance from God's altar so the

sacrifice could not yet be made; but in David's heart it was already done, as was the anticipated rescue.

> i. "So sure is he of deliverance, that, as often in similar psalms, his thoughts are busied in preparing his sacrifice of thanks before the actual advent of the mercy for which it is to be offered." (Maclaren)

> ii. **Render praises**: "*Thank offerings* can be a term for literal sacrifices (*e.g.* Leviticus 7:12) and for songs of gratitude (*e.g.* Psalm 26:7)." (Kidner)

> iii. "Reader, what hast thou *vowed* to God? To renounce the devil and all his works, the pomps and vanities of this wicked world, and all the sinful desires of the flesh; to keep God's holy word and commandment; and to walk before him all the days of thy life. These things hast *thou vowed*; and these *vows* are *upon thee*. Wilt thou *pay* them?" (Clarke)

b. **You have delivered my soul from death**: On his way to Gath, in Gath, and on his way from Gath, David's life was in constant danger. God and God alone **delivered** His life from his enemies, and **kept** his **feet from falling**.

c. **That I may walk before God in the light of the living**: David knew that this was *why* God spared his life. It wasn't so that David could do his own thing or live unto himself. It was so that he could live rightly **before God**.

> i. "Thus in this short psalm, we have climbed from the ravenous jaws of the enemy into the light of Jehovah's presence, a path which only faith can tread." (Spurgeon)

> ii. "The fact that Jesus seems to have used the last words of verse 13 in John 8:12 makes us think of verse 13 in light of the deliverance Jesus brings to those who trust him and the 'life' as his gift of salvation by the Holy Spirit." (Boice)

Psalm 57 – From the Cave to Above the Heavens

The title of this psalm is **To the Chief Musician. Set to "Do Not Destroy."** **A Michtam of David when he fled from Saul into the cave.** *Derek Kidner says of* **Do not Destroy:** *"This may well be a tune-indication: cf. Isaiah 65:8, where the phrase is identified as a popular saying (perhaps a snatch of vintage song), and borrowed to become a reassuring word from God. Yet notice also David's instructions about Saul, 'Destroy him not' (1 Samuel 26:9)."*

Charles Spurgeon noted, "There are four of these 'Destroy not' psalms, namely, the 57th, 58th, 59th, and 75th. In all of them there is a distinct declaration of the destruction of the wicked and the preservation of the righteous."

This is another **Michtam**, *or Golden Psalm. The* **cave** *was probably at Adullam, mentioned in 1 Samuel 22:1, though the caves of En Gedi (1 Samuel 24:1) are also a possibility. Adullam seems to be the best fit; therefore we can say that Psalm 34 is also associated with this period of David's life.*

A. A trusting soul set among lions.

1. (1-3) The trusting soul.

Be merciful to me, O God, be merciful to me!
For my soul trusts in You;
And in the shadow of Your wings I will make my refuge,
Until *these* calamities have passed by.
I will cry out to God Most High,
To God who performs *all things* for me.
He shall send from heaven and save me;
He reproaches the one who would swallow me up. Selah
God shall send forth His mercy and His truth.

    a. **Be merciful to me, O God, be merciful to me:** The need was so great that David repeated the request. When he fled from Saul into the cave, he had been through several near-death terrors (see Psalm 56). David came to Adullam Cave (1 Samuel 22) alone, discouraged, and in continued danger.

b. **For my soul trusts in You**: David did not say this to *earn* the mercy of God; mercy can't be earned. He said it to tell God that He was David's only hope. His **soul** trusted in God and nothing else; there *was* nothing else to trust in.

> i. "How can the Lord be unmerciful to a trustful soul? Our faith does not deserve mercy, but it always wins it from the sovereign grace of God when it is sincere." (Spurgeon)

c. **In the shadow of Your wings I will make my refuge**: Using a familiar image David expressed his trust and hope in God for defense. The idea is of how a mother bird shields her young chicks from predators, from the elements, and from dangers by gathering them under her wings.

> i. This figure of speech is also used in three other psalms (Psalms 17:8, 36:7, and 63:7). Jesus used this same word picture to show his love and desired care for Jerusalem in Matthew 23:37.

> ii. "Even as the parent bird completely shields her brood from evil, and meanwhile cherishes them with the warmth of her own heart, by covering them with her wings, so do thou with me, most condescending God, for I am thine offspring, and thou hast a parent's love in perfection." (Spurgeon)

> iii. Morgan connected this with Psalm 55:6 (*Oh, that I had wings like a dove! I would fly away and be at rest*). "There the desire was for the inefficient wings of a dove for flight. Here the sense is of the sufficient wings of God for refuge until calamities are past." (Morgan)

> iv. **I will make my refuge**: We should not focus so much on what David exactly meant by **wings** that we miss the greater fact: God was his **refuge**. "We should notice that David does not call the cave his refuge, though it was a refuge in a certain physical sense. Rather it is God whom he calls his refuge." (Boice)

d. **I will cry out to God Most High…He shall send from heaven and save me**: David came to the cave alone, and God was his only help. Yet he was confident, knowing as a military man the strategic value of high ground in battle. He looked for help from the **Most High** who occupied the greatest high ground of all: **heaven**.

> i. **God Most High**: "It could well have brought memories of God's good hand on Abram, another homeless man." (Kidner)

ii. **God who performs all things for me**: "It is a marvelous thing to consider God is literally willing to perform all things in us, and for us, if only we will let Him. The mischief is that most of us insist on performing all things in the energy of our own resolve, in the strength of our own power." (Meyer)

iii. **He shall send from heaven and save me**: "Were there no human agents or earthly means that he could employ, he would send his angels from heaven to rescue me from my enemies." (Clarke)

e. **He reproaches the one who would swallow me up**: God would speak against David's enemies, either the Philistines or the servants of Saul. For God to speak against them would be enough to protect David and defeat them.

i. **Selah**: "The Selah at the end of the clause is unusual in the middle of a verse; but it may be intended to underscore, as it were, the impiety of the enemy, and so corresponds with the other Selah in Psalm 57:6, which is also in an unusual place, and points attention to the enemy's ruin, as this does to his wickedness." (Maclaren)

2. (4) The dangerous enemies.

My soul *is* among lions;
I lie *among* the sons of men
Who are set on fire,
Whose teeth *are* spears and arrows,
And their tongue a sharp sword.

a. **My soul is among lions**: David had many reasons to believe his enemies were much more powerful than he. In describing his great disadvantage, he hoped to appeal to the mercy of God.

i. "The allusions to lying down among lions may possibly have been suggested by the wild beasts prowling round the psalmist's shelter." (Maclaren)

ii. "Would any man take the Church's picture, saith Luther? Then let him paint a silly poor maid sitting in a wood or wilderness, compassed about with hungry lions, wolves, boars, and bears." (Trapp)

iii. Peter thought that the enemy of our soul was something like a lion against us: *Be sober, be vigilant; because your adversary the devil walks about like a roaring lion, seeking whom he may devour* (1 Peter 5:8). When we feel threatened by the devil, we may appeal to God as David did.

iv. Spurgeon gave comfort and advice to believers who felt they were **among lions**:

- If you are **among lions**, you will have fellowship with Jesus and His church.

- If you are **among lions**, you will be driven nearer to your God.

- If you are **among lions**, remember that God has them on a leash.

- If you are **among lions**, remember there is another Lion, of the Tribe of Judah.

b. **I lie among the sons of men who are set on fire, whose teeth are spears and arrows**: David spoke of his enemies in fearful terms, especially noting the power of their words against him (**their tongue a sharp sword**).

i. "The horrors of a lion's den, the burning of a fiery furnace, and the cruel onset of war, are the striking images by which David here describes the peril and wretchedness of his present condition." (Morison, cited in Spurgeon)

ii. "The fiercest of beasts, the most devouring of elements, and the sharpest of military weapons, are selected to represent the power and fury of David's enemies." (Horne)

3. (5) The God-exalting refrain.

Be exalted, O God, above the heavens;
***Let* Your glory *be* above all the earth.**

a. **Be exalted, O God, above the heavens**: David declared this to his own soul and unto the Lord Himself. He recognized that God was worthy to be **exalted** high above the sky (**the heavens**).

i. "The poet is in the shadow of the cave at first, but he comes to the cavern's mouth at last, and sings in the sweet fresh air, with his eye on the heavens, watching joyously the clouds floating therein." (Spurgeon)

ii. "*Above the heavens*, i.e. higher than the heavens, or to the highest degree possible; or above all the false gods which are supposed to reside in heaven." (Poole)

iii. "David wants God to be exalted in his own personal circumstances and by the way he trusts and praises him even in difficulties." (Boice)

b. **Let Your glory be above all the earth**: David correctly reasoned that his problems all came from earth; he would glorify God **above all the earth**. God was worthy of David's praise and focus more than any crisis or danger on the earth.

i. "The good man interjects a verse of praise; and glorious praise *too*, seeing it comes up from the lion's den and from amid the coals of fire." (Spurgeon)

B. From the danger of the pit to praise above the heavens.

1. (6) The enemy's trap and what became of it.

They have prepared a net for my steps;
My soul is bowed down;
They have dug a pit before me;
Into the midst of it they *themselves* **have fallen. Selah**

a. **My soul is bowed down; they have dug a pit before me**: In the previous lines David's soul soared above the heavens. Now he is back down, in danger of going into the pit his enemies prepared to trap him.

b. **Into the midst of it they themselves have fallen**: The **pit** prepared by enemies has instead trapped those who dug it. From his circumstances as he came to the cave, we sense David said this with the anticipation of faith. It had not yet happened, but he knew that it would.

2. (7-10) Praise from a steadfast heart.

My heart is steadfast, O God, my heart is steadfast;
I will sing and give praise.
Awake, my glory!
Awake, lute and harp!
I will awaken the dawn.
I will praise You, O Lord, among the peoples;
I will sing to You among the nations.
For Your mercy reaches unto the heavens,
And Your truth unto the clouds.

a. **My heart is steadfast, O God, my heart is steadfast**: The psalm began with David twice appealing for mercy; now David twice expressed his **steadfast** confidence in God. Though alone in the cave and troubles behind and ahead, he could allow his **heart** to be **steadfast** in God.

i. "Fixity of heart is the secret of songs." (Morgan)

b. **I will sing and give praise**: The steadfast heart led to a singing heart. Perhaps David wished he had a **lute and harp** with him in the cave to accompany his singing of praise.

i. "With lip and with heart will I ascribe honour to thee. Satan shall not stop me, nor Saul, nor the Philistines. I will make Adullam ring with music, and all the caverns thereof echo with joyous song." (Spurgeon)

ii. **Lute and harp**: "The *psaltery* [**lute**] was a stringed instrument, usually with twelve strings, and played with the fingers. The *harp* or lyre was a stringed instrument, usually consisting of ten strings. Josephus says that it was struck or played with a key. It appears, however, that it was sometimes played with the fingers." (Barnes, cited in Spurgeon)

iii. **Awake, lute and harp**: "*Rabbi Solomon Jarchi tells us that David had a harp at his bed's head, which played of itself when the north wind blew on it; and then David arose to give praise to God.* This account has been treated as a *ridiculous fable* by grave Christian writers." (Clarke)

c. **I will sing to You among the nations**: Even from the cave, David could envision his song of praise extending to the **nations** and **among the peoples**.

i. "Faith lifts us high above the personal sense of pain, and creates a passion for the exaltation of God among the nations." (Morgan)

ii. "These words, or their near-equivalent in Psalm 18:49, are taken with full seriousness in Romans 15:9 as a prophecy which had to be fulfilled." (Kidner)

d. **Your mercy reaches unto the heavens, and Your truth unto the clouds**: A cave narrows and darkens the vision of most people, but David's heart and song soared **unto the clouds**. He exalted the **mercy** and **truth** of God even from difficult circumstances.

i. "A hard and ungrateful heart beholds even in prosperity only isolated drops of divine grace; but a grateful one like David's, though chased by persecutors, and striking the harp in the gloom of a cave, looks upon the mercy and faithfulness of God as a mighty ocean, waving and heaving from the earth to the clouds, and from the clouds to the earth again." (Tholuck, cited in Spurgeon)

ii. "The resurrection of Jesus from the grave, foreshadowed in the deliverance of David from the hand of Saul, was a transaction which caused the heavens and all the powers therein, to extol the mercy and truth of God." (Horne)

3. (11) The God-exalting refrain.

Be exalted, O God, above the heavens;
***Let* Your glory *be* above all the earth.**

a. **Be exalted, O God, above the heavens**: The refrain is repeated because of its goodness and for emphasis. It's important to remember that David's circumstances were not much better when he sang this song. He was delivered from the immediate danger at Gath, but a cave was a long way from the throne of Israel which God had promised him. David didn't wait for his circumstances to change before he praised God **above the heavens**.

b. **Let Your glory be above all the earth**: We sense the freedom in David's spirit. Though in a cave, his soul glorified God **above all the earth**.

i. Kidner observed regarding the repeated refrain: "Sung now not with the defiant faith of verse 5, but with grateful love."

Psalm 58 – Words to and Against the Wicked Judges

This psalm is titled **To the Chief Musician. Set to "Do Not Destroy." A Michtam of David.** *The phrase* **Do Not Destroy** *may refer to the tune, to David's determination to not destroy Saul, or to David's plea that God would not allow him to be destroyed.*

We have noted that **Michtam** *indicates* golden *and that they are golden psalms. Some commentators give an alternate meaning of Michtam, that of engraving. One commentator used that thought to picture David writing or scratching these psalms on the walls of his refuge caves.*

"*The proper meaning of the root of Michtam is* to engrave, *or to stamp a* metal. *It therefore, in strictness, means, an engraving or sculpture. Hence in the Septuagint, it is translated* στηλογραφία [stelographia], *an inscription on a column. I would venture to offer a conjecture in perfect harmony with this view. It appears by the titles of four out of these six psalms, that they were composed by David while flying and hiding from the persecutions of Saul. What, then, should hinder us from imagining that they were inscribed on the rocks and on the sides of the caves which so often formed his place of refuge? This view would accord with the strict etymological meaning of the word, and explain the rendering of the Septuagint.*" (Jebb, cited in Spurgeon)

A. Speaking to the wicked rulers.

1. (1-2) A challenge to wicked judges.

Do you indeed speak righteousness, you silent ones?
Do you judge uprightly, you sons of men?
No, in heart you work wickedness;
You weigh out the violence of your hands in the earth.

a. **Do you judge uprightly, you sons of men**: David directed this psalm against those who were rulers or judges in some sense. Some think they were leaders aligned with Saul who passed judgment on the fugitive David, condemning him to a death sentence as a traitor. David challenged these rulers and the uprightness of their decisions.

i. We picture David as a fugitive, perhaps at Adullam Cave. He hears from a messenger that some assembled court of leaders close to King Saul has met and judicially condemned him as a traitor, worthy of death. David is outraged at the injustice of it and proclaims this psalm.

ii. "Saul having attempted the life of David, the latter was obliged to flee from the court, and take refuge in the deserts of Judea. Saul, missing him, is supposed by Bishop *Patrick* to have called a council, when they, to ingratiate themselves with the monarch, adjudged David to be guilty of treason in aspiring to the throne of Israel. This being made known to David was the cause of this psalm." (Clarke)

iii. John Trapp had his own idea: "David here talketh to Abner and the rest, who, to please Saul, pronounced David a rebel, and condemned him absent for an enemy to the state." (Trapp)

iv. "Rather than limiting the sense of 'judge' to legal disputes, it may be well to be guided by the usage of the same Hebrew root in Psalm 58:11 and in Psalm 98:9b: 'govern' or 'rule.'" (VanGemeren)

v. David was outraged at corruption, perhaps because he now felt the sting of it. It's human nature to not care much about government and legal corruption until it personally hurts us.

b. **Do you indeed speak righteousness, you silent ones**: There is some question about the best way to translate the original here given as **silent ones**. Taking the text as it is, David challenged those leaders who should have defended him or other innocents but instead stayed **silent**.

i. "The interrogation, are *ye indeed*, expresses wonder, as at something scarcely credible. Can it be so? Is it possible? Are you really silent, you, whose very office is to speak for God, and against the sins of men?" (Alexander, cited in Spurgeon)

ii. "The problem is that these judges did not speak up for the right course of action when evil was being planned." (Boice)

iii. Some translations (such as the NIV) follow a different manuscript tradition and translate **silent ones** as *rulers*.

c. **No, in your heart you work wickedness**: After questioning the words and justice of his enemies, David examined their intentions and their actions. Their intention was to **work wickedness** and in their actions they dispensed **violence** in the earth.

i. "The Psalmist doth not say, they had wickedness in their heart, but they did work it there: the heart is a shop within, an under-ground shop; there they did closely contrive, forge, and hammer out their wicked purposes, and fit them into actions." (Caryl, cited in Spurgeon)

ii. David said they **weigh out the violence** against others; with careful thought and deliberation they gave it out. "As righteous judges ponder the law, balance the evidence, and weigh the case, so the malicious dispense injustice with malice aforethought in cold blood." (Spurgeon)

2. (3-5) A description of the wicked rulers.

The wicked are estranged from the womb;
They go astray as soon as they are born, speaking lies.
Their poison *is* like the poison of a serpent;
***They are* like the deaf cobra *that* stops its ear,**
Which will not heed the voice of charmers,
Charming ever so skillfully.

a. **The wicked are estranged from the womb**: David diagnosed the problem of the judges; they were **wicked** at the root, in their nature, from birth. David understood this of all humanity including himself (Psalm 51:5).

i. "The description in verses 3ff. is close enough to what is quoted in Romans 3:10ff. to warn the reader that he faces a mirror, not only a portrait." (Kidner)

ii. "G.K. Chesterson said that the doctrine of original sin is the only philosophy that has been empirically validated by thirty-five hundred years of human history." (Boice)

iii. "Sinful, indeed, we are all by nature, and a birth-blot we bring into the world with us, making us strangers and strayers from God." (Trapp)

iv. In the next few verses, "Figure is heaped on figure in a fashion suggestive of intense emotion." (Maclaren)

b. **They go astray as soon as they are born, speaking lies**: Their corrupt nature was evident early in life, especially in their words. No one has to *teach* a child how to lie; with some poetic hyperbole we can say they **are born, speaking lies**.

i. "To be untruthful is one of the surest proofs of a fallen state, and since falsehood is universal, so also is human depravity." (Spurgeon)

c. **Their poison is like the poison of a serpent**: The **lies** are not harmless; they are like **poison**. The words of judges and rulers have special power to oppress others, and their **poison** is more deadly. The words of these judges were as dangerous as a deadly, unpredictable **cobra**.

> i. "The wicked are as dangerous as the venomous cobra that bites his trainer when touched and handled by him." (VanGemeren)

B. Speaking to God who judges the wicked.

1. (6-8) David calls upon God to ruin the wicked.

Break their teeth in their mouth, O God!
Break out the fangs of the young lions, O LORD!
Let them flow away as waters *which* run continually;
When* he bends *his bow,
Let his arrows be as if cut in pieces.
***Let them be* like a snail which melts away as it goes,**
***Like* a stillborn child of a woman, that they may not see the sun.**

a. **Break their teeth in their mouth, O God**: David prayed that God would take vengeance on these dangerous judges. The power of serpents and **lions** was in their **fangs**; David asked God to take away their deadly bite.

> i. "The imprecatory nature of the prayer may seem strange to our ears, but the radical nature of evil requires a response from the God of justice." (VanGemeren)

> ii. "If they have no capacity for good, at least deprive them of their ability for evil." (Spurgeon)

> iii. **Fangs**: "*The great teeth,* called *the grinders,* which are more sharp and strong than the rest, and more used in breaking and tearing what they are about to eat." (Poole)

b. **Let them flow away as waters which run continually**: David asked for the rapid and complete dispersion of these men and their power – **like a snail which melts as it goes away**.

> i. "Let them be minished away like the waters which sometimes run in the desert, but are soon evaporated by the *sun,* or absorbed by the *sand.*" (Clarke)

> ii. "A slug does not actually melt away as it moves along the ground leaving its slimy trail behind. But it seems to." (Boice)

c. **Like a stillborn child**: With a severe and startling image, David prayed for the death of his enemies, or rather that they had never been born to see the light of day.

i. "Their life comes never to ripeness, their aims are abortive, their only achievement is to have brought misery to others, and horror to themselves. Such men as Herod, Judas, Alva, Bonner, had it not been better for them if they had never been born?" (Spurgeon)

2. (9-11) David's confidence in God's judgment.

Before your pots can feel *the burning* **thorns,**
He shall take them away as with a whirlwind,
As in His living and burning wrath.
The righteous shall rejoice when he sees the vengeance;
He shall wash his feet in the blood of the wicked,
So that men will say,
"Surely *there is* **a reward for the righteous;**
Surely He is God who judges in the earth."

a. **Before your pots can feel the burning thorns**: The Hebrew of these lines is difficult but the thought may be that David considered how quickly a bunch of dry **thorns** burn in a fire under cooking **pots**. David prayed that God's judgment would come upon his enemies like a flash of fire.

b. **The righteous shall rejoice when he sees the vengeance**: David thought of the happiness coming to the **righteous** at God's judgment on these unjust and oppressive rulers, as if **the righteous** walked the victorious field of battle with God (**his feet in the blood of the wicked**).

i. "If it is right in God to destroy, it cannot be wrong in His servants to rejoice that He does. Only they have to take heed that their emotion is untarnished by selfish gratulation, and is not untinged with solemn pity for those who were indeed doers of evil, but were themselves the greatest sufferers from their evil." (Maclaren)

ii. "It is a sickly sentimentality and a wicked weakness that have more sympathy with the corrupt oppressors than with the anger of God." (Morgan)

iii. When it comes to rejoicing in God's victory over those who wickedly oppress others, "The New Testament will, if anything, outdo this language in speaking of the day of reckoning (*e.g.* Revelation 14:19f.; 19:11ff.), while repudiating carnal weapons for the spiritual war (Revelation 12:11)." (Kidner)

iv. "It is hard, but not impossible, to take all that is expressed in the psalm, and to soften it by some effluence from the spirit of Him who wept over Jerusalem, and yet pronounced its doom." (Maclaren)

c. **Surely there is a reward for the righteous; surely He is God who judges the earth**: David desired the world to see there was a moral order under God where righteousness is rewarded and wickedness is judged. He longed for the justice that these wicked rulers denied.

i. "All men shall be forced by the sight of the final judgment to see that there is a God, and that he is the righteous ruler of the universe. Two things will come out clearly after all – there is a God and there is a reward for the righteous." (Spurgeon)

ii. **A reward for the righteous**: "Yes, child of God, there is a reward for thee. It is not in vain that thou hast washed thy hands in innocency. But it will not come in the coinage or honour of this age, else it would be evanescent and perishable. God is already giving thee of the eternal and divine – peace, joy, blessedness; and one day thou shalt be fully vindicated." (Meyer)

Psalm 59 – Praise to My High Tower Against Assassins

The title of this psalm is **To the Chief Musician. Set to "Do Not Destroy." A Michtam of David when Saul sent men, and they watched the house in order to kill him.** *This refers to the incident in 1 Samuel 19:11-12, which was when the murderous intent of King Saul against David was openly revealed, and David began his long season of living as a fugitive.*

A. David describes the bloodthirsty assassins.

1. (1-2) A prayer for deliverance and defense.

Deliver me from my enemies, O my God;
Defend me from those who rise up against me.
Deliver me from the workers of iniquity,
And save me from bloodthirsty men.

a. **Deliver me from my enemies, O my God**: Many were David's perils, many were his enemies, and many were the psalms that begin with this thought. We think it strange that the man after God's heart, Israel's greatest earthly king, had so many enemies. The idea is less strange when we think of how many enemies the Son of David had.

i. David cried out, **O my God**, meaning it in the most reverent way. Through this psalm David declared his close and personal connection with God.

- My God (Psalm 59:1).
- My Defense (Psalm 59:9, 17).
- My God of mercy (Psalm 59:10, 17).
- My Strength (Psalm 59:9, 17).

ii. We wish that those who thoughtlessly exclaim **O my God** today would change and do so with the heart and sense of personal trust that David had.

b. **Defend me**: The sense of this ancient Hebrew word is *to lift up*, as into a safe and defended place. It says, "Lift me up to Your high tower where I am even higher above **those who rise up against me**." This idea is repeated three more times in the psalm (59:9, 16, 17).

i. "The word protect [**defend**] (59:1), like the kindred word 'fortress' [*defense*] (59:9, 16, 17), contains the thought of what is set high up, out of reach." (Kidner)

ii. "He is a high tower or place of refuge and retreat to the soul in trouble and danger." (Morgan)

c. **Save me from bloodthirsty men**: David was the target of a focused assassination plot that came from the highest levels of Israel's government. Many felt they could advance their favor before King Saul by shedding David's blood. Knowing the danger, David looked to God for rescue and defense.

2. (3-5) Describing the need.

For look, they lie in wait for my life;
The mighty gather against me,
Not *for* my transgression nor *for* my sin, O LORD.
They run and prepare themselves through no fault *of mine*.
Awake to help me, and behold!
You therefore, O LORD God of hosts, the God of Israel,
Awake to punish all the nations;
Do not be merciful to any wicked transgressors. Selah

a. **For look, they lie in wait for my life**: The circumstances of 1 Samuel 19:11-12 must have amazed David. Assassins came against his own home, hoping to surprise him in the routines of daily life. David saw **the mighty gather against** him and looked to God for help.

b. **Not for my transgression nor for my sin, O LORD**: David didn't make a claim to sinless perfection. He simply understood and said to God that there was no justified reason at all for Saul to send the bloodthirsty assassins against him.

i. **They run and prepare themselves**: "The zeal and diligence of the wicked in the cause of unrighteousness might well reprove the languor and tardiness of saints in the work of faith and labour of love. In the church of God nothing is the source of more mischief than the want of true zeal and liveliness." (Plumer, cited in Spurgeon)

c. **Awake to help me, and behold**: David feared he would die if God were asleep to his need. He asked God to be active for him and to look (**behold**) upon his crisis.

d. **O Lord God of hosts, the God of Israel**: David appealed to God with a variety of His names and titles.

- He was *Yahweh*, the covenant God of Israel (**Lord**).

- He was *Elohim Sabaoth*, the commander of heavenly armies (**God of hosts**).

- He was *Elohi Israel*, the God of His chosen people (**God of Israel**).

  i. "The petitions in Psalm 59:5 are remarkable, both in their accumulation of the Divine names and in their apparent transcending of the suppliant's need.... Each name suggests something in God which encourages hope, and when appealed to by a trusting soul, moves Him to act." (Maclaren)

e. **Awake to punish all the nations**: The hope of God setting things right in David's cause made the psalmist think of God setting things right on a global scale. David looked to the God of angelic armies (**Lord God of hosts**) to judge the nations and all **wicked transgressors**.

  i. "The psalmist looks for his own deliverance as one instance of that world-wide manifestation of Divine justice which will 'render to every man according to his deeds.'" (Maclaren)

  ii. **Selah**: "'*Selah*,' assuredly God will have them in derision; '*Selah*,' assuredly God shall shiver their bones, shake their best actions, and discover their impurity; '*Selah*,' assuredly God's hand shall be heavy upon them, and they shall not discern it to be his hand till they are consumed. '*Selah*,' assuredly, verily, amen, this is a faithful, an infallible truth; as the Lord liveth it shall be so." (Wright, cited in Spurgeon)

3. (6-7) The proud arrogance of David's enemies.

At evening they return,
They growl like a dog,
And go all around the city.
Indeed, they belch with their mouth;
Swords *are* in their lips;
For *they say*, "Who hears?"

a. **At evening they return, they growl like a dog**: The men sent to watch David's house and kill him were determined. They didn't give up quickly and they growled like dangerous dogs, going **all around the city** to find and murder David.

i. "David called them dogs, and no doubt a pretty pack they were, a cursed cursing company of curs." (Spurgeon)

ii. "*They make a noise like a dog;* either when he is hungry and pursuing his prey, and howls for meat; or when he is enraged, and grins and snarls where he cannot or dare not bite." (Poole)

iii. "There is some uncertainty over the word *growl*, which is the expression used for the Israelites' 'murmuring' – one might almost say 'whining' in the wilderness, and makes excellent sense." (Kidner)

b. **They belch with their mouth; swords are in their lips**: Perhaps David actually saw and heard such a **belch** as he watched those who watched him. He heard their sharp words against him, and their disregard for God or David or any authority (**Who hears?**).

i. **They belch**: "The word rendered (A.V. [King James Version] and R.V. [Revised Version]) 'belch' means to gush out, and is found in a good sense in Psalm 19:1. Here it may perhaps be taken as meaning 'foam,' with some advantage to the truth of the picture." (Maclaren)

ii. "The root idea is of bubbling up and bursting out; so in terms of dogs JB [Jerusalem Bible] has 'See how they slaver at the mouth.'" (Kidner)

iii. **Who hears**: "David doth not hear us, either to discover, and so to prevent our plots; or to punish us for them; and God either doth not hear or not regard what we say and do against David; and therefore we may speak and act what we think fit." (Poole)

B. God's response to the bloodthirsty men.

1. (8-10) David's strong confidence in God.

But You, O Lord, shall laugh at them;
You shall have all the nations in derision.
I will wait for You, O You his Strength;
For God *is* my defense.
My God of mercy shall come to meet me;
God shall let me see *my desire* on my enemies.

a. **But You, O Lord, shall laugh at them**: David's danger from the assassins was real and fearful. Yet he understood that they were nothing against God. The Lord could simply **laugh** at them and their arrogant claim that God did not hear or care about their evil.

b. **You shall have all the nations in derision**: David saw God's laugh against the men who waited outside his house to kill him in connection with God's triumph over **all the nations**. All who opposed God would be held **in derision**.

c. **God is my defense**: The word **defense** has the idea of a high tower or fortress. David believed that God was like a strong, high tower for him. It seemed impossible for David to survive against such a powerful conspiracy against him, but God would be his **defense**, his high tower.

> i. "'*For God is my defence*,' my high place, my fortress, the place of my resort in the time of my danger. If the foe be too strong for me to cope with him, I will retreat into my castle, where he cannot reach me." (Spurgeon)

> ii. "There is perhaps no more beautiful description of what God is to His tried people. The phrase suggests at once strength and peace. A tower against which all the might of the foe hurls itself in vain." (Morgan)

d. **My God of mercy shall come to meet me**: David didn't only believe that the LORD was the **God of mercy** in a distant, theoretical sense. He could confidently say, **My God of mercy**. He knew that God would be merciful to him and that God would **meet** him, even lead him, in his need.

> i. **Shall come to meet me**: "The word *meet* (59:10a) is vivid: It is based on the idea of what is 'in front' of someone, usually in the sense of confronting them by coming to meet them, as in the beautiful phrase of Psalm 21:3. But it can alternatively imply going in front to lead the way." (Kidner)

> ii. Meyer considered that Psalm 59:9-10 uses three titles for God that are precious for the troubled believer: **my God of mercy**, **my defense** [high tower], and **strength**.

> iii. "Meditate on these three attributes. He is the God of your mercy, the Fountain from which pure mercy flows, and nothing but mercy; He is your High Tower, whom you may put between yourself and Saul's hate, He is your Strength, not that you receive strength from Him, but that you appropriate Him as your strength." (Meyer)

> iv. **God shall let me see *my desire* on my enemies**: "Observe that the words, '*my desire*,' are not in the original. From the Hebrew we are taught that David expected to see his enemies without fear. God will enable his servant to gaze steadily upon the foe without trepidation; he shall be calm, and self-possessed, in the hour of peril." (Spurgeon)

2. (11-13) David asks that his enemies be defeated to bring God glory.

Do not slay them, lest my people forget;
Scatter them by Your power,
And bring them down,
O Lord our shield.
For the sin of their mouth *and* the words of their lips,
Let them even be taken in their pride,
And for the cursing and lying *which* they speak.
Consume *them* in wrath, consume *them,*
That they *may* not *be;*
And let them know that God rules in Jacob
To the ends of the earth. Selah

a. **Do not slay them, lest my people forget; scatter them**: David didn't only want the defeat of his enemies. He wanted them defeated in a way that would do the most good for God's **people**. If those enemies were kept alive but scattered, the lesson would last longer.

i. **Lest my people forget** reminds us that whenever David prayed for the destruction of his enemies (and sometimes he prayed quite severely), he had in mind not only his personal deliverance but also what the display of Divine justice would teach God's **people**.

ii. "Hereby it most plainly appears that David, in these and the like imprecations against his enemies, was not moved thereunto by his private malice, or desire of revenge, but by the respect which he had to God's honour and the general good of his people." (Poole)

b. **For the sin of their mouth and the words of their lips, let them even be taken in their pride**: David seemed especially offended at the proud words he overheard from the men who hoped to ambush him. With **cursing and lying** they boasted of David's death and their own advancement through it.

c. **Consume them in wrath, consume them, that they may not be**: Just a few lines before David prayed that God would **not slay them**; now he repeated the prayer **consume them** twice for emphasis. There is no contradiction; we see that such prayers simply expressed David's desire that God "get them," and he didn't care much about how God got them.

d. **Let them know that God rules in Jacob to the ends of the earth**: What David did care about was God's honor and glory. David prayed that the way God dealt with these bloodthirsty assassins would tell **the ends of the earth** something about God's righteous rule in the world.

i. **Let them know that God rules in Jacob to the ends of the earth**: These words are very similar to what David said to Goliath in 1

Samuel 17:46, an event that happened not very long before Saul sent the assassins after David. He discerned that these enemies acted very Goliath-like.

3. (14-15) The abiding danger.

And at evening they return,
They growl like a dog,
And go all around the city.
They wander up and down for food,
And howl if they are not satisfied.

a. **At evening they return, and growl like a dog**: The line from Psalm 59:6 is repeated for emphasis. We sense David peeking through a window at the assassins surrounding his house and seeing them for the pack of dangerous dogs that they are.

b. **They wander up and down for food, and howl if they are not satisfied**: As David watched them, he noticed them **wander** the streets around his house the way hungry dogs hunt for food.

4. (16-17) Singing praise despite the danger.

But I will sing of Your power;
Yes, I will sing aloud of Your mercy in the morning;
For You have been my defense
And refuge in the day of my trouble.
To You, O my Strength, I will sing praises;
For God *is* my defense,
My God of mercy.

a. **But I will sing of Your power**: The murdering dogs howl in the street, but David will **sing** of God's **power** and **mercy**. They wait for him in the evening, but David was confident that with God as his **defense** and **refuge**, he would survive until **morning** and survive singing.

i. "While the wicked are howling, growling, and snarling (vv. 14-15), the servant of God praises the Lord instead." (VanGemeren)

b. **To You, O my Strength, I will sing praises**: Though a conspiracy to kill him still existed in the highest places of the kingdom, David's heart was filled with songs of praise instead of dark fears. He started the psalm asking God for His defense (Psalm 59:1); at the end of the psalm he was so confident that **God is my defense** that he could sing about it.

i. It is easy to read **I will sing** and **I will sing aloud** and **I will sing praises** and assume that the same wording is repeated. Kidner observed that these three phrases used three different words. "Three different words are used for this, which might be rendered 'I will sing...I will shout (59:16); I will raise a psalm (59:17)." (Kidner)

ii. When King Saul sent assassins to David's house, he openly revealed his desire to kill David. From then on, for the next many years (perhaps 10 to 15 years), David had to live as a fugitive, constantly in danger of his life. It's interesting to notice that David entered that period singing praises and was still able to pour out his heart to God in song at the end of that period (2 Samuel 1:17-27).

Psalm 60 – From Defeat to Victory in God

This psalm is titled **To the Chief Musician. Set to "Lily of the Testimony." A Michtam of David. For teaching. When he fought against Mesopotamia and Syria of Zobah, and Joab returned and killed twelve thousand Edomites in the Valley of Salt.**

Lily of the Testimony *may refer to an instrument or to a tune.*

This is a **Michtam**, *a golden psalm of David, intended* **for teaching**, *to instruct his present and future generations, especially about relying upon God and nothing else in conflict.*

The historical markers **against Mesopotamia and Syria of Zobah, and Joab returned and killed twelve thousand Edomites in the Valley of Salt** *place it sometime in the earlier part of King David's reign, when he subjected neighboring nations. 2 Samuel 8:1-8 records David's victories over Philistia, Moab, and Syria. 2 Samuel 10:1-19 tells of David's victories over Ammon and Syria. 1 Chronicles 18:11-13 gives us David's victories over Edom (and specifically in the* **Valley of Salt***), Moab, Ammon, Philistia, and Amalek.*

The victories described in 2 Samuel and 1 Chronicles do not mention the kind of setbacks lamented in this psalm. It reminds us that the historical record often condenses events, and that the successes were real, yet not always immediate.

A. The defeated nation.

1. (1-3) A plea for mercy from God who has afflicted His people.

O God, You have cast us off;
You have broken us down;
You have been displeased;
Oh, restore us again!
You have made the earth tremble;
You have broken it;
Heal its breaches, for it is shaking.

146

You have shown Your people hard things;
You have made us drink the wine of confusion.

a. **O God, You have cast us off; You have broken us down**: David and the armies of Israel fought against foreign armies and experienced some measure of defeat. David knew that when the Lord fought for Israel, victory was assured; if there was defeat, it was likely because of God's displeasure. Therefore David appealed to what he believed to be the ultimate cause, not the immediate cause.

i. Worse than defeat was the sense of separation from God. "God's people live a meaningless existence without his presence. They take defeat seriously, because divine abandonment is the most miserable condition." (VanGemeren)

ii. "But for this psalm and its title we should have had no inkling of the resilience of David's hostile neighbours at the peak of his power." (Kidner)

b. **Oh, restore us again**: If in some way God had caused the defeat of Israel, it did not discourage David from appealing to Him that His favor be restored. This cry, **restore us again**, immediately brings hope to the matter.

i. "To be cast off by God is the worst calamity that can befall a man or a people; but the worst form of it is when the person is not aware of it and is indifferent to it. When the divine desertion causes mourning and repentance, it will be but partial and temporary." (Spurgeon)

c. **You have made the earth tremble**: David felt as if the whole earth shook at the defeat of God's people, yet the God who could shake the earth could also **heal its breaches**.

d. **You have shown Your people hard things; You have made us drink the wine of confusion**: Israel's defeat was hard to understand, and there were many other aspects of their situation that caused David **confusion**. Still, there was a kind of comfort in understanding that God was the author of it all, because what God does in judgment or discipline, He can restore in love and mercy.

i. "*Thou hast showed thy people hard things,* God will be sure to plough his own ground, whatsoever becometh of the waste; and to weed his own garden, though the rest of the world should be let alone to grow wild." (Trapp)

ii. **The wine of confusion**: "We reel as *drunken* men; we are *giddy*, like those who have drank too much wine; but *our giddiness* has been occasioned by the *astonishment* and *dismay* that have taken place in consequence of the prevalence of our enemies, and the unsettled state of the land." (Clarke)

iii. "So far gone was Israel, that only God's interposition could preserve it from utter destruction. How often have we seen churches in this condition, and how suitable is the prayer before us, in which the extremity of the need is used as an argument for help." (Spurgeon)

2. (4-5) Hope in His deliverance.

You have given a banner to those who fear You,
That it may be displayed because of the truth. Selah
That Your beloved may be delivered,
Save *with* Your right hand, and hear me.

a. **You have given a banner to those who fear You**: David felt that God had cast off and broken Israel, yet he would not stop flying the **banner** of allegiance and trust in God. The **truth** about God – who He is and what He has done – demanded that this banner be **displayed**.

i. "He gave them an ensign, which would be both a rallying point for their hosts, a proof that he had sent them to fight, and a guarantee of victory." (Spurgeon)

ii. The concept of the **banner** was connected to Israel's reliance upon God and His victory for them. "When Amalek fought against Israel in Rephidim, victory came to the people of God as Moses, supported by Aaron and Hur, prayed on the mount and Joshua went forth to battle. After the victory Moses built an altar, and called the name of it 'Jehovah Nissi,' that is, Jehovah our Banner." (Morgan)

iii. **Selah**: "Note the 'Selah' at this point, suggesting especial attention to this fact. For the sake of that banner the cry for deliverance is raised." (Morgan)

b. **That Your beloved may be delivered**: Claiming himself as God's **beloved**, despite the present defeat, David understood that his rescue would be found in *greater* allegiance to God, not less.

i. **Beloved**: "The Hebrew word belongs to the language of love poetry; it appeals to the strongest of bonds, the most ardent of relationships." (Kidner)

B. The victorious God.

1. (6-8) God's word of triumph over the nations.

God has spoken in His holiness:
"I will rejoice;
I will divide Shechem

And measure out the Valley of Succoth.
Gilead *is* Mine, and Manasseh *is* Mine;
Ephraim also *is* the helmet for My head;
Judah *is* My lawgiver.
Moab *is* My washpot;
Over Edom I will cast My shoe;
Philistia, shout in triumph because of Me."

a. **I will rejoice**: Speaking as an inspired prophet, David understood the words God Himself spoke. God Himself would **rejoice** in His Lordship over Israel and His victory over the nations.

b. **I will divide Shechem and measure out the Valley of Succoth**: With these and the following lines, God proclaimed how the land of Israel was His special possession. The specific mentions of **Shechem**, of the **Valley of Succoth**, of **Gilead**, of **Manasseh**, of **Ephraim**, and of **Judah** show that God did not speak symbolically, but geographically. Though He is Lord over all the earth, He has a special care and regard for the land of Israel.

i. As the nations battled, it was as if David understood the LORD to step forward and settle the disputes with His authority. "It is no longer a matter of rivals fighting for possession, but of the lord of the manor parceling out his lands and employments exactly as it suits him." (Kidner)

ii. "Ephraim is called a 'helmet' (literally, 'the strength of my head'), symbolic of force; Judah is a 'scepter' (cf. Genesis 49:10), symbolic of dominon and governance." (VanGemeren)

iii. "Note the repeated *mine* and *my*, for everything is His, not theirs, and those to whom He gives it are His tenants and stewards. Yet it is theirs all the more securely for that." (Kidner)

c. **Moab is My washpot; over Edom I will cast My shoe**: God also said that He would exalt Himself over the surrounding nations. Both Moab and Edom were noted for their pride (Isaiah 16:6, Obadiah 3). Here God gives them places of humble service.

i. "The picture of Moab coming with a washbasin for the warrior to wash his feet represents her subjugation to servant status." (VanGemeren)

ii. "*Will I cast out my shoe*, i.e. I will use them like slaves; either holding forth my shoes, that they may pluck them off; or throwing my shoes at them, either in anger or contempt, as the manner of many masters was and is in such cases." (Poole)

2. (9-12) Renewed trust in the God who helps.

Who will bring me *to* the strong city?
Who will lead me to Edom?
Is it **not You, O God,** *who* **cast us off?**
And You, O God, *who* **did not go out with our armies?**
Give us help from trouble,
For the help of man *is* **useless.**
Through God we will do valiantly,
For *it is* **He** *who* **shall tread down our enemies.**

a. **Who will lead me to Edom? Is it not You, O God, who cast us off**: David knew that their previous defeat was because God did not fight for them, **who did not go out with our armies**. He trusted that God would **lead** Israel to victory over **the strong city**.

i. **The strong city**: "When David speaks of '*the* fortified city' he can only mean Petra, the most inaccessible and apparently impregnable mountain stronghold of Edom. Only God could give victory over a fortress like that, and David knew it. So he cries to God, acknowledging that 'the help of man is worthless.'" (Boice)

b. **Give us help from trouble, for the help of man is useless**: David had seen many brave men accomplish great things on the field of battle. Yet for David and for Israel, the help of man was not enough; indeed, it was **useless**. God's help would lead them to victory.

i. "*For vain is the help of man.* As they had lately experimented in *Saul,* a king of their own choosing, but not able to save them from those proud Philistines." (Trapp)

ii. "The king is not looking for a military solution to his problems, such as alliances with other kings, because he knows that their 'help is worthless.'" (VanGemeren)

c. **Through God we will do valiantly, for it is He who shall tread down our enemies**: David understood that it wasn't God's desire for Israel to leave off fighting and passively see what God would do. Instead, they would fight, but fight **through God**. Their fighting through God would be brave and valiant, and in it they would see God **tread down our enemies**. The psalm that began in defeat would end in victory.

i. **We will do valiantly**: "Divine working is not an argument for human inaction, but rather is it the best excitement for courageous effort." (Spurgeon)

ii. "For our part, there will be valiant deeds; for God's part, there will be not only His hand on ours, but His foot on the enemy." (Kidner)

Psalm 61 – Hope and Help When My Heart is Overwhelmed

This psalm is titled **To the Chief Musician. On a stringed instrument. A Psalm of David.** *David was often in trouble; we don't know the life circumstances which prompted this psalm. It does seem to come after he came to the throne. Because of a reference to* the end of the earth, *some have thought it comes from the time of Absalom's rebellion or on his military campaign near the Euphrates (2 Samuel 8:3-4). Those are possible, but by no means certain settings for this psalm.*

On a stringed instrument: *"The word* Neginah *(the singular of* Neginoth*) may be understood to be synonymous with the* kinnor *or harp: that is to say, the instrument of eight strings, probably played with a bow or plectrum." (John Jebb, cited in Charles Spurgeon)*

A. The prayer.

1. (1-2) Crying out for rescue when overwhelmed.

Hear my cry, O God;
Attend to my prayer.
From the end of the earth I will cry to You,
When my heart is overwhelmed;
Lead me to the rock that is higher than I.

a. **Hear my cry, O God; attend to my prayer**: This was wise praying from David. He understood that though God hears all prayer in one sense, in the sense of answering and responding favorably, God does not **hear** or **attend** to all prayer. Opening his prayer this way, David did not presume a response from God, but actively asked for the response.

i. "Pharisees may rest in their prayers; true believers are eager for an answer to them: ritualists may be satisfied when they have '*said* or sung' their litanies and collects, but living children of God will never rest till their supplications have entered the ears of the Lord God of Sabaoth." (Spurgeon)

b. **From the end of the earth I will cry to You**: From what we know, David did not travel far outside the Promised Land. Yet figuratively he was at the end of human understanding and strength and resources; there was a real and powerful sense in which this prayer was offered **from the end of the earth**.

> i. "Though the phrase 'from the ends of the earth' may denote a geographical distance away from the land (cf. Psalm 46:9; Deuteronomy 28:49), it is also a metaphor for despair, alienation, and spiritual distance from the Lord." (VanGemeren)

> ii. David did not say, *from the end of the earth I will give up hope* or *from the end of the earth I will deny that You love me*. At the limit of his wisdom, endurance, and ability, David said, **I will cry to You**.

> iii. "Observe that David never dreamed of seeking any other God; he did not imagine the dominion of Jehovah to be local: he was at the end of the promised land, but he knew himself to be still in the territory of the Great King." (Spurgeon)

c. **When my heart is overwhelmed; lead me to the rock that is higher than I**: David knew there would be times when his heart was **overwhelmed**. In those moments he needed at least three things.

- He needed **the rock**, a place of stability and security, something strong enough to stand against crashing waves or quaking earth.

- He needed a rock **that is higher than I**, a place above himself, above his wisdom, above his abilities.

- He needed God to **lead** him to that rock. David was unable to get to the firm-footed place above his crisis on his own.

> i. **Overwhelmed**: The same word is translated *faints* in Jonah 2:7. "Here David had the added trial of depression or exhaustion; *cf.* the same word...[is found] in the title of Psalm 102, where the condition is subsequently described at some length." (Kidner)

> ii. We are not told why David was **overwhelmed**, and it is better that we do not know. If we knew his specific circumstances, we would be strongly tempted to limit God's rescue only to those in the same situation. God wanted this prayer to be prayed by His people no matter the reason their **heart is overwhelmed**.

> iii. **To the rock**: "The thought of God being a rock is prominent in the Davidic psalms because David had used the rocks of the Judean

wilderness as places of refuge and protection." (Boice)

iv. "His imagination sees towering above him a great cliff, on which, if he could be planted, he might defy pursuit or assault. But he is distant from it, and the inaccessibility which, were he in its clefts, would be his safety, is now his despair. Therefore he turns to God and asks Him to bear him up in His hands, that he may set his foot on that rock." (Maclaren)

d. **To the rock that is higher than I**: Assuming David wrote this as king, humanly speaking he had reached the top of the ladder. He still realized that wasn't enough, and needed something higher than himself.

i. **That is higher than I**: "Thus his prayer was for elevation above self in God." (Morgan)

ii. Ultimately Jesus Christ is the **Rock that is higher than I**. "Higher than I, because of His divine origin; higher, because of His perfect obedience; higher, because of His supreme sufferings; higher, because of his ascension to the right hand of power." (Meyer)

2. (3-4) Present trust based on past faithfulness.

For You have been a shelter for me,
A strong tower from the enemy.
I will abide in Your tabernacle forever;
I will trust in the shelter of Your wings. Selah

a. **For You have been a shelter for me, a strong tower from the enemy**: David remembered that God had answered such prayers in the past. In the past God *Himself* had been a **shelter** and **strong tower** for David.

b. **I will abide in Your tabernacle forever**: The word **tabernacle** is simply the word for *tent*. David had one of two (or perhaps both) ideas in mind:

- The *tent of God* as a refuge for the weary traveler, the place where protection and hospitality are given to the honored guest.

- The *tent of God* as the tabernacle of meeting, the center of Israel's sacrifice and worship.

  i. "The imagery of dwelling in the tent goes back to the desert experience (cf. Exodus 33:7-11; Numbers 11:16-17) when the Lord resided among the tribes of Israel in a tent." (VanGemeren)

  ii. "He saith not, I shall abide in my palace, but in thy tabernacle, which he more highly esteemed." (Trapp)

c. **I will trust in the shelter of Your wings**: Again there may be one of two ideas or the conscious reference to both ideas.

- **Wings** as the near and protected place that a mother bird gives to her offspring, protecting her chicks under **the shelter** of her **wings**.

- **Wings** as that which marked and surrounded the interior of God's tabernacle of meeting and the mercy seat of the ark of the covenant, which included the designs of cherubim and their **wings**.

d. **A shelter...a strong tower...Your tabernacle...the shelter of Your wings**: With image after image, David built upon the idea of *the rock that is higher than I* first stated in Psalm 61:2. No one image could fully express the greatness of God's help to David.

B. The answer to the prayer.

1. (5-7) God's care for King David.

For You, O God, have heard my vows;
You have given *me* the heritage of those who fear Your name.
You will prolong the king's life,
His years as many generations.
He shall abide before God forever.
Oh, prepare mercy and truth, *which* may preserve him!

a. **For You, O God, have heard my vows**: David probably referred to past vows of grateful allegiance to God, which he continued to honor. God **heard** these vows and responded to them, giving David rule over God's people (**the heritage of those who fear Your name**).

i. **You, O God, have heard my vows**: "Often have I purposed to be wholly thine, – to serve thee alone, – to give up my whole life to thy service: and thou hast heard me, and taken me at my word; and given me that heritage, the privilege of enjoying thee in thy ordinances, which is the lot of them that *fear thy name*." (Clarke)

b. **You will prolong the king's life**: David confidently expected God's blessing upon his reign. It was not because he thought so highly of himself; it was because he thought so highly of the God who keeps His promises.

i. "Long 'life' (literally, 'days') is an idiom for the prosperity of the reigning monarch as well as for the preservation of his dynasty, similar to the British 'God save the queen.'" (VanGemeren)

ii. **His years as many generations**: "Thus he speaks, partly because his kingdom was not like Saul's, a matter of one age, expiring with his life, but established to him and his heirs for ever; and partly because Christ, his Son and Heir, should actually and in his own person possess the kingdom for ever." (Poole)

c. **He shall abide before God forever**: David could only say this in reference to himself in a very limited way. He could say it without limitation of the Messiah that was promised to come from his lineage (2 Samuel 7:11-16).

> i. **He shall abide before God forever**: "Literally, 'He shall sit for ever before the faces of God.' He shall ever appear in the presence of God for us." (Clarke)
>
> ii. "The psalm is…[so] Messianic that the everlasting kingdom of the Christ alone fulfils its prayer." (Maclaren)
>
> iii. "The promises of the Lord have found their focus in the messiahship of Jesus the Christ, whose rule is established by the promise and reward of the Father (Ephesians 4:7-13)." (VanGemeren)

d. **Oh, prepare mercy and truth, which may preserve him**: David himself needed this **mercy and truth**, but he also knew that his Greater Son, the promised Messiah, would also rely upon God's **mercy and truth**.

> i. "Let these two (thy mercy and thy truth) be the supporters of his throne, let them be of his lifeguard, let them be his due and prepared portion." (Trapp)
>
> ii. "As men cry, '*Long live the king*,' so we hail with acclamation our enthroned Immanuel, and cry, '*Let mercy and truth preserve him*.' Eternal love and immutable faithfulness are the bodyguards of Jesus' throne." (Spurgeon)

2. (8) Praising God forever.

So I will sing praise to Your name forever,
That I may daily perform my vows.

a. **So I will sing praise to Your name forever**: David began the psalm desperately crying out to God with a heart that was fainting and overwhelmed. The song ends with praise, honoring the character of God as expressed in His **name**, and doing so **forever**.

b. **That I may daily perform my vows**: David knew he had an unending obligation to thank and honor God. It could and should be done **daily** and that **forever**.

> i. "God daily performs his promises, let us daily perform our vows; he keeps his covenant, let us not forget ours." (Spurgeon)
>
> ii. **Forever…daily**: "Here the word *ever* carries the mind illimitably forward, while *day after day* directs it first to what lies immediately ahead." (Kidner)

Psalm 62 – My Only Rock, My Only Salvation

The title of this psalm is **To the Chief Musician. To Jeduthun. A Psalm of David.**

The Chief Musician *is thought by some to be the Lord* G OD *Himself, and others suppose him to be a leader of choirs or musicians in David's time, such as Heman the singer or Asaph (1 Chronicles 6:33, 16:5-7, and 25:6).*

Jeduthun *(mentioned also in the titles of Psalms 39 and 77) was one of the musicians appointed by David to lead Israel's public worship (1 Chronicles 16:41; 25:1-3). Charles Spurgeon wrote regarding Jeduthun: "The sons of Jeduthun were porters or doorkeepers, according to 1 Chronicles 16:42. Those who serve well make the best of singers, and those who occupy the highest posts in the choir must not be ashamed to wait at the posts of the doors of the Lord's house."*

A. Waiting upon God, who is my rock and defense.

1. (1-2) David's soul silently waits for God.

> **Truly my soul silently *waits* for God;**
> **From Him *comes* my salvation.**
> **He only *is* my rock and my salvation;**
> **He is my defense;**
> **I shall not be greatly moved.**

> a. **Truly my soul silently waits for God**: The emphasis in this line is of *surrendered silence* before God and God *alone*. The word **truly** is often translated *alone* or *only* and seems to have that sense here.

> > i. "It is hard to see this in the English text, because the Hebrew is almost untranslatable, but in the Hebrew text the word *only* or *alone* occurs five times in the first eight verses (in verses 1, 2, 4, 5, 6), and once in verse 9." (Boice) Kidner said of this Hebrew word *ak*, "It is an emphasizer, to underline a statement or to point to a contrast; its insistent repetition gives the psalm a tone of special earnestness."

156

ii. "The words have all been said – or perhaps no words will come – and the issue rests with Him alone." (Kidner)

iii. "The natural mind is ever prone to *reason,* when we ought *to believe;* to be *at work,* when we ought to be *quiet;* to go our own way, when we ought steadily to walk on in God's ways." (Müller, cited in Spurgeon)

iv. "This is why God keeps you waiting. All that is of self and nature must be silence; one voice after another cease to boast; one light after another be put out; until the soul is shut up to God alone." (Meyer)

b. **From Him comes my salvation**: In many psalms David began by telling his great need or describing his present crisis. Here, David began by declaring his great confidence in and trust upon God.

i. Psalm 62 seems to come from a time of trouble, yet it *asks God for nothing*. It is full of faith and trust, but has no fear, no despair, and no petition.

ii. "There is in it throughout not one single word (and this is a rare occurrence), in which the prophet expresses *fear* or *dejection;* and there is also no prayer in it, although, on other occasions, when in danger, he never omits to pray." (Amyraut, cited in Spurgeon)

c. **He only is my rock and my salvation**: David trusted in God alone for his strength and stability. The description is of a man completely focused upon God for His help, firmly resolved to look nowhere else.

i. "Because God *only* is our Rock, let us ever be silent *only* for God." (Morgan)

ii. **He is my defense**: Or, *fortress*. "The tried believer not only abides in God as in a cavernous rock; but dwells in him as Warrior in some bravely defiant tower or lordly castle." (Spurgeon)

2. (3-4) David complains to his enemies and of his enemies.

How long will you attack a man?
You shall be slain, all of you,
Like a leaning wall and a tottering fence.
They only consult to cast *him* down from his high position;
They delight in lies;
They bless with their mouth,
But they curse inwardly. Selah

a. **How long will you attack a man**: David's faith was in God alone, but he had words for his enemies. He rebuked them for their crazy persistence in attacking him, and warned them of judgment to come (**you shall be slain**).

b. **Like a leaning wall and a tottering fence**: David's image is clear enough, but there is disagreement among translators and commentators as to whom this applies. The New King James Version presents the opponents of David as the **leaning wall and a tottering fence**. Others think that David himself was the **leaning wall**, in his weakness unfairly set upon by his enemies.

> i. Spurgeon gave the sense of the first: "Boastful persecutors bulge and swell with pride, but they are only as a bulging wall ready to fall in a heap; they lean forward to seize their prey, but it is only as a tottering fence inclines to the earth upon which it will soon lie at length." (Spurgeon)

> ii. The English Standard Version gives the second sense: *How long will all of you attack a man to batter him, like a leaning wall, a tottering fence.*

c. **They only consult to cast him down**: David described his enemies as those who only think through a matter if it involves bringing down a man of God. They were liars, especially in the sense of being two-faced (**they bless with their mouth, but they curse inwardly**).

3. (5-7) David's calm confidence in God alone.

My soul, wait silently for God alone,
For my expectation *is* from Him.
He only *is* my rock and my salvation;
***He is* my defense;**
I shall not be moved.
In God *is* my salvation and my glory;
The rock of my strength,
***And* my refuge, *is* in God.**

a. **My soul, wait silently for God alone**: In the opening lines of the psalm, David said that this *was* the state of his soul. Here he spoke to his **soul**, telling it to remain in that place of trust in and surrender to God. David's complete **expectation** was upon God.

> i. "David now urges on himself the silence which he simply stated in verse 1." (Kidner)

> ii. **For God alone**: "They trust not God *at all* who trust him not *alone*. He that stands with one foot on a rock, and another foot upon a quicksand, will sink and perish, as certainly as he that standeth with both feet upon a quicksand. David knew this, and therefore calleth earnestly upon his soul (for his business lay most within doors) to trust only upon God." (Trapp)

b. **He only is my rock and my salvation**: David assured himself by repeating the lines from Psalm 62:2. It *was* true for David and he wanted it to *remain* true.

> i. **He is my defense**: "Not my defender only, but my actual protection." (Spurgeon)

c. **I shall not be moved**: David repeated the idea from Psalm 62:2, but with this small variation. In verse 2 he wrote, *I shall not be greatly moved*. In this verse he seems to come to an even stronger position: **I shall not be moved**.

> i. "There may be deep meaning in the slight omission of 'greatly' in the second refrain. Confidence has grown." (Maclaren)

d. **My refuge is in God**: The emphasis again reflects David's decision to trust in nothing or no one else. God alone is his **salvation**, his **glory**, his **rock**, his **strength**, and his **refuge**. We sense David was tempted to trust many different things, but he refused and kept his expectation in God alone.

> i. "Observe how the Psalmist brands his own initials upon every name which he rejoicingly gives to his God – *my* expectation, *my* rock, *my* salvation, *my* glory, *my* strength, *my* refuge; he is not content to know that the Lord is all these things; he acts in faith towards him, and lays claim to him under every character." (Spurgeon)

B. David teaches others and teaches himself.

1. (8) Teaching the people to trust in God.

Trust in Him at all times, you people;
Pour out your heart before Him;
God *is* a refuge for us. Selah

a. **Trust in Him at all times, you people**: David felt what was good for him was good for others, also. As a leader of God's people he spoke wisdom to them, reminding them that God was worthy **at all times** of their **trust in Him**.

> i. "The comforts which David had found, he exhorteth others to seek, in faith and prayer." (Spurgeon)

b. **Pour out your heart before Him**: God's strength and stability made David rightly think of Him as a **rock**. Yet God was not insensitive or unfeeling like a rock. God invites His people to **pour out** their heart – their sorrows, their joys, their trust, and their doubt, all of it – **before Him**.

> i. "Pour it out as water. Not as milk, whose colour remains. Not as wine, whose savour remains. Not as honey, whose taste remains. But

as water, of which, when it is poured out, nothing remains." (Le Blanc, cited in Spurgeon)

c. **God is a refuge for us**: He welcomes the poured-out heart as the cities of refuge welcomed the hunted man in ancient Israel.

2. (9-10) Teaching the people what not to trust in.

Surely men of low degree *are* a vapor,
Men of high degree *are* a lie;
If they are weighed on the scales,
They *are* altogether *lighter* than vapor.
Do not trust in oppression,
Nor vainly hope in robbery;
If riches increase,
Do not set *your* heart *on them*.

a. **Surely men of low degree are a vapor, men of high degree are a lie**: This psalm speaks much of trusting in God alone. Now David explained why it was important to *not* set trust in man. David understood that whether they are men of **low degree** or **high degree**, they are **altogether lighter than vapor**. There is no substance there worthy of trust.

i. "Common men can give no help. They are vanity, and it is folly to trust in them; for although they may be *willing*, yet they have no *ability* to help you: 'Rich men are a lie.' They promise much, but perform nothing; they cause you to *hope*, but mock your *expectation*." (Clarke)

ii. However, it is possible that David did not intend the reader to understand a distinction between **men of low degree** and **men of high degree**; it may simply be an expression of Hebrew poetic repetition and parallelism. "The distinction of 'lowborn men' and 'the highborn' is based on the different words for 'man' in the MT [Masoretic Text]: *adam* and *ish* (62:9; cf. 49:2). But it is equally possible to treat both [parts] of 62:9 as a general reference to mankind: 'mankind is but a breath; mankind is but a lie.'" (VanGemeren)

iii. "The point, then, is not so much that we have nothing to *fear* from man (as in Psalm 27:1ff.), as that we have nothing to hope from him." (Kidner)

b. **Do not trust in oppression, nor vainly hope in robbery**: David had seen men advance through cruel or dishonest ways. He warned the people against this, understanding that the results never justify the evil used to get the results.

c. **If riches increase, do not set your heart on them**: As a king, David ended up being a very wealthy man, though most of his earlier years were lived in deep poverty. David knew what it was to see **riches increase**, and he knew the foolishness of setting one's **heart on them**. It's possible to hold great wealth without trusting in those riches, but it isn't easy.

i. "If they grow in an honest, providential manner, as the result of industry or commercial success, do not make much account of the circumstance; be not unduly elated, do not fix your love upon your money-bags." (Spurgeon)

ii. There are at least three ways in which one may **set** the **heart** on riches.

- To take excessive pleasure in riches, making them the source of joy for life.
- To place one's hope and security in riches.
- To grow proud and arrogant because of riches.

iii. "Whether rightly or wrongly won, they are wrongly used if they are trusted in." (Maclaren)

iv. "Riches are themselves transient things; therefore they should have but our transient thoughts." (Caryl, cited in Spurgeon)

v. "As we must not rest in men, so neither must we repose in money. Gain and fame are only so much foam of the sea." (Spurgeon)

vi. "1 Timothy 6:17ff. may be alluding to this verse in its own careful treatment of the subject." (Kidner)

3. (11-12) Teaching himself about God's power and mercy.

God has spoken once,
Twice I have heard this:
That power *belongs* to God.
Also to You, O Lord, *belongs* mercy;
For You render to each one according to his work.

a. **God has spoken once, twice I have heard this: that power belongs to God**: This truth was deeply ingrained in David's soul. Through repetition he understood that **power belongs to God** and to none other. This is why David was so determined to trust in God and God alone.

i. Since **power belongs to God**, David refused to look for strength anywhere else. Since **power belongs to God**, David did not long for power unto himself. Since **power belongs to God**, David did not become arrogant as a ruler, knowing any power he held was as God's representative.

b. **Also to You, O Lord, belongs mercy**: Gratefully, David understood that God's nature was much more than **power**. He also is rich in **mercy**. Just as men could and should look to God for **power**, so they should look to Him for **mercy**.

i. **Mercy** translates one of the great words of the Old Testament, *hesed*. It may perhaps be better translated as *love, lovingkindness,* or *loyal love*. David knew **power belongs to God**, but that God is a God of love who is loyal and good to His people.

ii. "The second attribute used to be translated 'mercy', but verse 12 makes it particularly clear that this word (*hesed*) has its basis in what is true and dependable. It is closely linked with covenant-keeping, hence the modern translations, *steadfast love* or 'true love.'" (Kidner)

iii. "David says that he has learned two lessons: that God is strong and that God is loving." (Boice)

iv. This meant that David had no expectation of mercy from man. If it came he was pleased, but he knew that ultimately this great covenant love [**mercy**] belonged to God.

v. "This tender attribute sweetens the grand thought of his power: the divine strength will not crush us, but will be used for our good; God is so full of mercy that it belongs to him, as if all the mercy in the universe came from God, and still was claimed by him as his possession." (Spurgeon)

vi. "This is the only truly worthy representation of God. Power without love is brutality, and love without power is weakness. Power is the strong foundation of love, and love is the beauty and the crown of power." (Perowne, cited in Boice)

vii. "The power of God is more than the strength of the adversaries; the mercy of God is equal to dealing with all the need of the failing soul." (Morgan)

c. **For You render to each one according to his work**: We don't normally think of this as an expression of God's **mercy**. In some ways it sounds more like God's *judgment*. Yet David had in mind the good person whose goodness is despised by this world. The God of mercy would reward their goodness (even on a relative measure) as the world ignored or rejected it.

i. "Man neither helps us nor rewards us; God will do both." (Spurgeon)

ii. "To all mankind, therefore, the prophet here recommendeth meditation on these two most interesting subject; the 'power' of God to punish sin, and his 'mercy' to pardon it. Fear of the former will beget desire of the later." (Horne)

Psalm 63 – Love Better than Life

The title of this psalm is, **A Psalm of David when he was in the wilderness of Judah.** *Most commentators believe it to belong either to David's wilderness years before he came to the throne of Israel, or to his brief exile from the throne in the rebellion of Absalom. The wilderness years when hunted by King Saul are preferred, but not held with absolute certainty.*

Charles Spurgeon added a note of interest: "Chrysostom tells us that among the primitive Christians it was decreed and ordained that no day should pass without the public singing of this psalm."

A. Praise from the wilderness.

1. (1-2) David's thirst for God.

O God, You *are* my God;
Early will I seek You;
My soul thirsts for You;
My flesh longs for You
In a dry and thirsty land
Where there is no water.
So I have looked for You in the sanctuary,
To see Your power and Your glory.

a. **O God, You are my God**: This may seem like senseless repetition, a tautology. It is not; David declared to *Elohim* that He was David's *El*, David's God in the most fundamental sense. In a day when pagans thought there were many gods and each nation had their own gods, David sweeps such ideas aside and proclaimed his allegiance to *Elohim*.

i. "The simplicity and boldness of *Thou art my God* is the secret of all that follows, since this relationship is the heart of the covenant, from the patriarchs to the present day (Genesis 17:8c; Hebrews 8:10c)." (Kidner)

b. **Early will I seek You**: Appreciating God as God, it is entirely reasonable to **seek** Him, and to seek Him as a priority of the day. The thirst of David's soul demanded to be satisfied **early** in the day.

> i. "What first lays hold of the heart in the morning is likely to occupy the place all the day. First impressions are the most durable, because there is not a multitude of ideas to drive them out, or prevent them from being deeply fixed in the moral feeling." (Clarke)

> ii. "The word '*early*' has not only the sense of early in the morning, but that of eagerness, immediateness. He who truly longs for God longs for him now." (Spurgeon)

> iii. **My flesh longs for You**: "*Longeth;* or, *languisheth*, or *pineth away*. The desire of my soul after thee is so vehement and insatiable, that my very body feels the effects of it, as it commonly doth of all great passions." (Poole)

> iv. "Most people do not even know that it is God their souls truly desire. They are seeking satisfaction in other things." (Boice)

c. **So I have looked for You in the sanctuary**: David sought God at the tabernacle as earnestly as a thirsty man looks for water **in a dry and thirsty land**. The Wilderness of Judah is largely desert, so this was a picture of longing that came easily to David's mind.

> i. "There was no desert in his heart, though there was a desert around him." (Spurgeon)

> ii. **In a dry and thirsty land**: "Learn from this, and do not say, 'I will get into communion with God when I feel better,' but long for communion now. It is one of the temptations of the devil to tell you not to pray when you do not feel like praying. Pray twice as much then." (Spurgeon)

d. **To see Your power and Your glory**: David sought God at the tabernacle to connect in some way with God's **power** and **glory**. Significantly, David was *not* at the tabernacle when he sang this song; he was in the Wilderness of Judah. Yet he knew that's God's **sanctuary** was not only a place, but also a spiritual concept that could be entered by faith no matter where a person was.

> i. "Our misery is that we thirst so little for these sublime things, and so much for the mocking trifles of time and sense." (Spurgeon)

2. (3-6) The greatness of God's love stirs praise.

Because Your lovingkindness *is* better than life,
My lips shall praise You.

Thus I will bless You while I live;
I will lift up my hands in Your name.
My soul shall be satisfied as with marrow and fatness,
And my mouth shall praise You with joyful lips.
When I remember You on my bed,
I meditate on You in the *night* watches.

a. **Because Your lovingkindness is better than life**: This is the reason why David was so motivated to pursue God. The **lovingkindness** (*hesed*) of God was **better**, more meaningful to David, than **life** itself. This means that David both knew and experienced something of God's **lovingkindness** that many believers today do not know and experience.

- People regard life as natural; David regarded God's great love as natural.

- People enjoy life; David enjoyed God's great love.

- People value life; David valued God's great love.

- People will sacrifice to live; David would sacrifice for God's great love.

- People want to give life to others; David wanted to give God's great love.

- People despair without the sense of life; David despaired without the sense of God's great love.

i. Life and literature are filled with people who loved someone or something more than their own life, and it could be said of them that they held love **better than life**. Yet that *is not* what David sang of here. David meant that the *love of God to him* was more precious than his own life.

ii. "Now you know at what a high rate men value their lives; they will bleed, sweat, vomit, purge, part with an estate, yea, with a limb, yea, limbs, to preserve their lives.... Now, though life be so dear and precious to a man, yet a deserted soul prizes the returnings of divine favour upon him above life, yea, above many lives." (Brooks, cited in Spurgeon)

iii. "To dwell with God is better than life at its best; life at ease, in a palace, in health, in honour, in wealth, in pleasure; yea, a thousand lives are not equal to the eternal life which abides in Jehovah's smile." (Spurgeon)

iv. "He knew a pearl of far greater price, namely, the 'loving-kindness' of Jehovah, on which is suspended not only the life which now is, but that which is to come." (Horne)

v. **Better than life**: "Many men have been weary of their lives, as is evident in Scripture and history; but no man was ever yet found that was weary of the love and favour of God." (Brooks, cited in Spurgeon)

b. **My lips shall praise You**: In light of David's experience of God's great love, he determined to vocally praise God. David thought that he would be ungrateful and rude to not praise and thank the God who loved him so greatly.

i. "If we have nothing to say about God's goodness, the probable cause is our want of experience of it." (Maclaren)

ii. "May I ask a question of every professed Christian? Have you spoken with God this morning? Do you allow a day to pass without converse with God? Can it be right for us to treat the Lord with mute indifference?" (Spurgeon)

iii. Psalm 63 speaks of praise and devotion given to God in gratitude, out of a rich sense of being blessed. Spurgeon noted that we should not limit our thanks and praise to such seasons: "Even when our heart is rather desiring than enjoying we should still continue to magnify the Most High, for his love is truly precious; even if we do not personally, for the time being, happen to be rejoicing in it. We ought not to make our praises of God to depend upon our own personal and present reception of benefits; this would be mere selfishness: even publicans and sinners have a good word for those whose hands are enriching them with gifts; it is the true believer only who will bless the Lord when he takes away his gifts or hides his face." (Spurgeon)

c. **Thus I will bless You**: David did not mean this in the sense that a greater person bestows a blessing on a lesser. David meant this in the sense that it blessed and honored God when His creatures praised Him and thanked Him appropriately.

d. **I will lift up my hands in Your name**: The lifting of the hands was not only the common posture of prayer among the ancient Hebrews, it was especially appropriate for praise. It displayed the anticipation of gratefully receiving from God, and the sense of surrender to Him.

e. **My soul shall be satisfied as with marrow and fatness**: David spoke of a satisfaction that too few people know, even among believers. He spoke of the deep satisfaction that comes in a surrendered seeking of God, of receiving His great love, of praising God without reservation.

i. "There is in the love of God a richness, a sumptuousness, a fulness of soul-filling joy, comparable to the richest food with which the body can be nourished." (Spurgeon)

f. **When I remember You on my bed, I meditate on You in the night watches**: David thought that there were not enough hours in the day to think upon God's greatness and goodness. Therefore he also used the **night watches** to **meditate** upon God.

i. **Night watches**: "An expression which stresses the slow progress of the hours." (Kidner)

ii. "Solitude and stillness render the 'night watches' a fit season for meditation on the so often experienced mercies of God; which, when thus called to remembrance, become a delicious repast to the spirit, filling it with all joy, and peace, and consolation." (Horne)

B. Thankful confidence in God.

1. (7-8) Thanks for help already given.

Because You have been my help,
Therefore in the shadow of Your wings I will rejoice.
My soul follows close behind You;
Your right hand upholds me.

a. **Because You have been my help**: Many of David's psalms are simple cries for help. Since this psalm was composed from the Wilderness of Judah, there was certainly help David could ask for. Yet, Psalm 63 has no cry for help but gives thanks and praise for God's faithfulness in many times when God had **been my help** for David.

b. **Therefore in the shadow of Your wings I will rejoice**: The idea of the shelter of **shadow** of God's wings is repeated many times in the psalms. Sometimes it has the idea of *protection*, as a mother bird shelters her young chicks. Other times it has the idea of *presence*, as in the wings of the cherubim that surround the throne of God. Here the idea of *presence* seems to best fit the context.

c. **My soul follows close behind You; Your right hand upholds me**: This speaks of the partnership and connection the believer experiences with God. David's **soul** was close to God, following Him as one followed a Master or Teacher. God responded with care and strength for David, upholding him with His mighty **right hand** (the hand of skill and strength).

i. **My soul follows close**: "Press toward the mark. Let there be no needless space between the Master and thee." (Meyer)

ii. The connection expressed by **my soul follows close** is truly close. The words translated **follow close** have the sense of joining or gluing together, as in Genesis 2:24.

iii. "The primary sense of [the Hebrew word is] to glue together; from thence it signifies figuratively *to associate,* to adhere to, to be united with; and particularly to be firmly united with strong affection." (Chandler, cited in Spurgeon)

2. (9-10) Trust despite the trouble.

But those *who* seek my life, to destroy *it*,
Shall go into the lower parts of the earth.
They shall fall by the sword;
They shall be a portion for jackals.

a. **But those who seek my life, to destroy it**: David's deep communion with God did not take away his problems. There were still those who wanted to kill him. According to its title, Psalm 63 was written from *the Wilderness of Judah* and David was in the wilderness hiding from a conspiracy to kill him.

b. **They shall fall by the sword**: David trusted God to deal with his enemies, especially with King Saul. In God's time and in God's way, David's enemies did **fall by the sword**, which has the sense of being killed in battle.

i. "He knows that the 'steadfast love' of God which he praised in verse 3, is strong with justice (*cf.* 62:12)." (Kidner)

ii. **A portion for jackals**: "If the body of a human being were to be left on the ground, the *jackals* would certainly leave but little traces of it; and in the olden times of warfare, they must have held high revelry in the battle-fields after the armies had retired. It is to this propensity of the *jackal* that David refers – himself a man of war, who had fought on many a battle-field, and must have seen the carcasses of the slain mangled by these nocturnal prowlers." (Wood, cited in Spurgeon)

iii. "*Jackals* make sense here, rather than the 'foxes' of some older translations (one Hebrew word serves for both). They are the final scavengers, consuming the remains of the kill rejected by the larger beasts." (Kidner)

3. (11) The king's confidence.

But the king shall rejoice in God;
Everyone who swears by Him shall glory;
But the mouth of those who speak lies shall be stopped.

a. **But the king shall rejoice in God**: David was not yet on Israel's throne and that promise still waited many years for fulfillment. Yet it was a promise of God (first expressed in 1 Samuel 16), so by faith David could dare to think of himself as **the king**, and in that daring faith **rejoice in God**.

i. "*The king;* I, who am already anointed king, and who shall be actually king, when these mine enemies are fallen by the sword. He speaks of himself in the third person, either out of modesty or out of prudence." (Poole)

b. **Everyone who swears by Him shall glory; but the mouth of those who speak lies shall be stopped**: The sense of **swears by Him** is to trust in God and place one's confident love in Him; men normally take oaths upon what they hold dear. The contrast to trusting God is to **speak lies**; we resort to lies when we don't trust God. One of these paths has a future of **glory** and the other path will **be stopped**.

i. "Two things are necessary for such triumph as this. These are indicated in the opening words of the psalm. First, there must be the consciousness of personal relationship, 'O God, Thou art my God'; and, second, there must be earnest seeking after God: 'Early will I seek Thee.' Relationship must be established. Fellowship must be cultivated." (Morgan)

Psalm 64 – Secret Plots and Sudden Shots

This psalm is titled **To the Chief Musician. A Psalm of David.** *As with many of David's psalms, it concerns a crisis that made him cry out to God. It is impossible to connect this psalm to a specific event in David's life with certainty.*

A. The wicked attack.

1. (1-4) Word weapons of the wicked.

Hear my voice, O God, in my meditation;
Preserve my life from fear of the enemy.
Hide me from the secret plots of the wicked,
From the rebellion of the workers of iniquity,
Who sharpen their tongue like a sword,
And bend *their bows to shoot* their arrows—bitter words,
That they may shoot in secret at the blameless;
Suddenly they shoot at him and do not fear.

a. **Hear my voice, O God, in my meditation**: This is an interesting turn of phrase. Either David meant that his meditation was vocal so that God could hear his voice, or that God would hear the silent expression of his heart as his voice. Either way, as with many times in the psalms, David cried out to God for help.

i. "He can but pray, but he can pray; and no man is helpless who can look up. However high and closely engirdling may be the walls that men or sorrows build around us, there is always an opening in the dungeon roof, through which heaven is visible and prayers can mount." (Maclaren)

b. **Preserve my life from fear of the enemy**: The word **fear** is commonly translated *dread* and speaks of something greater than the normal fear of battle. David knew how crippling this kind of *dread* could be and prayed to be kept from it.

170

i. "In the second line, note the word *dread*, which is paralyzing, whereas fear can be sobering and healthy." (Kidner)

ii. "Every sentence reveals the relentless fury and remorseless subtlety and cruelty of the foes by whom he was surrounded. Conscious of all this he had one fear, and that was that he should be afraid of them." (Morgan)

iii. "We need to pray as the psalmist does, not so much for the deliverance from enemies as for deliverance from fear of them." (Morgan)

c. **Hide me from the secret plots of the wicked**: David knew there were dangerous enemies plotting his destruction. He felt powerless to make them stop, so he prayed. The New International Version gives a good sense of this in translating, *Hide me from the conspiracy of the wicked*.

i. "This is the singer's distress. The warfare is unequal. His foes are not out in the open, but under cover." (Morgan)

ii. "Their methods cannot afford to be those of honest opposition ('the open statement of the truth', 2 Corinthians 4:2; *cf.* 'I opposed him to his face', Galatians 2:11)." (Kidner)

d. **Who sharpen their tongue like a sword, and bend their bows to shoot their arrows – bitter words**: The **secret plots** against David consisted in words and lies against him, all pushing towards his destruction and death. This was not a case of words merely hurting; this was an active conspiracy to kill.

i. "In the context of this war of lies and innuendo, the *ambush* will be either the prepared situation which 'frames' an innocent man, or the shelter of anonymity from which a rumour can be launched *without fear*." (Kidner)

ii. "An open liar is an angel compared with this demon. Vipers and cobras are harmless and amiable creatures compared with such a reptile. The devil himself might blush at being the father of so base an offspring." (Spurgeon)

e. **Suddenly they shoot at him and do not fear**: David knew that his enemies fired their **bitter words** as arrows against him, and when they did, it didn't bother them in the least. They did not fear either David or God.

i. Psalm 64 emphasizes the devious nature of David's enemies. They use **secret plots**. They **shoot in secret**. They attack **suddenly**. Especially because David mentions an attack by **arrows** from a hidden or **secret position**, his enemies act like the ancient version of snipers.

ii. "The key word in Psalm 64 is *suddenly*, meaning 'unexpectedly' or 'without warning.'" (Boice)

iii. David knew how dangerous it was in battle if a hidden archer worked as a sniper. If he could see and confront his enemy one-on-one, a warrior such as David liked his chances. The hidden sniper was of great concern, to be put down by an arrow he never saw coming.

iv. David's enemies didn't use literal arrows, but they attacked him secretly, anonymously, without the courage to say things to his face. They shot at him like a sniper shoots at a man who has no way to defend himself.

2. (5-6) The secret plotting of an evil matter.

They encourage themselves *in* an evil matter;
They talk of laying snares secretly;
They say, "Who will see them?"
They devise iniquities:
"We have perfected a shrewd scheme."
Both the inward thought and the heart of man are deep.

a. **They encourage themselves in an evil matter**: It would be bad enough that an individual purposed this against David, but it was worse than that. Many people had conspired against him, planning secret traps and **snares**, unafraid before God or man (**Who will see them?**).

i. "They foolishly believe that they are not accountable to anyone, as is expressed by their confident question." (VanGemeren)

ii. **They encourage themselves**: "Good men are frequently discouraged, and not unfrequently discourage one another, but the children of darkness are wise in their generation and keep their spirits up, and each one has a cheering word to say to his fellow villain." (Spurgeon)

b. **We have perfected a shrewd scheme**: They were proud in their evil plotting. They boasted of their sins, showing the dark depth of their **thought** and **heart**.

i. **They devise iniquities**: "They search the devil's skull for new inventions; who is ready enough to lend them his seven heads to plot and his ten horns to push at good people." (Trapp)

ii. **The inward thought and heart of man are deep**: "The Hebrew literally speaks of men's hearts as being 'deep,' the idea being that they are almost bottomless in their supply of evil deeds and cunning." (Boice)

B. God responds.

1. (7-9) God answers back with His own arrow.

But God shall shoot at them *with* an arrow;
Suddenly they shall be wounded.
So He will make them stumble over their own tongue;
All who see them shall flee away.
All men shall fear,
And shall declare the work of God;
For they shall wisely consider His doing.

a. **But God shall shoot at them with an arrow**: The evil men opposing David acted as if they had all the arrows, but David knew that God was his defense, and God was well-armed. God had an arrow of His own, and **suddenly they shall be wounded**.

i. David's enemies shot at him like snipers, from hidden and high positions. David's friend was **God**, in a higher and more hidden position. They shot their poisonous words at David unexpectedly, without warning [*suddenly*, Psalm 64:4]. God would shoot back at them unexpectedly, without warning – **suddenly**. God had them in His sights.

ii. **Suddenly they shall be wounded** reminds us that often the judgment of God comes upon the wicked unexpectedly, without any warning. They think everything is fine until they are **wounded**.

iii. "The brevity of God's countermeasures, after the elaborate scheming of the wicked, tells its own decisive tale." (Kidner)

b. **He will make them stumble over their own tongue**: They used their lies and slanders to attack David, but God would find a way to make their own words their ruin. They would trip in the very way they hoped to trap David.

c. **All men shall fear, and shall declare the work of God**: David was confident that God would use His dealings against these wicked men as a lesson to others. When they saw the evil plotters wounded by God, they would learn.

i. Previously the wicked asked, "Who will see them?" (Psalm 64:5). The answer is, *everyone will see them*, because God will use them to teach a lesson to **all men**.

ii. *When Your judgments are in the earth, the inhabitants of the world will learn righteousness.* (Isaiah 26:9b)

iii. "Those who might have been bold in sin shall be made to tremble and to stand in awe of the righteous Judge." (Spurgeon)

2. (10) Resolution for the righteous.

The righteous shall be glad in the LORD, and trust in Him.
And all the upright in heart shall glory.

    a. **The righteous shall be glad in the LORD**: God's dealing with the wicked would be a lesson to all men, but it would be special joy to the righteous. They had special reason to **be glad** that God was vindicated and His servant was protected.

        i. "As sorrow, sooner or later, will be the portion of Messiah's enemies, so joy is the high privilege of his friends and disciples." (Horne)

    b. **And trust in Him**: It would not only bring joy, but also increase faith. God's faithful answer to prayer would demonstrate that He is worthy of **trust**, and build the faith of the **righteous**.

        i. "Their observation of providence shall increase their faith; since he who fulfils his threatenings will not forget his promises." (Spurgeon)

        ii. "So the answer of verse 1, to be preserved from panic, is more than answered. The judgment is still future, but joy can break out already. It is a sober joy, with the facts faced at their worst, but also at their overwhelming best." (Kidner)

Psalm 65 – At the Temple, In the Earth

The title of this psalm is **To the Chief Musician. A Psalm of David. A Song.**
Charles Spurgeon observed this about the uncommon pairing of **Psalm** *and* **Song**
*for this composition: "The Hebrew calls it a Shur and Mizmor, a combination of
psalm and song, which may be best described by the term, 'A Lyrical Poem.' In this
case the psalm may be said or sung, and be equally suitable."*

*We don't know the occasion of this psalm, but because of its thankfulness and praise
connected to flocks and grain, many think it was composed for a harvest festival,
perhaps the Feast of Tabernacles in the fall season.*

A. God in His temple.

1. (1-3) Why praise waits for God in Jerusalem.

Praise is awaiting You, O God, in Zion;
And to You the vow shall be performed.
O You who hear prayer,
To You all flesh will come.
Iniquities prevail against me;
***As for* our transgressions,**
You will provide atonement for them.

> a. **Praise is awaiting You, O God, in Zion**: The psalmist David described
> a wonderful picture, the idea that **praise** was waiting to be given unto God
> in Jerusalem. The sense is that when God came to meet His people, He
> would be received in an atmosphere of praise.

> > i. "The word translated 'waiteth' [**awaiting**] comes from a root
> > meaning to be dumb.... This does not mean that there is no praise, but
> > on the contrary that praise is so complete that at first it can find no
> > utterance." (Morgan)

ii. "Literally, 'Praise is silence for thee'.... It may sometimes be the height of worship, in other words, to fall silent before God in awe at His presence and in submission to His will." (Kidner)

iii. "Certainly, when the soul is most filled with adoring awe, she is least content with her own expressions, and feels most deeply how inadequate are all mortal songs to proclaim the divine goodness." (Spurgeon)

b. **To You the vow shall be performed**: God's people would gather together in Jerusalem to thank God for answering their prayers and to give sacrifices and praise in fulfillment of vows made.

i. Believers should take seriously their vows before God. In addition to vows and promises made to God, our baptism is itself a vow to God. Our association with God's people is a vow. These should be regarded with a solemn and serious dependence upon God.

ii. "A vow unkept will burn the conscience like a hot iron. Vows of service, of donation, of praise, or whatever they may be, are no trifles; and in the day of grateful praise they should, without fail, be fulfilled to the utmost of our power." (Spurgeon)

iii. At Mount Zion the Son of David fulfilled the greatest vow, coming to completely do the will of God (Psalm 40:6-8) and giving His life as a sacrifice and atonement for the sins of the world.

c. **O You who hear prayer, to You all flesh will come**: Praise awaits and vows are performed because God hears and answers prayer. This goodness of God draws not only Israel, but also **all flesh**. This starts a thought that will be developed later in the psalm.

d. **Iniquities prevail against me; as for our transgressions, You will provide atonement for them**: This shows a proper understanding of the sacrificial system in God's greater plan. David understood his personal struggle against sin, and how he sometimes failed in that struggle. He also understood that God's answer for **transgressions** is an atoning sacrifice that *God* provides.

i. David was humble enough to say, **iniquities prevail against me**. "No man was ever rejected by God for his confessed badness, as sundry have been for their supposed goodness." (Trapp)

ii. **Iniquities prevail against me**: "Our sins would, but for grace, prevail against us in the court of divine justice, in the court of conscience, and in the battle of life." (Spurgeon)

iii. David believed in the system of animal sacrifice established by the Law of Moses, but he also looked beyond that system to a perfect sacrifice that God Himself would provide. In this David looked to the Messiah and His perfect, atoning work on the cross fulfilling the promise, **You will provide atonement for them**.

2. (4) The goodness of God's house.

Blessed *is the man* You choose,
And cause to approach *You*,
***That* he may dwell in Your courts.**
We shall be satisfied with the goodness of Your house,
Of Your holy temple.

a. **Blessed is the man You choose, and cause to approach You**: In the connection between God and man, David knew that God was the cause of the connection. The connection begins when God chooses and then causes a man or a woman to come to Him, **that he may dwell in Your courts**.

i. Some think that the chosen man in David's mind is the priest. Yet he mentions the part of the house of God where all were welcome, the **courts**. "He mentioneth courts, because the people were permitted to go no further into God's house." (Poole)

ii. If there is a priest in view, then prophetically we can apply this in an ultimate sense to Jesus, our Great High Priest. "Blessed, above all blessing and praise, is the man Christ Jesus, elect, precious, chosen of God to be a high priest for ever." (Horne)

b. **We shall be satisfied with the goodness of Your house**: Once established and enjoyed, the connection between God and man brings satisfaction to men. They experienced God's house as a place of **goodness** received.

i. **The goodness of Your house** gives the image of God as a host for His people. "It happily dwells a guest in the house and is supplied with that which satisfies all desires. The guest's security in the house of his host, his right to protection, help, and food, are, as usual, implied in the imagery." (Maclaren)

B. God in His creation.

1. (5-8) The far-reaching greatness of God.

***By* awesome deeds in righteousness You will answer us,**
O God of our salvation,
***You who are* the confidence of all the ends of the earth,**
And of the far-off seas;
Who established the mountains by His strength,

Being clothed with power;
You who still the noise of the seas,
The noise of their waves,
And the tumult of the peoples.
They also who dwell in the farthest parts are afraid of Your signs;
You make the outgoings of the morning and evening rejoice.

a. **By awesome deeds in righteousness You will answer us, O God of our salvation**: This was an ongoing confidence in the continuation of God's goodness. God had answered prayer and provided atonement; David expected such **awesome deeds** in the future also.

b. **You who are the confidence of all the ends of the earth**: David again lifted his vision from beyond Israel to **the ends of the earth**, to **the far-off seas**. He understood that though Israel belonged to God in a special sense, He was and is the God of the whole earth.

c. **You who still the noise of the seas, the noise of their waves, and the tumult of the peoples**: God's might is shown in His ability to quiet not only the oceans but also the noise of the peoples of the world. His authority extended far beyond Israel, to **the farthest parts** of the earth.

i. Stormy and noisy seas put forth enormous energy. According to the National Oceanic and Atmospheric Administration (NOAA), an average hurricane releases energy equivalent to 6×10^{14} watts of electricity. This is 200 times world-wide electrical generating capacity. The National Aeronautics and Space Administration (NASA) says that in its lifetime an average hurricane can release as much energy as 10,000 nuclear bombs. Yet God can and does **still the noise of the seas, the noise of their waves**.

ii. Knowing this great power of God should build our faith when we see the **tumult of the peoples** and are concerned for God's salvation to reach **the ends of the earth**. We can think of those at the **ends of the earth** as those who are farthest off, least known, least thought of, most afflicted, and the hardest to reach.

iii. "The child of God in seasons of trouble should fly at once to him who stills the seas: nothing is too hard for him." (Spurgeon)

iv. "In pagan mythology the 'sea' connoted chaotic and life-threatening powers. However, Israel knew that the Lord created everything and established his rule over the 'roaring' seas and their waves." (VanGemeren)

v. **Established the mountains by His strength**: "Philosophers of the forget-God school are too much engrossed with their laws of upheaval to think of the Upheaver. Their theories of volcanic action and glacier action, etc., are frequently used as bolts and bars to shut the Lord out of his own world. Our poet is of another mind, and sees God's hand settling Alps and Andes on their bases, and therefore he sings in his praise." (Spurgeon)

d. **You make the outgoings of the morning and evening rejoice**: The exercise of God's authority over the earth does not bring it fear and oppression; it brings rejoicing to the day.

> i. **Outgoings of the morning and evening**: "What is pictured, then, may be either the glory of day and night (*cf.* Psalm 19:1f.; Job 38:7, 19f.), or the whole expanse of earth from east to west, praising the Creator." (Kidner)

2. (9-13) The blessed and grateful earth.

You visit the earth and water it,
You greatly enrich it;
The river of God is full of water;
You provide their grain,
For so You have prepared it.
You water its ridges abundantly,
You settle its furrows;
You make it soft with showers,
You bless its growth.
You crown the year with Your goodness,
And Your paths drip *with* abundance.
They drop *on* the pastures of the wilderness,
And the little hills rejoice on every side.
The pastures are clothed with flocks;
The valleys also are covered with grain;
They shout for joy, they also sing.

a. **You visit the earth and water it, You greatly enrich it**: God cares for the earth and makes sure it has what it needs. He provides rivers of **water**, and **grain** for the earth.

> i. "For people in that place and day, the coming of abundant rains to water the crops was literally the blessing of life rather than death. It is hard for most of us today to fully appreciate that." (Boice)

> ii. "Thou art the right Master-cultivator, who cultivates the land much more and much better than the farmer does. He does nothing more to it than break up the ground, and plough, and sow, and then lets it lie. But God must be always attending to it with rain and heat, and

must do everything to make it grow and prosper while the farmer lies at home and sleeps." (Luther, cited in Spurgeon)

iii. The idea is clear: *the earth is barren until God acts upon it*. God is faithful to send the rain and what is necessary for the cultivation of the earth, bringing forth a wonderful harvest. So, God's people should pray and expect God to move upon both His Church and the world, knowing that they will be barren unless God acts upon them.

iv. Isaiah 55:10-11 speaks of this analogy between the fruitfulness of the earth and the effectiveness of God's work, especially through His Word: *For as the rain comes down, and the snow from heaven, and do not return there, but water the earth, and make it bring forth and bud, that it may give seed to the sower and bread to the eater, so shall My word be that goes forth from My mouth; it shall not return to Me void, but it shall accomplish what I please, and it shall prosper in the thing for which I sent it.*

b. **You bless its growth**: The earth is full of living, growing things all established and blessed by God. This is another aspect of His power and care for the earth.

i. "How easy were it with God to starve us all!" (Trapp)

ii. David was only concerned for *God's work* in bringing forth grain. David wasn't a fool; he knew that man had his work to do. Yet, "This is beautiful as a description of God's part therein. Man's toil is not described. It is taken for granted, and is his prayer." (Morgan)

iii. **You crown the year with Your goodness**: "A full and *plentiful harvest* is the *crown* of the year; and this springs from the unmerited *goodness* of God. This is the *diadem* of the earth." (Clarke)

iv. **The little hills rejoice**: "Literally, *The hills gird themselves with exultation*. The metaphor appears to be taken from the frisking of lambs, bounding of kids, and dancing of shepherds and shepherdesses, in the joy-inspiring summer season." (Clarke)

c. **The pastures are clothed with flocks; the valleys also are covered with grain**: David looked out over the land and saw hills covered with livestock and valleys full of grain. It seemed that creation itself shouted for joy and sang to God.

i. "It would be hard to surpass this evocative description of the fertile earth, observed with loving exactness at one moment and poetic freedom at the next, culminating in the fantasy of hills and fields putting on their finest clothes and making merry together." (Kidner)

ii. "The voice of nature is articulate to God; it is not only a shout, but a song." (Spurgeon)

iii. The hills and valleys are happy and joyful before God because of His great power and care for them. David understood that the people of God have those same reasons to praise God, in addition to the even greater reasons of atonement and connection with God described earlier in the psalms.

Psalm 66 – How Everyone Can Praise God

This psalm is titled **To the Chief Musician. A Song. A Psalm.** *As with Psalm 65, it is described as both a* **Song** *and a* **Psalm**. *This is the first psalm since Psalm 50 to not be attributed to David.*

"This Psalm is said to be recited on Easter day, by the Greek church: it is described in the Greek Bible as A Psalm of the Resurrection, *and may be understood to refer, in a prophetic sense, to the regeneration of the world, through the conversion of the Gentiles." (Daniel Cresswell, cited in Spurgeon)*

A. Praising the God of all the earth.

1. (1-2) Singing to the honor of His name.

Make a joyful shout to God, all the earth!
Sing out the honor of His name;
Make His praise glorious.

> a. **Make a joyful shout to God, all the earth**: As in the previous and the next psalm, Psalm 66 has not only Israel in view but **all the earth**. The psalmist understood that God was not only God over Israel, but the whole world. It was good and appropriate for him to call everyone to **joyfully** praise God.

> > i. "Composers of tunes for the congregation should see to it that their airs are cheerful; we need not so much noise, as *joyful* noise." (Spurgeon)

> b. **Make His praise glorious**: Song is not the only way to praise God, but it is one of the chief ways. The psalmist encouraged all to **sing out the honor of His name**, and to do it in a way that made God's praise **glorious**.

> > i. "Praise requires concentration on the thing, person, or deity being praised. Thanks tend to be focused on what the *speaker has received*, and thus may become rather narrow and perfunctory. In the expression

182

of thanksgiving, the self may become the primary subject, but this is much less likely to happen in praise." (Tate, cited in Boice)

2. (3-4) How to praise God.

Say to God,
"How awesome are Your works!
Through the greatness of Your power
Your enemies shall submit themselves to You.
All the earth shall worship You
And sing praises to You;
They shall sing praises *to* Your name." Selah

a. **Say to God**: The psalmist gives practical guidance for the those who want to praise God, telling them specifically what to **say**. He doesn't mean this in a mechanical or unfeeling way, but as help to the hearts that truly want to praise God but needs some instruction as to *how*. It begins with what we **say to God**, words that we actually speak. There is a place for unspoken praise (Psalm 65:1) but spoken praise must not be neglected.

i. **Say to God**: "There was more required than to think of God. Consideration, meditation, speculation, contemplation upon God and divine objects, have their place and their season; but this is more than that, and more than admiration." (John Donne, cited in Spurgeon)

b. **How awesome are Your works**: One may begin to praise God by thinking upon the greatness of His work in creation, salvation, and restoration. Then, by telling God **how awesome** His **works** are.

c. **Through the greatness of Your power Your enemies shall submit themselves to You**: Praise may continue in the recognition of the great **power** of God, which brought forth the **awesome** works. This awesome and powerful God has **enemies**, but through His great power they will be conquered and brought to **submit themselves** to God. This praises God for the triumph of His power over all His **enemies**.

i. Several commentators note that the sense of **shall submit themselves to You** has the feel of an insincere, unwilling submission to God. "The Hebrew clearly intimates, it will be a forced and false submission. Power brings a man to his knee, but love alone wins his heart. Pharaoh said he would let Israel go, but he lied unto God; he submitted in word but not in deed. Tens of thousands, both in earth and hell, are rendering this constrained homage to the Almighty; they *only* submit because they cannot do otherwise; it is not their loyalty, but his power, which keeps them subjects of his boundless dominion." (Spurgeon)

ii. "True, he discerns that submission will not always be genuine; for he uses the same word to express it as occurs in Psalm 18:44, which represents 'feigned homage.'" (Maclaren)

iii. Philippians 2:10-11 has something of this sense: *That at the name of Jesus every knee should bow, of those in heaven, and of those on earth, and of those under the earth, and that every tongue should confess that Jesus Christ is Lord, to the glory of God the Father.*

d. **All the earth shall worship You**: God may be praised in the recognition of His ultimate triumph over **all the earth** and in His worthiness to receive the **worship** and **praises** they rightly bring to Him.

e. **They shall sing praises to Your name**: In the thinking of the ancient Jews, the **name** was more than a word; it was a true identifier, an indication of character. This speaks of something greater than the grudging submission of the previous lines; this is praise that knows something of the nature and character of God.

i. "Acceptable worship not only praises God as the mysterious Lord, but it is rendered fragrant by some measure of knowledge of his name or character. God would not be worshipped as an unknown God, nor have it said of his people, '*Ye* worship ye know not what.'" (Spurgeon)

ii. **Selah**: "A little pause, for holy expectation is well inserted after so great a prophecy, and the uplifting of the heart is also a seasonable direction. No meditation can be more joyous than that excited by the prospect of a world reconciled to its Creator." (Spurgeon)

B. Praising the God of Israel.

1. (5-7) Seeing the works of God that make Him worthy of praise.

Come and see the works of God;
He is **awesome** *in His* **doing toward the sons of men.**
He turned the sea into dry *land;*
They went through the river on foot.
There we will rejoice in Him.
He rules by His power forever;
His eyes observe the nations;
Do not let the rebellious exalt themselves. Selah

a. **Come and see the works of God**: The psalmist felt that perhaps others might be slow to think of God's awesome works (Psalm 66:3). He would help, describing how **He is awesome in His doing toward the sons of men.**

i. **Come and see**: "He taketh good people by the hand, as it were, leading them to the sight of God's stupendous proceedings." (Trapp)

b. **He turned the sea into dry land; they went through the river on foot**: The psalmist turned to the holy history of the Scriptures and remembered how God showed His power in bringing Israel through the Red Sea (Exodus 14:21) and through the Jordan River (Joshua 3:14-16).

i. The psalmist could have picked anything to describe the **works** of God, but chose two events that showed how God participates in human affairs. The God of all power is not a passive observer, but an active participant.

c. **There we will rejoice in Him**: In saying **we**, the psalmist identifies himself with Israel hundreds of years before his time, as if he were there. It was as if the psalmist stood beside the Jordan River, pointed to a spot and said, "**There**. That is where this happened. It wasn't a legend or a myth, but there is a **there** where it happened. Therefore **we will rejoice in Him**."

i. "God's work is never antiquated. It is all a revelation of eternal activities. What He has been, He is. What He did, He does. Therefore faith may feed on all the records of old time, and expect the repetition of all that they contain." (Maclaren)

ii. **Rejoice in Him**: "It is to be remarked that Israel's joy was in her God, and there let ours be. It is not so much what he has done, as what he is, that should excite in us a sacred rejoicing." (Spurgeon)

d. **His eyes observe the nations**: The psalmist called all the earth to observe the great works of God and give Him praise. It was also worth remembering that He observes **the nations**; they should look up to the One who looks at them.

e. **Do not let the rebellious exalt themselves**: In light of God's power, His participation in human affairs, and His eye upon the world, to be **rebellious** against Him is foolish. To **exalt** yourself against Him is madness.

2. (8-12) More reasons to praise God.

Oh, bless our God, you peoples!
And make the voice of His praise to be heard,
Who keeps our soul among the living,
And does not allow our feet to be moved.
For You, O God, have tested us;
You have refined us as silver is refined.
You brought us into the net;
You laid affliction on our backs.
You have caused men to ride over our heads;

We went through fire and through water;
But You brought us out to rich *fulfillment*.

a. **Oh, bless our God, you peoples**: The psalmist repeated his exhortation to all the earth, telling them to praise the God of Israel. He will give many more reasons to do so.

i. "Verse 8 reveals the conviction that Israel's fortunes embrace the world, as Abram was promised that they should." (Kidner)

ii. "We must not only publish God's praises, but provoke others also so to do." (Trapp)

b. **Who keeps our soul among the living**: God preserves His people, giving them life and secure position (**does not allow our feet to be moved**).

i. "Try us, O God; but enable us to stand the trial!" (Horne)

ii. "If God has enabled us not only to keep our life, but our position, we are bound to give him double praise. Living and standing is the saint's condition through divine grace. Immortal and immovable are those whom God preserves." (Spurgeon)

c. **For You, O God, have tested us**: God blesses His people, but sometimes the blessing is in a difficult testing. The psalmist praised God for life and secure position, but also recognized the hardships of life. He expressed the hardships and testing with many word pictures.

- **You have refined us as silver is refined**: We feel the heat rising until we have no strength and stability but are melted. The impure dross rises to the top and God, the Refiner expertly scrapes it away, knowing that the silver was pure enough when He can see His own reflection in our melted metal.

- **You have brought us into the net**: We felt the freedom of being able to swim wherever we pleased, and life was full of options and choices. Suddenly, that freedom seemed gone and our choices became few.

- **You laid affliction on our backs**: We used to walk easy and carefree, as if we did not have a single burden. Now our **backs** are loaded with **affliction**, and we find the weight difficult to bear.

- **You have caused men to ride over our heads**: We used to stand in battle and fight on equal footing with our enemies, if not better footing. Then we were cast down and felt them riding in triumph over us. Where once we seemed to only know victory, now we feel the sting of defeat.

- **We went through fire and through water**: We feel that we have been through it all, and it seems that no adversity has been kept from us.

    i. "The word translated *affliction* is unknown elsewhere, and its meaning uncertain; but it may derive from a root meaning 'to press,' an idea familiar with us in our modern metaphorical use of the word 'pressure.'" (Kidner)

    ii. "*To ride over our heads;* to ride upon our shoulders. By thy permission they have used us like slaves, yea, like beasts, to carry their persons or burdens. Compare Isaiah 51:23." (Poole)

d. **But You brought us out to rich fulfillment**: The psalmist said to God that he understood, that in some ultimate sense, their affliction was "from **You**" – it was allowed by God Himself. As they continued to trust in God, He vindicated Himself and their trust, not only delivering them from difficulty, but bringing them **out to rich fulfillment**. This **rich fulfillment** would never have come apart from the many difficulties.

    i. "The main end of our life is not to do, but to become. For this we are being moulded and disciplined each hour." (Meyer)

    ii. We remind ourselves that this is in a list giving all the earth reasons why God should be praised. We would think that such difficulties should be avoided if we want others to praise God, but the psalmist described life lived for God as it really is – and knew that understanding God as He really is will draw men and women to praise.

C. Praising the God of the individual believer.

1. (13-15) Praising God with sacrifices and the paying of vows.

I will go into Your house with burnt offerings;
I will pay You my vows,
Which my lips have uttered
And my mouth has spoken when I was in trouble.
I will offer You burnt sacrifices of fat animals,
With the sweet aroma of rams;
I will offer bulls with goats. Selah

a. **I will go into Your house with burnt offerings**: The psalmist determined to praise God by obeying His command regarding sacrifices, bringing them to the altar of God.

    i. "By its very nature a burnt offering was more serious, signifying something like the complete dedication or consecration of himself to God by the worshipper." (Boice)

b. **I will pay You my vows**: The psalmist had promised God certain sacrifices or gifts in gratitude for God's work when he **was in trouble**. He would not sin by failing to bring these.

i. **My vows**: "Only let us never forget that when made, they must be fulfilled. The reason is not in God, but in us. To fail to keep faith with God is to suffer deterioration of character." (Morgan)

c. **Burnt sacrifices of fat animals, with sweet aroma of rams; I will offer bulls with goats**: The psalmist would fulfill his vows to God with generous, expensive sacrifices, offering multiple animals. What he brought to God was of the best; they were **fat animals**.

i. "The qualifying animals the psalmist makes mention of are rams, bulls, and goats. The largess of the vow is unusual." (VanGemeren)

2. (16-19) Praising God with words.

Come *and* hear, all you who fear God,
And I will declare what He has done for my soul.
I cried to Him with my mouth,
And He was extolled with my tongue.
If I regard iniquity in my heart,
The Lord will not hear.
But certainly God has heard *me;*
He has attended to the voice of my prayer.

a. **Come and hear, all you who fear God**: The vow of the psalmist was not fulfilled through sacrifice alone. He also had an obligation to proclaim God's goodness, to **declare what He has done for my soul**. His actions spoke, but did not take away the need for his mouth to also speak.

i. "We may picture the scene of public worship, perhaps at Passover or at a victory celebration, in which the corporate praise gives way to the voice of this single worshipper, who stands with his gifts before the altar, and speaks of the God whose care is not only world- and nation-wide, but personal: *I will tell what he has done for me.*" (Kidner)

b. **I cried to Him with my mouth, and He was extolled with my tongue**: As the psalmist spoke to others about God's goodness, he described how he spoke to God. He offered both the sacrifice of animals and the sacrifice of praise.

c. **If I regard iniquity in my heart, the Lord will not hear**: No one should think that God could be persuaded merely through sacrifices or vows. It was important to make clear that the psalmist did not only sacrifice but also gave God the better: obedience. He did not hold on to **iniquity** in his **heart**.

i. "*Iniquity;* any sin whatsoever, and especially idolatry, which is oft expressed by this word, to which the Israelites were very prone, and to which they had most powerful temptations." (Poole)

ii. "The prayer which is 'heard,' is the prayer of the penitent, heartily grieved and wearied with sin, hating and longing to be delivered from it." (Horne)

d. **Certainly God has heard me**: When he cried out to God, God heard. He answered, giving more reasons to praise Him.

3. (20) The conclusion of praise.

Blessed *be* **God,**
Who has not turned away my prayer,
Nor His mercy from me!

a. **Blessed be God, who has not turned away my prayer**: We often take the privilege of prayer for granted. The psalmist understood how wonderful it was that God received his prayer, and how it made God more to be praised.

b. **Nor His mercy from me**: This was a final and wonderful reminder that the answer to prayer did not come from what the psalmist deserved, but as a gift from the great love and mercy [*hesed*] of God.

i. "The final word of gratitude is not for the answered request alone, but for what it signifies: an unbroken relationship with God." (Kidner)

ii. Thomas Fuller (cited by Spurgeon) composed a syllogism from Psalm 66:19-20. It works something like this:

- If I regard iniquity in my heart, God will not hear my prayer.
- God has heard my prayer.

We would expect the next line to be, *Therefore, there is no iniquity in my heart*. Yet the psalmist completed the syllogism in an unexpected way, praising the **mercy** of God. "I looked that he should have clapped the crown on his own, and he puts it on God's head. I will learn this excellent logic." (Fuller)

iii. "This is the conclusion of David's syllogism, in this and the two former verses; and herein his logic is better than Aristotle's." (Trapp)

Psalm 67 – A Missionary Psalm

The title tells us the audience of the psalm: **To the Chief Musician. On Stringed Instruments. A Psalm. A song.** *Some believe that* **the Chief Musician** *is the Lord* GOD *Himself, and others suppose him to be a leader of choirs or musicians in David's time, such as Heman the singer or Asaph (1 Chronicles 6:33, 16:5-7, and 25:6).*

This wonderful psalm is sometimes forgotten or neglected when God's people think of their favorite psalms. Though Martin Luther wrote five large volumes of exposition on Psalms, he skipped Psalm 67 entirely. Nevertheless, this psalm has a heart to see God's way, God's salvation, and God's praise extended through all the earth.

A. A request and reason for blessing.

1. (1) A request for blessing.

God be merciful to us and bless us,
***And* cause His face to shine upon us. Selah**

a. **God be merciful to us and bless us**: These words come from the Aaronic Blessing of Numbers 6:24-26, where the High Priest of Israel would pronounce this beautiful blessing upon the people.

i. Paul wrote in Romans 15:16: *That I might be a minister of Jesus Christ to the Gentiles, ministering the gospel of God, that the offering of the Gentiles might be acceptable, sanctified by the Holy Spirit.* This was priestly language, and we might say that Paul saw himself as a priest. He did his priestly service through *evangelism*, not animal sacrifice. 1 Peter 2:9-10 tells us that all believers are also a priesthood. We offer a priestly service to the world, and we primarily do it through evangelism.

b. **God be merciful to us**: The psalmist first knew his need for mercy. This sets our heart in the right frame of mind: sinners who need the mercy of God. One may need more mercy than another, but we all need mercy.

i. "The best saints and the worst sinners may unite in this petition." (Spurgeon)

c. **And bless us**: Beyond the mercy of God – which He could show simply by leaving us alone, by *not* destroying us – we want God to **bless us** also. It would be quite a sight to see a guilty criminal before a judge, pleading for mercy, and receiving it – and then asking for a *blessing*! But God's love towards us is that great.

d. **And cause His face to shine upon us**: To have the glorious, happy face of God shining upon us is the greatest gift we could have. To know that as God looks upon you, He is well pleased – not because of who you are, or what you have done, but because you are in Jesus Christ – there is no greater source of peace and power in life.

i. "An Oriental monarch revealed in his facial expression either his pleasure or displeasure with the party that sought an audience with him." (VanGemeren)

ii. "A shining face is the opposite of an angry or scowling face, and a face turned toward someone is the opposite of a face turned away in indifference or disgust. A shining face implies favor...and it implies the friendliness of warm personal relationships too." (Boice)

iii. "Why should he fret when God smiles? What matters though all the world should censure, if Jehovah countenances his servant. A look of approval from God creates a deep, delightful calm within the soul." (Spurgeon)

e. **Selah**: The idea in the Hebrew for this word (occurring 74 times in the Old Testament) is for a *pause*. Most people think it speaks of a reflective pause, a pause to meditate on the words just spoken. It may also be a musical instruction, for a musical interlude of some kind.

i. Think about the greatness of:

- God's mercy.
- God's blessing.
- The approval of God's shining face.

ii. "These three petitions include all that we need here or hereafter." (Spurgeon)

2. (2) The reason for blessing.

That Your way may be known on earth,
Your salvation among all nations.

a. **That Your way may be known on earth**: The reason the psalmist asked for this high and great blessing wasn't a selfish reason. He asked for this blessing for the sake of God's glory *and* for the sake of the perishing multitudes.

    i. When people see the work of God in the lives of His people – His blessing active upon them – it is one way God makes His way **known on earth**. When it seems that God is silent or dead in the lives of His people, it is a great hindrance to making His way **known on earth**.

    ii. "It may be said without fear of contradiction that the greatest hindrance to evangelism in the world today is the failure of the church to supply evidence in her own life and work of the saving power of God." (Stott, cited in Boice)

b. **Your way**: Not simply the truth of God or the word of God to be published abroad – but for **Your way**; the **way** of the Lord, to **be known on earth**.

    i. This reminds us of the idea behind the great missionary passage of Matthew 28:19-20: *Go therefore and make disciples of all the nations, baptizing them in the name of the Father and of the Son and of the Holy Spirit, teaching them to observe all things that I have commanded you; and lo, I am with you always, even to the end of the age.* Jesus didn't tell them only to evangelize and save souls, but to *make disciples of all the nations*, and to teach them *to observe all things that I have commanded you*.

    ii. Of course, we need to *know* God's Word to walk in His **way**; but walking in His **way** is more than knowing His Word.

c. **May be known on earth**: The psalmist had a beautiful *scope* in mind: not just Jerusalem, not just Judea, not just all of Israel, not just all the Middle East, not just all the Mediterranean world, not just his continent or hemisphere, but all the **earth**.

    i. God wants us to have the *same heart* and the *same vision* – for all the **earth**.

d. **Your salvation among all nations**: Of all of the *ways* of God, this is the most precious and needful. We should see a perishing world and long for God's **salvation among all nations**.

    i. Again, this is the *reason* for blessing. Are you a member of the "bless me" club, always crying out to God, "Bless me, bless me, bless me"? But your cry is essentially a selfish one, the kind of cry a self-interested child makes. Yes, we unashamedly ask God to bless us – but not only for ourselves, but so His **way** will be made known in all the earth, and His **salvation** among all nations.

ii. "Since Pentecost Israel's ancient prayer is being fulfilled more magnificently than they could ever have imagined." (VanGemeren)

B. A call to praise God.

1. (3) A prayer to God for all peoples.

Let the peoples praise You, O God;
Let all the peoples praise You.

a. **Let the peoples praise You, O God**: We notice that this is first and foremost a *prayer to God*. It is fine to call upon the peoples to praise God; but it is also fine to ask God to bring the nations to Himself.

i. When we pray like this, we pray according to the heart of God, Who desires that none perish but all come to repentance (2 Peter 3:9), and Who has ordained a great multitude from all nations, tribes, peoples and tongues to praise Him before His throne (Revelation 7:9).

b. **Let all the peoples praise You**: It wasn't big enough to pray **Let the peoples praise You**; the psalmist took it a step deeper: **Let *all* the peoples praise You!**

i. "It is in fact a prayer of great vision and daring." (Kidner)

ii. We don't only want the earth to know God's *way*; we don't even want it to stop with the nations knowing His *salvation*. We want all the peoples to **praise** Him. There is something wonderful about *a lot* of people praising God. Our walk with God is incomplete until we are praising Him.

iii. Do we have the same heart? Or will we write off *some* peoples, instead of having God's heart for **all the peoples**?

2. (4-5) A joyful anticipation of the Kingdom of God.

Oh, let the nations be glad and sing for joy!
For You shall judge the people righteously,
And govern the nations on earth. Selah
Let the peoples praise You, O God;
Let all the peoples praise You.

a. **Let the nations be glad and sing for joy**: Why? Why should the nations be so happy? Because God is coming to **judge the people righteously, and govern the nations on earth**. Jesus is coming back, and it should make us even more excited about bringing the nations God's *way*, God's *salvation*, and God's *praise*.

i. God forbid that knowing that Jesus is coming soon should make us *less* passionate about evangelism and missions. It should make us much *more* passionate.

b. **Govern the nations on earth**: It's a fact. It's going to happen. Jesus Christ is going to reign on planet earth as King of Kings and Lord of Lords. We want to get the nations ready for it.

i. "Because he would 'judge the people righteously'; breaking the yoke of the oppressor, and the iron rod of the prince of this world; becoming himself an advocate in the cause of his church; introducing her into the glorious liberty of the children of God, whose service is perfect freedom." (Horne)

c. **Selah**: This is worthy of reflection – the connection between being passionate about the return of Jesus and a passion to spread the gospel.

d. **Let the peoples praise You**: The idea of Psalm 67:3 is so important that the psalmist repeated it. "These words are no vain repetition, but are a chorus worthy to be sung again and again." (Spurgeon)

i. "Let them praise thee (that pronoun 'thee' is emphatical and exclusive), and not their gods of gold and silver." (Trapp)

ii. This will have an ultimate fulfillment in heaven, where people from every tribe and tongue will praise God. "In that day our joy will be even greater because great multitudes from all the nations of the earth will be praising God with us." (Boice)

C. The answer to this prayer.

1. (6a) Blessing for the earth.

Then **the earth shall yield her increase;**

a. **Then the earth shall yield her increase**: This idea may be present in the psalm because the song was written in the harvest season. The abundance of harvest lifted the thoughts of the psalmist to the greatest harvest yet to come.

i. "If it was a harvest festival song, as the first part of verse 6 would indicate, then the local occasion is graciously submerged in a far wider outlook." (Morgan)

b. **Then the earth shall yield her increase**: When the earth knows God's way, God's salvation, and God's praise, then she will **yield her increase**. The fruit will come forth; the appointed purpose for the earth will be fulfilled. Praise God!

i. God *created* us to know His way, His salvation, and His praise. When we do this the **earth** itself is happy, because the people of the earth are doing what God created them to do. God's natural order for creation and mankind is then honored, and blessing is the result. It is just like using something for the exact use and in the exact way that the manufacturer designed.

c. **Shall yield her increase**: This also tells us that the earth will *never* **yield her increase**, find its fruitfulness and fulfillment, *until* she knows God's way, God's salvation, and God's praise.

i. "*Let the people praise thee, O God; let all the people praise thee!* What then? '*Then shall the earth yield her increase; and God, even our own God, shall bless us.*' Our unthankfulness is the cause of the earth's unfruitfulness. While man is blessing God for his mercies, He is blessing man *with* his mercies." (William Seeker, in 1660, cited in Spurgeon)

2. (6b-7a) Blessing for the one who prayed.

God, our own God, shall bless us.
God shall bless us,

a. **God, our own God, shall bless us**: When we share God's heart and vision for the world, we **shall** be blessed. We *must* be blessed.

i. So we see a glorious circle. We are blessed; we use that blessing to pray for and reach a hurting world, and as that aligns us with the heart of God, we are blessed even more, so we use that blessing for all the earth…and it just goes on and on.

ii. It's worth looking at our lives and seeing if we have broken the circle anywhere. Have we stopped believing that God blesses? Have we stopped seeking to extend that blessing? Have we stopped seeing God's heart in it all? If we don't break the circle, we really move from glory to glory.

iii. "Let God (the psalm encourages us to pray), who brings much out of little and distributes it in love, bring such blessing on us as to make us, in our turn, the blessing of the world!" (Kidner)

iv. **God, our own God**: "We never love God aright till we know him to be ours, and the more we love him the more do we long to be fully assured that he is ours." (Spurgeon)

b. **God shall bless us**: It is repeated twice in a row to emphasize the confident expectation. God promised to bless the nations of the earth through the seed of Abraham, and we know this is and will be fulfilled in Jesus Christ.

i. "There is a constant circular course and recourse from the sea, unto the sea; so there is between God and us; the more we praise him, the more our blessings come down; and the more his blessings come down, the more we praise him again; so that we do not so much bless God as bless ourselves. When the springs lie low, we pour a little water into the pump, not to enrich the fountain, but to bring up more for ourselves." (Thomas Manton, cited in Spurgeon)

ii. "If a psalm was ever written round the promises to Abraham that he would be both blessed and made a blessing, it could well have been such as this." (Kidner)

3. (7b) Conclusion: The answer to the prayer.

And all the ends of the earth shall fear Him.

a. **All the ends of the earth**: If the psalmist had not yet been strong enough, here he makes the point even clearer. God's heart and plan is for **all the ends of the earth**.

b. **All the ends of the earth shall fear Him**: God gets the respect, the honor, the praise, the glory, He is worthy of. *We* may never get respect; we may never face anything but hardship; we may end up poor and broken and persecuted and even laying down our lives – and be more blessed than ever, because God has used us in a great way.

Psalm 68 – The Victorious Procession of God to Zion

The title of this psalm is **To the Chief Musician. A Psalm of David. A Song.** *Most commentators believe this psalm is connected with the coming of the ark of the covenant into Jerusalem (2 Samuel 6), celebrating not only that event, but also the faithfulness of God to give Israel victory over her enemies, and to make Jerusalem secure enough to bring the ark into the city.*

George Horne described how this psalm was assigned to Pentecost in the Anglican liturgy, no doubt because it describes gifts given upon ascension and is quoted in Ephesians 4. "This beautiful, sublime, and comprehensive, but very difficult Psalm, is one of those which the church has appointed to be used on Whitsunday."

The composition of this psalm makes it a challenge for commentators, both from the Hebrew and in translation. Adam Clarke wrote, "I know not how to undertake a comment on this psalm: it is the most difficult in the whole Psalter."

A. The God of triumph.

1. (1-3) God triumphs over His enemies.

Let God arise,
Let His enemies be scattered;
Let those also who hate Him flee before Him.
As smoke is driven away,
So drive *them* away;
As wax melts before the fire,
***So* let the wicked perish at the presence of God.**
But let the righteous be glad;
Let them rejoice before God;
Yes, let them rejoice exceedingly.

a. **Let God arise, let His enemies be scattered**: Using the phrasing of Numbers 10:35, David proclaimed the triumph of God over all His enemies. When God goes forth, no opponent can stand against Him. They are all **scattered**. Since Moses said those words when the ark of the covenant led Israel from Mount Sinai, David knew it was appropriate to say the same words as the ark came to Jerusalem, its resting place.

i. As David brought the ark of the covenant to Jerusalem (2 Samuel 6), he made a dramatic historical connection. To relate it to American history, it would be like a modern American President beginning a speech with the phrase, *Four score and seven years ago* – which would immediately be recognized as the first few words of Abraham Lincoln's Gettysburg Address, originally spoken in 1863.

ii. Numbers 10 describes the departure of Israel from Mount Sinai towards the Promised Land. As they marched, the ark of the covenant led the way. *So it was, whenever the ark set out, that Moses said: "Rise up, O LORD! Let Your enemies be scattered, and let those who hate You flee before You."* (Numbers 10:35)

iii. The idea was simple, both with Moses in the exodus and David with Israel in the land. It expressed the confidence and the need of God's people: "God, go before us and take care of our enemies. It's too dangerous ahead without You." This spirit of confident dependence is appropriate for every believer.

iv. This is also a fitting prayer by which to remember the glory and strength of the resurrected Jesus. When Jesus rose up, all His enemies scattered. None dared oppose Him. If we are set in Jesus, they scatter before us also because all our victory is found in His resurrected glory.

v. **Let those also who hate Him flee before Him**: "Athanasius telleth us that evil spirits may be put to flight by the psalm; and that Antony, the hermit, fought against the devil with this verse, and worsted him." (Trapp)

b. **As smoke is driven away, so drive them away**: God's enemies have no ability to stand against Him, shown by the images of vanishing **smoke** and melting **wax**. David prayed that the **wicked** would **perish** just as easily.

i. "Wax is hard by itself, but put it to the fire, how soft it is. Wicked men are haughty till they come into contact with the Lord, and then they faint for fear; their hearts melt like wax when they feel the power of his anger." (Spurgeon)

ii. Ephesians 6:10-18 is the great New Testament passage on spiritual conflict and how God equips the believer for success in that conflict. A repeated theme in that passage is the idea of *standing* against spiritual attack and opposition (*that you may be able to stand...that you may be able to withstand in the evil day, and having done all, to stand...stand therefore*). What David described here with vanishing **smoke** and melting **wax** is the exact *opposite* of standing in the sense Ephesians 6 meant it.

c. **But let the righteous be glad**: What is disaster and calamity for the wicked is gladness and extra rejoicing for the righteous. We can't help but be glad in God's victory.

2. (4-6) Singing praise to the God of triumph.

Sing to God, sing praises to His name;
Extol Him who rides on the clouds,
By His name YAH,
And rejoice before Him.
A father of the fatherless, a defender of widows,
Is **God in His holy habitation.**
God sets the solitary in families;
He brings out those who are bound into prosperity;
But the rebellious dwell in a dry *land.*

a. **Sing to God, sing praises to His name**: There is an aspect of this that is the simple repetition and parallelism of Hebrew poetry. Yet there is a slightly more developed thought in the phrase **sing praises to His name**, having the idea of praising God with knowledge of His character, and knowing Him personally.

b. **Extol Him who rides on the clouds, by His name YAH, and rejoice before Him**: David gave us two specific reasons to **rejoice** in God. He **rides on the clouds**, in victory and triumph over all the earth. Also, He has revealed Himself to humanity in the name *Yahweh*, showing His love and loyalty to His people.

i. **Extol Him**: "The root *s-l-l* [extol] usually denotes the act of constructing a road or highway (cf. Isaiah 57:14; 62:10), but is used here metaphorically with the sense of 'lift up' or 'extol.'" (VanGemeren)

ii. **Who rides on the clouds**: "By the ascription 'who rides on the clouds,' the psalmist contrasts the all-sufficiency of the God of Israel with the powers of Baal whom the Canaanites worshipped as 'the Rider on the clouds.'" (VanGemeren)

iii. "The name JAH is an abbreviation of the name Jehovah; it is not a diminution of that name, but an intensified word, containing in it the essence of the longer, august title. It only occurs here in our version of Scripture, except in connection with other words such as *Hallelujah*." (Spurgeon)

iv. "*Yah*, probably a contraction of the word *Yehovah*; at least so the ancient versions understood it. It is used but in a few places in the sacred writings. It might be translated *The Self-existent*." (Clarke)

c. **A father of the fatherless, a defender of widows**: God's greatness isn't only defined by military-like triumphs. It is also seen in His compassionate concern and care for the weak and needy. The name *Yahweh* is connected to God as the *Becoming One* (Exodus 3:13-14), the God who becomes what His people need. The **fatherless** need a **father**; Yahweh is there. The **widows** need a **defender**; God is there.

> i. "He is the God who acts on behalf of those who look for protection and vindication: the fatherless, the widows, the lonely (NEB [New English Bible], 'the friendless'), and the exiles ('prisoners') [**those who are bound**]." (VanGemeren)

> ii. "The kings and other rulers of this world do not act like this. They surround themselves with the noblest and richest of their lands, those who can enhance their glory and strengthen their power. The highest glory of God is that he cares for the miserable and surrounds himself with them." (Boice)

> iii. "Does not James 1:27, refer to this verse, for we have '*the fatherless*,' '*the widow*,' and then the '*holiness*,' of the God we serve?" (Bonar, cited in Spurgeon)

d. **God sets the solitary in families**: God sees those who live without a close family connection and cares to provide them with **families**. They may be without husband or wife, without father or mother, or without brother or sister nearby; God cares and has family connections among His people for the **solitary**.

> i. Since this is God's will for the **solitary**, they should look for and cultivate such relationships.

e. **He brings out those who are bound into prosperity; but the rebellious dwell in a dry land**: God can help even those who in their poverty have been subjected to some kind of bondage or servitude; God can bring them **into prosperity**. This is not a promised blessing for the **rebellious**.

> i. "The most oppressed in Egypt were chained and imprisoned, but the divine Emancipator brought them all forth into perfect liberty. He who did this of old continues his gracious work." (Spurgeon)

B. God wins the battle for His people.

1. (7-10) The mighty presence of God with Israel in the wilderness.

O God, when You went out before Your people,
When You marched through the wilderness, Selah
The earth shook;
The heavens also dropped *rain* at the presence of God;
Sinai itself *was moved* at the presence of God, the God of Israel.
You, O God, sent a plentiful rain,
Whereby You confirmed Your inheritance,
When it was weary.
Your congregation dwelt in it;
You, O God, provided from Your goodness for the poor.

a. **O God, when You went out before Your people**: Having introduced the idea in the first line of the psalm, David continued his thoughts on God's presence with and care for Israel **through the wilderness** on the way to Canaan. **You went out before Your people** emphasizes the idea that God was *with* Israel; He did not abandon them despite the many ways they provoked Him.

i. **Marched through the wilderness**: "We may speak, if we will, of the '*wanderings* of the children of Israel,' but we must not think them purposeless strayings; they were in reality a well-arranged and well considered march." (Spurgeon)

b. **The earth shook**: As God was with Israel in the wilderness, they were protected. His *might* was on their side. No other nation could defeat them when they walked with God.

c. **The heavens also dropped rain at the presence of God**: As God was with Israel in the wilderness they were provided for. They would never suffer hunger or thirst as they walked in God's **presence**.

i. As part of that provision, God sent them **a plentiful rain** in a needy time. This care for them was a way God **confirmed** the special place Israel had in His heart and plan. They were His **inheritance**.

ii. "*Send a plentiful rain*; either, 1. In the wilderness, where they oft wanted water, and were by God's extraordinary care supplied with it. Or rather, 2. In the land of Canaan, which he calls God's inheritance in the next words." (Poole)

d. **Sinai itself was moved at the presence of God**: As God was with Israel in the wilderness, they experienced the revelation of His power and glory. Mighty mountains shook at the very presence of God.

i. "Verse 8 quotes the allusion to Sinai from the Song of Deborah, Judges 5:4f." (Kidner)

2. (11-14) Proclaiming God's victory over the kings.

The Lord gave the word;
Great *was* the company of those who proclaimed *it*:
"Kings of armies flee, they flee,
And she who remains at home divides the spoil.
Though you lie down among the sheepfolds,
***You will be* like the wings of a dove covered with silver,**
And her feathers with yellow gold."
When the Almighty scattered kings in it,
It was *white* as snow in Zalmon.

a. **Kings of armies flee, they flee, and she who remains at home divides the spoil**: This was the word of victory that God **gave**, the word of triumph that was **proclaimed** by a great **company** of people. The message was that God has won a great victory over mighty enemies (**kings**), and His people, even His weak people, benefited even though they did not directly fight (**she who remains at home divides the spoil**).

i. *This is the message of the Gospel, the Good News of Jesus Christ*. God won a great victory through the Person and work of Jesus Christ, and His people gain everything through that victory in a battle they did not directly fight. This is the message that we as a great company are to proclaim.

ii. "The words in the original are very significant, and do note two things. First, the word which you read '*company*,' in the Hebrew it is 'army...great was the army of preachers.' An army of preachers is a great matter; nay, it is a great matter to have seven or eight good preachers in a great army; but to have a whole army of preachers that is glorious." (Bridge, cited in Spurgeon)

iii. **Great was the company**: "The Hebrew word is of the feminine gender, because it was the manner of the Hebrews, that when the men returned victorious from the battle, the women went out to meet them with songs of triumph." (Poole)

iv. The text tells us a **great...company** of women proclaimed the good news of God's victory. It is significant that God chose women to be the first messengers of the good news of the victory of Jesus' resurrection (Matthew 28:1-10, Luke 24:1-10). The New Testament says that women should not be in positions of doctrinal authority (1 Timothy 2:9-14), but they certainly can and should proclaim the good news of God's victory in Jesus Christ.

v. **She who remains at home divides the spoil**: "Thus, in the spiritual war, apostles, confessors, and martyrs went out to the battle, fought and conquered…the benefits of victory extended to thousands and millions, who, without being exposed to their conflicts and torments, have enjoyed the fruit of their labours." (Horne)

b. **You will be like the wings of a dove covered with silver**: The people of God come from humble circumstances (they **lie down among the sheepfolds**), but they share in God's great victory over their enemies and are graced with great blessings and gifts.

i. "*The wings of a dove*, flashing *silver* and *gold*, have been taken to refer to Israel basking in prosperity (Delitzsch), to the enemy in flight (Briggs), to the glory of the Lord manifested at the battle (Weiser), or even to a particular trophy seized from the enemy (*cf.* NEB [New English Bible]); but could it not depict the women of 68:12b preening themselves in their new finery, peacocking around, as we might have put it?" (Kidner)

c. **It was white as snow in Zalmon**: **Zalmon** is another name for Mount Ebal in central Israel, which many would consider more of a high hill than an actual mountain. The meaning of this line is not entirely clear and has been the source of much speculation.

i. "According to Judges 9:48, Zalmon ('the Dark One') is one of the mountains by Shechem." (VanGemeren)

ii. "Whether the rout of kings there was caused by a blizzard, or whether the battlefield was 'snowed' with weapons and garments (or, later, with bones), or the fleeing armies compared to snowflakes, we cannot tell." (Kidner)

iii. "Others take the point of comparison to be the change from trouble to joy which follows the foe's defeat, and is likened to the change of the dark hillside to a gleaming snow field." (Maclaren)

3. (15-18) Victory on the mountains.

A mountain of God *is* the mountain of Bashan;
A mountain *of many* peaks *is* the mountain of Bashan.
Why do you fume with envy, you mountains of *many* peaks?
***This is* the mountain *which* God desires to dwell in;**
Yes, the LORD will dwell *in it* forever.
The chariots of God *are* twenty thousand,
***Even* thousands of thousands;**
The Lord is among them *as in* Sinai, in the Holy *Place*.
You have ascended on high,

You have led captivity captive;
You have received gifts among men,
Even *from* the rebellious,
That the LORD God might dwell *there.*

a. **A mountain of God is the mountain of Bashan**: **Bashan** was farther north in Israel, in the region of what today is called the Golan Heights. **Bashan** was an impressive mountain, even **a mountain of God** and part of Israel's heritage. Yet it and the other mountains seem to **fume with envy** when they see how God has favored Zion.

i. "In comparison with these, Mount Zion was the merest hill: yet Zion, as if to their baleful *envy*, was God's choice." (Kidner)

b. **This is the mountain which God desires to dwell in**: God chose Jerusalem even though there were higher and more spectacular mountains. Yet as He often chooses the weak to confound the strong and the foolish to mystify the wise, He chose Zion over Bashan.

i. "This low, little, barren hill of Zion; and God's election maketh the difference, as it did of Aaron's rod from the rest, and doth still of the church from the rest of the world. The Lamb Christ is on Mount Zion." (Trapp)

c. **The chariots of God are twenty thousands**: By God's command (Deuteronomy 17:16), ancient Israel never had many chariots. They were still protected because God fought for Israel and He had power greater than **thousands of thousands** of chariots.

i. "The presence of God is the strength of the church; all power is ours when God is ours. Twenty thousand chariots shall bear the gospel to the ends of the earth; and myriads of agencies shall work for its success." (Spurgeon)

d. **You have ascended on high, You have led captivity captive**: David had in mind God's victory over the people and what happened after the battle was over. After the battle was over, God dealt with His enemies (**led captivity captive**) and He **received gifts** of tribute and submission from them. This was an even greater confirmation of God's ownership of the land (**that the LORD God might dwell there**).

i. "The expression is emphatical. He has conquered and triumphed over all the powers which held us in captivity, so that captivity itself is taken captive." (Newton, cited in Spurgeon)

ii. With the direct leading of the Holy Spirit, the Apostle Paul quoted Psalm 68:18 and applied it to Jesus, keeping the context but changing one key word. Paul quoted, *When He ascended on high, He led captivity captive, and gave gifts to men* (Ephesians 4:8). Paul applied this to the ascension of Jesus into heaven and His sending of the power and the gifts of the Holy Spirit to His Church. The one word Paul changed by the inspiration of the Holy Spirit was **received gifts** to *gave gifts*.

C. Praise to the God who wins the battle for His people.

1. (19-23) God's rescue in battle and victory over the enemy.

Blessed *be* **the Lord,**
Who **daily loads us** *with benefits,*
The God of our salvation! Selah
Our God *is* **the God of salvation;**
And to GOD the Lord *belong* **escapes from death.**
But God will wound the head of His enemies,
The hairy scalp of the one who still goes on in his trespasses.
The Lord said, "I will bring back from Bashan,
I will bring *them* **back from the depths of the sea,**
That your foot may crush *them* **in blood,**
And the tongues of your dogs *may have* **their portion from** *your* **enemies."**

a. **Blessed be the Lord, who daily loads us with benefits**: It is undeniably true that God **daily** gives **benefits** to His people. Yet many think the sense of this verse is more accurately translated, *Blessed be the Lord, who daily beareth our burden* (Revised Standard Version).

b. **Our God is the God of salvation; and to GOD the Lord belong escapes from death**: This psalm speaks much of the ark coming to Jerusalem, but that only happened after David defeated Israel's surrounding enemies. David thought of how God rescued him in those conflicts. In doing so He used the somewhat uncommon but wonderful phrasing of *Yahweh Adonai* (**GOD the Lord**).

c. **God will wound the head of His enemies**: In describing God's victory, David used an image from Genesis 3:15 where God promised that the Messiah would strike a fatal head wound against Satan. The victory would be total, with God's people walking as winners over the field of battle (**that your foot may crush them in blood**).

i. "*The hairy scalp*, i.e. his most fierce and terrible enemies. For in ancient times many people used to wear long and shaggy hair, that their looks might be more terrible to their enemies." (Poole)

2. (24-27) The procession of the ark.

They have seen Your procession, O God,
The procession of my God, my King, into the sanctuary.

The singers went before, the players on instruments *followed* after;
Among *them were* the maidens playing timbrels.
Bless God in the congregations,
The Lord, from the fountain of Israel.
There *is* little Benjamin, their leader,
The princes of Judah *and* their company,
The princes of Zebulun *and* the princes of Naphtali.

a. **The procession of my God, my King, into the sanctuary**: After the great triumph over their enemies, David and Israel could bring the ark of the covenant into Jerusalem (2 Samuel 6). This was not *David's* parade, but **Your procession, O God**. Honor went to Him.

i. "As the ark, the throne of the invisible God, leads the procession up to its resting place, its progress is a victory march completing the exodus." (Kidner)

ii. **From the fountain of Israel**: "Reuchlin was wont to say, that the Latins drank out of cisterns, the Greeks out of ponds, but the Hebrews out of the fountain itself." (Trapp)

b. **There is little Benjamin, their leader**: In the procession of the ark, the small tribe of **Benjamin** had a prominent role. This showed wonderful grace on David's part because his predecessor King Saul was from the tribe of Benjamin, and many kings of David's day would refuse to give them any honor at all.

i. "*Little Benjamin*. That tribe is called *little*, partly because it was the youngest, as being descended from Jacob's youngest son Benjamin; and principally because it was exceedingly diminished, and almost extinguished, under the judges." (Poole)

ii. "The fact that there are only four tribes may be explained by the principle of poetic selectivity." (VanGemeren)

3. (28-31) Confidence for future victories.

Your God has commanded your strength;
Strengthen, O God, what You have done for us.
Because of Your temple at Jerusalem,
Kings will bring presents to You.
Rebuke the beasts of the reeds,
The herd of bulls with the calves of the peoples,
Till everyone submits himself with pieces of silver.
Scatter the peoples *who* delight in war.
Envoys will come out of Egypt;
Ethiopia will quickly stretch out her hands to God.

a. **Strengthen, O God, what You have done for us**: David was grateful for the wonderful victory but also knew that many challenges were still ahead. He prayed that God would pour strength into the victory of the past, using it as a foundation for what He would do in the future.

b. **Because of Your temple at Jerusalem, kings will bring presents to You**: David was confident that in the end, God and His covenant people would survive and thrive despite their enemies among the nations. In the end others would come in tribute to Israel, not the other way around.

i. Ultimately, this speaks of "A time still in the future when Jesus will actually reign on earth, the millennium, though there is certainly a kind of fulfillment now through Christians' obedience to the Great Commission and the resulting advance of worldwide Christianity." (Boice)

c. **Rebuke the beasts of the reeds**: Since **reeds** were often associated with the Nile River, David prayed that God would keep them safe against the Egyptians and Ethiopians. He asked God to do that until they, like all the nations, come in submitted tribute to Jerusalem (**till everyone submits himself with pieces of silver...envoys will come out of Egypt**).

i. "The 'beast' and the 'bulls' denote the oppressors, troublers, and seducers of the nations. They must come to an end, as the nations that have loved warfare and tribute will be 'humbled' and despoiled." (VanGemeren)

ii. "*Egypt, Ethiopia:* he names only these, as the great and ancient enemies of God, and of his people, and as a most wicked, and idolatrous, and incorrigible sort of men; see Jeremiah 13:23, Amos 9:7; but by them he synecdochically understands all other nations and people of the like character." (Poole)

iii. "Old foes shall be new friends. Solomon shall find a spouse in Pharaoh's house. Christ shall gather a people from the realms of sin. Great sinners shall yield themselves to the sceptre of grace, and great men shall become good men, by coming to God." (Spurgeon)

4. (32-35) All the kingdoms of the earth praise the God of Israel.

Sing to God, you kingdoms of the earth;
Oh, sing praises to the Lord, Selah
To Him who rides on the heaven of heavens, *which were* of old!
Indeed, He sends out His voice, a mighty voice.
Ascribe strength to God;
His excellence *is* over Israel,
And His strength *is* in the clouds.

O God, *You are* **more awesome than Your holy places.**
The God of Israel *is* **He who gives strength and power to** *His* **people.**
Blessed *be* **God!**

> a. **Sing to God, you kingdoms of the earth**: Knowing the ultimate victory of God, David invited the nations to worship Him *now*. It was far better for them to do it now out of a willing, surrendered heart than to do it later as conquered enemies of God.

> > i. "We have too much sinning against God, but cannot have too much singing to God." (Spurgeon)

> > ii. **The heaven of heavens, which were of old**: "This Hebrew word [of old] answers to *olam*, which looks not only backward to time past; but forward to the future." (Poole)

> b. **Ascribe strength to God; His excellence over Israel**: The nations would only benefit from recognizing and surrendering to God's **strength** and noting His rule over Israel.

> c. **O God, You are more awesome than Your holy places**: David thought of the land of Israel as God's holy place, belonging to Him in a special way. Yet David had the sophistication to understand that God was greater than any **holy place**, whether it be land, a mountain, or a temple.

> d. **The God of Israel is He who gives strength and power to His people**: The God who is actively involved in the life and victory of His people is worthy of praise.

> > i. This psalm has been much loved by generals and soldiers: "To the Crusaders, setting out for the recovery of the Holy Land; to Savonarola and his monks, as they marched to the 'Trial of Fire' in the Piazza at Florence; to the Huguenots, who called it 'The song of battles'; to Cromwell, at Dunbar, as the sun rose on the mists of the morning and he charged Leslie's army." (Kirkpatrick, cited in Morgan)

> > ii. Whatever victory they may have won and inspiration they received from this psalm, their victories did not last. The lasting victory still waits for the Messiah's great kingdom.

Psalm 69 – Rescued from Deep Waters

This psalm is titled **To the Chief Musician. Set to "The Lilies." A Psalm of David.**

As with Psalm 45, this psalm is **Set to "The Lilies."** *The phrase may refer to the general beauty of the composition, to the tune, or even to a six-stringed instrument known as the Shoshannim (the literal translation of the Hebrew).*

"Perhaps in no psalm in the whole psalter is the sense of sorrow profounder or more intense than in this. The soul of the singer pours itself out in unrestrained abandonment to the overwhelming and terrible grief which consumes it." (G. Campbell Morgan)

A. Drowning in disapproval.

1. (1-3) Drowning in a flood of trouble.

Save me, O God!
For the waters have come up to *my* neck.
I sink in deep mire,
Where *there is* no standing;
I have come into deep waters,
Where the floods overflow me.
I am weary with my crying;
My throat is dry;
My eyes fail while I wait for my God.

> a. **Save me, O God**: David had many times in his life where this prayer was needed. He felt he was about to drown (**the waters have come up to my neck**). Centuries later, the Son of David heard a drowning disciple cry out, *Save me!* (Matthew 14:30)
>
>> i. Sometimes we feel like things rush in on us, like drowning in a flood. Other times we feel as if the water level slowly rises until we are overwhelmed. Each has its own type of fear and misery.

b. **I sink in deep mire**: In other psalms David rejoiced at being set upon a rock (Psalm 40:2). Here he is in the opposite position, sinking down in the mud and the **mire, where there is no standing**.

i. We can picture Jesus sinking down into the **deep mire** of humanity's sin and guilt, coming truly to the **deep waters, where the floods overflow**. No wonder it was said of Jesus before He went to the cross, *He began to be sorrowful and deeply distressed* (Matthew 26:37).

ii. Spurgeon described several kinds of **deep mire** the believer may sink into:

- The deep mire of unbelief.
- The deep mire of trial and difficulty.
- The deep mire of inward corruption.
- The deep mire of the devil's temptation and oppression.

c. **I am weary with my crying**: David was worn out with all the energy spent in his crying and crying out as he waited for God to rescue him.

i. **My throat is dry**: "We are, it is to be feared, more likely to be hoarse with talking frivolities to men than by pleading with God." (Spurgeon)

2. (4) The problem described.

Those who hate me without a cause
Are more than the hairs of my head;
They are mighty who would destroy me,
***Being* my enemies wrongfully;**
Though I have stolen nothing,
I *still* must restore it.

a. **Those who hate me without a cause are more than the hairs of my head**: This begins the description of the real problems David poetically described in the previous verses. He lived under the great stress of knowing there were many people who simply hated him, and **without cause**.

i. "Nothing can be conceived more overwhelming than the strange and inexplicable suffering resulting from loyalty to God and zeal for His honor. Undeserved reproach is the most stupendous grief possible to the sensitive soul." (Morgan)

ii. It's hard for us to believe that such a wonderful, godly man as David would be so hated. This is human nature, and was even more evident in the hatred **without cause** directed to Jesus Christ, David's Greater Son.

iii. Jesus specifically referred to Psalm 69:4 when He spoke to His disciples the night before His crucifixion. He said, *But this happened that the word might be fulfilled which is written in their law, "They hated Me without a cause."* (John 15:25)

iv. "There were those among the scribes and Pharisees, the priests and the Levites, who simply hated him. The reason is not far to find. Until he came and stood beside them, they looked like good men.... They hated him freely; they hated him without cause in himself. The only cause was in their evil hearts." (Barnhouse, cited in Boice)

b. **They are mighty who would destroy me**: Among the many who hated David were some who went beyond the feelings of hatred to active efforts to **destroy** him. Those set on David's destruction were **mighty**; they could make it happen.

i. "The burdened heart finds some ease in describing how heavy its burden is, and the devout heart receives some foretaste of longed-for help in the act of telling God how sorely His help is needed." (Maclaren)

c. **Though I have stolen nothing, I still must restore it**: The fundamental *injustice* of David's misery increased his sense of despair.

i. "Though innocent, he was treated guilty. Though David had no share in plots against Saul, yet he was held accountable for them." (Spurgeon)

ii. David could only imperfectly say, **I have stolen nothing**, but his Greater Son could say it in a remarkable way. The devil tried to take what was not his – God's honor and glory in heaven. Adam took what was not his – the fruit forbidden to him. Moses took what was not lawful for him to take – the life of an Egyptian foreman. David took what was not his – Bathsheba into his bed. Yet Jesus *refused* to take what was rightfully His; *He did not consider it robbery to be equal with God* (Philippians 2:6), choosing to set aside Divine privileges that were rightfully His. For this, Jesus was condemned by humanity: *He ought to die, because He made Himself the Son of God* (John 19:7).

3. (5-12) Living with the constant disapproval of man.

O God, You know my foolishness;
And my sins are not hidden from You.
Let not those who wait for You, O Lord GOD of hosts, be ashamed
because of me;
Let not those who seek You be confounded because of me, O God of
Israel.

Because for Your sake I have borne reproach;
Shame has covered my face.
I have become a stranger to my brothers,
And an alien to my mother's children;
Because zeal for Your house has eaten me up,
And the reproaches of those who reproach You have fallen on me.
When I wept *and chastened* my soul with fasting,
That became my reproach.
I also made sackcloth my garment;
I became a byword to them.
Those who sit in the gate speak against me,
And I *am* the song of the drunkards.

a. **You know my foolishness; and my sins are not hidden from You**: In many of the psalms, David proclaimed his innocence compared to his adversaries. In Psalm 69 David confessed his sin and failings, appealing to God's mercy.

i. "[By] *Foolishness* he means lesser sins, committed through ignorance or inconsiderateness, and by *sins* those of a grosser nature." (Poole)

ii. **My sins are not hidden from You**: "It ought to render confession easy, when we are assured that all is known already." (Spurgeon)

iii. **My sins are not hidden from You**: We may spiritually apply this to Jesus, noting the public nature of His humiliation on the cross. Nailed to the cross, likely with no clothing at all before a mocking public, Jesus accomplished His great work on the cross with nothing **hidden**. He had no sins of His own to bear, but the bearing of our **sins** was not **hidden from** either God or man.

b. **Let not those who seek You be confounded because of me**: David's concern was not only the effect it had upon himself, but especially the effect it had upon the people of God. The thought of embarrassing those who seek God was painful to David.

i. "He feared lest other believing and loyal souls should be deflected from faith, and dishonoured because of what they saw of his sufferings." (Morgan)

ii. "It ought to be the prayer of every Christian, especially if he be a minister of the gospel, that his sufferings in the world may not give just offence to the brethren, or the church." (Horne)

iii. **O Lord God of hosts**: "This phrase includes three designations for God. He is the Lord of the universe [**Lord**, *Adonai*], the Lord of the covenant [**God**, *Yahweh*], and the Divine Warrior [**of hosts**, *Zaboath*]." (VanGemeren)

c. **Shame has covered my face**: Among the other problems caused by David's sin, he also had to deal with damaged relationships with his **brothers**.

> i. "Unless this aversion of his brethren had pained him, he would not have complained of it. It would not have pained him unless he had felt a special affection for them." (Musculus, cited in Spurgeon)

> ii. How strange it was that Jesus' own brothers rejected Him and treated Him as **a stranger** (John 7:5, Mark 3:21). If any should have stood by Him and defended Him to the death, it should have been His own brothers.

d. **Because zeal for Your house has eaten me up, and the reproaches of those who reproach You have fallen on me**: David's sin was not the only cause of his problems. He was also rejected and spoken against because of his **zeal** for God and His **house**.

> i. The **zeal** connected to God's **house** for David was evident in his desire to build God a temple (2 Samuel 7:1-3) and in the diligent preparation he made for the temple that his son Solomon would actually build (1 Chronicles 22:1-5).

> ii. When Jesus drove the moneychangers out of the temple courts at the beginning of His ministry, His disciples remembered this very passage from Psalm 69:9 (John 2:17).

> iii. "*Eaten me up;* exhausted and wasted my natural moisture and vital spirits, which is oft effected by grief and anger, and fervent love and desire; of which passions zeal is composed." (Poole)

> iv. "Some men are eaten up with lechery, others with covetousness, and a third class with pride, but the master-passion with our great leader was the glory of God, jealousy for his name, and love to the divine family." (Spurgeon)

e. **The reproaches of those who reproach You have fallen on me**: David was happy to identify himself with God, counting it an honor to bear the disapproval of those who disapproved of Yahweh.

> i. The Apostle Paul referenced Psalm 69:9 in speaking of the sacrificial nature of Jesus in Romans 15:3: *For even Christ did not please Himself; but as it is written, "The reproaches of those who reproached You fell on Me."*

f. **When I wept and chastened my soul with fasting, that became my reproach**: David was rejected because of his foolishness and sins (Psalm 69:5). When he repented, then people disapproved of that.

i. **I also made sackcloth my garment**: "[This was] A fashion at solemn fasts among the Easterlings; as if they thought the coarsest clothing too good for them; and but for shame would have gone stark naked." (Trapp)

ii. **I became a byword to them**: The idea is becoming a proverb, a label. In our world this is a deliberate strategy, to dismiss people simply by giving them a label so that you don't have to think about or engage their ideas. Faithful believers know the sting of this today. They are derided as *religious nuts* and *fundamentalists* and *radicals* and *haters*.

g. **Those who sit in the gate speak against me, and I am the song of the drunkards**: David became the target of scorn and disapproval from almost everyone, from the leaders of the city to the city drunks.

i. "*Of the drunkards;* of the scum of the people; of all lewd and debauched persons. Thus both high and low conspired against him." (Trapp)

ii. "To this day the tavern makes rare fun of the tabernacle, and the ale-bench is the seat of the scorner." (Spurgeon)

iii. The High Priest and the thief on the cross both reviled Jesus.

B. The prayer for rescue.

1. (13-15) The appeal to God.

But as for me, my prayer *is* to You,
O Lᴏʀᴅ, *in* the acceptable time;
O God, in the multitude of Your mercy,
Hear me in the truth of Your salvation.
Deliver me out of the mire,
And let me not sink;
Let me be delivered from those who hate me,
And out of the deep waters.
Let not the floodwater overflow me,
Nor let the deep swallow me up;
And let not the pit shut its mouth on me.

a. **As for me, my prayer is to You**: With the constant disapproval from men, David naturally and wisely turned to God. He would seek God and make his prayer to the One who would hear **in the multitude of Your mercy**.

i. **In the acceptable time**: "It was a time of rejection with man, but of acceptance with God. Sin ruled on earth, but grace reigned in heaven." (Spurgeon)

b. **Let not the floodwater overflow me**: With poetic repetition, David returned to the image of him drowning, asking God to rescue him from those who **hate** him.

2. (16-18) Asking for speedy deliverance.

Hear me, O LORD, for Your lovingkindness *is* good;
Turn to me according to the multitude of Your tender mercies.
And do not hide Your face from Your servant,
For I am in trouble;
Hear me speedily.
Draw near to my soul, *and* redeem it;
Deliver me because of my enemies.

a. **Hear me, O Lord, for Your lovingkindness is good**: Appealing to God because of his loyal love (**lovingkindness**, *hesed*), David once again asked for the **multitude** of God's **tender mercies**.

b. **Do not hide Your face from Your servant, for I am in trouble**: By presenting himself to God as His **servant** and in **trouble**, David hoped to appeal to God's compassion.

3. (19-21) The plea for compassion.

You know my reproach, my shame, and my dishonor;
My adversaries *are* all before You.
Reproach has broken my heart,
And I am full of heaviness;
I looked *for someone* to take pity, but *there was* none;
And for comforters, but I found none.
They also gave me gall for my food,
And for my thirst they gave me vinegar to drink.

a. **You know my reproach, my shame, and my dishonor**: The appeal to God's compassion continued, especially because David bore much reproach in his loyalty to God (Psalm 69:9b).

i. Adam Clarke wrote of Psalm 69:19-20: "This is one of the most forcible appeals to mercy and compassion that was ever made. The language of these two verses is inimitable; and the sentiment cannot be mended. I can devise no comment that would not lessen their effect." (Clarke)

ii. **My adversaries are all before You**: Spurgeon pictured these words in the heart of Jesus in His great suffering: "The whole lewd and loud company is now present to thine eye: Judas and his treachery; Herod and his cunning; Caiaphas and his counsel; Pilate and his vacillation; Jews, priests, people, rulers, all, thou seest and wilt judge." (Spurgeon)

b. **I looked for someone to take pity, but there was none**: David asked God for help because there was **none** to help him.

c. **They also gave me gall for my food, and for my thirst they gave me vinegar to drink**: Instead of help, David found cruelty from his enemies. They gave him bitter things to eat (**gall for my food**) and sour **vinegar to drink**.

i. "*Gall*, or *poison*, or *bitter herbs* [hemlock], Hosea 10:4." (Poole)

ii. "Such are the comforts often administered by the world to an afflicted and deserted soul." (Horne) As believers we must have special care that we are *not like* the world in this respect, and that we do not increase the misery of those who are already laid low.

iii. This is another line in Psalm 69 that is referred to in the New Testament, specifically in the suffering of Jesus. On the cross they gave Him **vinegar to drink**. This is described in Matthew 27:34; John 19:28-29 is even more clear with John adding that this was done *that the Scripture might be fulfilled*.

iv. "What David was offered in metaphor, Jesus was offered in fact, according to Matthew 27:34, 48, where the Greek words for gall and *vinegar* are those that the LXX [Septuagint] uses here." (Kidner)

4. (22-28) Asking for the defeat of his enemies.

Let their table become a snare before them,
And their well-being a trap.
Let their eyes be darkened, so that they do not see;
And make their loins shake continually.
Pour out Your indignation upon them,
And let Your wrathful anger take hold of them.
Let their dwelling place be desolate;
Let no one live in their tents.
For they persecute the *ones* You have struck,
And talk of the grief of those You have wounded.
Add iniquity to their iniquity,
And let them not come into Your righteousness.
Let them be blotted out of the book of the living,
And not be written with the righteous.

a. **Let their table become a snare before them, and their well-being a trap**: David hurt under the scorn of those who sat comfortably while he was in misery. He prayed that their ease would become a trap.

i. In the section from Psalm 69:22-28, it's hard to know if David meant, "This is what I want God to do to them" or "This is what I know God will do to them." In either sense the point is clear. "He denounceth ten plagues, or effects of God's wrath, to come upon them for their wickedness." (Dickson, cited in Spurgeon)

ii. "*Their table* figuratively sets forth their prosperity, the abundance of all things. It represents peace and security, as in Psalm 33:5; Job 36:16." (Venema, cited in Spurgeon)

iii. This peril waiting for those who rejected the man after God's heart as described in Psalm 69:22-23 was quoted by the Apostle Paul in Romans 11:9-10 as appropriate to those among his own people who rejected Jesus.

b. **Let their eyes be darkened, so that they do not see**: David's enemies had distorted vision when they looked at him; he prayed the distortion would become permanent blindness.

c. **Pour out Your indignation upon them**: David asked God to fulfill a series of curses upon his enemies, ending with the wish that they would **be blotted out of the book of the living, and not be written with the righteous**.

i. **Let their dwelling place become desolate**: This line is twice referred to in the New Testament. Jesus quoted it in sadness over Jerusalem (Matthew 23:38) and Peter quoted it as descriptive of the desolation of Judas (Acts 1:20).

ii. **Add iniquity to their iniquity**: "Punish one sin with another (by giving them up to a reprobate sense, to an incurable hardness), and plague them soundly for their sin. The same Hebrew word signifieth both sin and punishment; these two are tied together with chains of adamant." (Trapp)

iii. **Let them be blotted out of the book**: "But to blot names therefrom is not only to kill, but to exclude from the national community, and so from all the privileges of the people of God." (Maclaren)

iv. Most draw a contrast between these severe prayers of David and what seems to be a more loving approach to enemies taught in the New Testament. "But the very juxtaposition of David cursing his tormentors and Jesus praying for His, brings out the gulf between type and antitype, and indeed between accepted attitudes among saints of the Old Testament and the New." (Kidner)

v. That more loving approach is often given example in the great forgiveness Jesus showed even for those who nailed Him to the cross. G. Campbell Morgan had a somewhat contrary analysis: "He said, 'Father, forgive them, for they know not what they do.' That was a prayer inspired by His freedom from all personal vindictiveness. Neither in that prayer, nor in any of His teachings, can we find a word of tolerance for those who do evil, knowing that it is evil." (Morgan)

5. (29-33) Lifting up the poor and humble one.

But I *am* poor and sorrowful;
Let Your salvation, O God, set me up on high.
I will praise the name of God with a song,
And will magnify Him with thanksgiving.
***This* also shall please the Lord better than an ox *or* bull,**
Which has horns and hooves.
The humble shall see *this and* be glad;
And you who seek God, your hearts shall live.
For the Lord hears the poor,
And does not despise His prisoners.

a. **Let Your salvation, O God, set me up on high**: David did not only pray for the downfall of his enemies. He also asked God to rescue him from drowning in the mire of hateful men and to establish him **up on high**.

i. **I am poor and sorrowful**: "Literally, *I am laid low, and full of pain* or *grief*. Hence the prayer, 'Let thy salvation, O God set me on high!' My oppression has laid me *low*; thy salvation shall make me *high*!" (Clarke)

b. **I will praise the name of God with a song**: Moving to greater confidence, the psalmist vowed to **praise** and **magnify** God for His rescue. This sincere praise honored God even more than an animal sacrifice.

i. **Which has horns and hooves**: "A bullock was in its prime for sacrifice, under the law, when it began to put forth its 'horns and hoofs.'" (Horne)

c. **You who seek God, your hearts shall live**: The trial of the psalmist would not be wasted. He would become a lesson to others who **seek God** and show them how their **hearts shall live**.

6. (34-36) The triumphant conclusion.

Let heaven and earth praise Him,
The seas and everything that moves in them.

For God will save Zion
And build the cities of Judah,
That they may dwell there and possess it.
Also, the descendants of His servants shall inherit it,
And those who love His name shall dwell in it.

a. **Let heaven and earth praise Him**: As low as this psalm began, it soars to the highest praise in the end. **Heaven and earth** are not big enough to give God the praise He is due. **The seas and everything that moves in them** will also bring Him praise.

b. **For God will save Zion and build the cities of Judah**: The vision is lifted high above the problems of one man. Now David prayed for blessing for Jerusalem and Judah, **that they may dwell there and possess it**.

i. Some believe that the specific mention of **the cities of Judah** and no mention of broader Israel means this psalm, or this portion of the psalm, must date to either the days of the divided monarchy or of the Babylonian exile. This is not at all necessary. First, it is not unusual that David would have special regard for the land of his own tribe, **Judah**. Second, it may have been composed in the seven years and six months when David was king over Judah, before he was king over the other 11 tribes (2 Samuel 2:1-11).

c. **Those who love His name shall dwell in it**: Scorned by his enemies, David knew that he and others who **love His name** would **inherit** the land and **dwell in it**.

Psalm 70 – Help Quickly, O Lord

This psalm is titled **To the Chief Musician.** *A* **Psalm** *of* **David. To bring to remembrance.** *This psalm certainly has the sense of* **remembrance**, *in that it is almost the same as Psalm 40:13-17.*

"This prayer is the shield, spear, thunderbolt and defense against every attack of rear, presumption [and] lukewarmness...which are especially dominant today." (Martin Luther, cited in James Montgomery Boice)

A. The plea for deliverance.

1. (1) Answer me quickly, O God.

Make haste, O God, to deliver me!
Make haste to help me, O Lord!

a. **Make haste, O God, to deliver me**: David asked God to bring help with **haste**, knowing that if deliverance was too long delayed, it was of no help at all. Therefore he asked with a sense of urgency. Many of our prayers would prevail more with God if they were offered with more urgency.

i. "The petitions in this form of the psalm emphasize the urgency of the matter. There is not a moment to lose; or so it appears." (Kidner)

b. **Make haste to help me, O Lord**: David repeated the request for emphasis, but slightly changed his address to Deity. In the repetition he used the name *Yahweh* (**Lord**), the covenant name of God. By the additional name he hoped to secure additional speed in the reply.

i. G. Campbell Morgan believed that such prayers were flawed in their understanding of God. "It reveals a mistaken conception of God. God never needs to be called upon to hasten. He is never tarrying uselessly or carelessly." (Morgan)

ii. However, Morgan explained that God still wants to hear such imperfect prayers. "We may use any terms in our prayers, if they are directed to Him, knowing that He will understand, and in

His understanding, interpret our faulty terms by His own perfect knowledge, and give us His best answers to our deepest need." (Morgan)

iii. "Let us take it and use it, knowing that He would far rather have in our song an expression of an honest questioning than any affectation of a confidence not possessed. Moreover, He would rather have from us such a song than silence." (Morgan)

2. (2-3) David prays against his adversaries.

Let them be ashamed and confounded
Who seek my life;
Let them be turned back and confused
Who desire my hurt.
Let them be turned back because of their shame,
Who say, "Aha, aha!"

a. **Let them be ashamed and confounded who seek my life**: This was the help that David sought. David prayed that God would turn back his enemies and cause them to be **confused**.

i. "The psalmist prays for his enemies' fall and shame in accordance with the principles of justice and with the promise of God to curse those who cursed his own." (VanGemeren)

b. **Let them be turned back because of their shame**: This was a bold request, because many times our enemies seem to have no sense of **shame** as they attack and oppose us.

i. "The kindest thing we can pray for people who do wrong is that their plans will fail, for it may be that in their frustration they will see the folly and true end of evil and be reached for God." (Boice)

ii. "Rest assured, the enemies of Christ and his people shall have wages for their work; they shall be paid in their own coin; they loved scoffing, and they shall be filled with it." (Spurgeon)

c. **Who say to me, "Aha! Aha!"**: This has the sense of scornful mocking. It was bad enough that David's enemies wanted him dead; they also poured ridicule on him.

i. "*Heach! heach*! a note of supreme contempt." (Clarke)

B. Praise added to the plea.

1. (4) Calling God's people to praise.

Let all those who seek You rejoice and be glad in You;
And let those who love Your salvation say continually,
"Let God be magnified!"

a. **Let all those who seek You rejoice and be glad in You**: David called the people of God – those who **seek** Him and **love** His **salvation** – to be happy in Him. We sense that it would be impossible for David to do this unless he also found some measure of joy and gladness in God, despite his urgent problem.

b. **Let those who love Your salvation say continually, "Let God be magnified"**: David thought that to praise God was to *magnify* Him – that is, to make Him larger in one's perception. Magnification does not actually make an object bigger, and we can't make God bigger. Still, to magnify something or someone is to *perceive* it as bigger, and we must do that regarding God.

> i. **Those who love Your salvation**: "All men are lovers as well as seekers; for all men love. Some love money more than God's salvation; others love pleasure, even the pleasures of sin, more than God's salvation; and others love bustle and business more than God's salvation." (Frame, cited in Spurgeon)

> ii. **Let God be magnified**: "It does not say, let God be magnified by me if he will please to make me successful in business, and happy, and healthy, but it leaves it open. Only let God be magnified, and he may do what he wills with me." (Spurgeon)

> iii. "Nor is there any limit as to place or persons. My heart says, 'Let God be magnified among the Wesleyans! The Lord be magnified among the Independents! The Lord be magnified among the Episcopalians! The Lord be magnified among the Baptists!'" (Spurgeon)

> iv. "The doxology, '*Let* the Lord's name be magnified,' is infinitely more manly and ennobling than the dog's bark of '*Aha, aha.*'" (Spurgeon)

2. (5) The plea repeated: Help quickly, O God.

But I *am* poor and needy;
Make haste to me, O God!
You *are* my help and my deliverer;
O LORD, do not delay.

a. **But I am poor and needy**: David could combine his sense of great joy in God with a realistic appraisal of his present need. Secure in the truth that God cared for and thought about him, David again appealed to God to be his **help** and **deliverer**, and he needed God to do this without **delay**.

> i. **Poor and needy**: "I am a poor man, and a beggar – an *afflicted beggar*; a sense of my poverty causes me to beg." (Clarke)

ii. Spurgeon thought that the sense of being **poor and needy** was also appropriate for a congregation seeking God's blessing. "We are praying for a display of the Holy Spirit's power in this church, and, in order to have successful pleading in this matter, it is necessary that we should unanimously make the confession of our text, 'I am poor and needy.' We must own that we are powerless in this business." (Spurgeon)

iii. **Poor and needy**: "With such a Father and such a Friend, poverty becometh rich, and weakness itself is strong." (Horne)

iv. The request is repeated again for emphasis: **Make haste to me, O God!** "But God is making haste. On the wings of every hour, quicker than light leaps from world to world, He is on his way. Delays are not denials, but are necessary to the perfecting of his arrangements." (Meyer)

b. **You are my help and my deliverer**: David appealed to God on the grounds that he had *no other* **help** or **deliverer**. He would not look to self or the gods of the nations. God would answer this complete dependence upon Him.

Psalm 71 – Older in Years, Strong in Faith

Many commentators believe this is a psalm of David and is his prayer and trust in God in his latter years under the crisis of Absalom's rebellion. Since there is no title and the text of the psalm does not say this, we will not speculate and treat Psalm 71 as if it were written under those circumstances. Instead, we regard it as an anonymous composition.

"We have here THE PRAYER OF THE AGED BELIEVER, *who in holy confidence of faith, strengthened by a long and remarkable experience, pleads against his enemies, and asks further blessings for himself." (Charles Spurgeon)*

Of interest in this psalm are the many references and allusions to other psalms.

- Psalm 71:1-3 is quoted almost exactly from Psalm 31:1-3.

- The thoughts of Psalm 71:5 seem to be suggested by Psalm 22:9-11.

- Do not be far from me *(Psalm 71:12a)* echoes Psalm 22:11.

- My God, make haste to help me! *(Psalm 71:12b) takes the thought of Psalm 70:1.*

- *Psalm 71:13 is similar to Psalm 35:26.*

- *Psalm 71:18 carries the thoughts of Psalm 22:22 and 22:30-31.*

- *Psalm 71:19 uses the phrasing of Exodus 15:11.*

It is reasonable to think the author of Psalm 71 made study and meditation upon God's Word a priority through his life, and the result is that he naturally used the phrases and vocabulary of the Scriptures to pray and praise.

"But imitative words are none the less sincere; and new thankfulness may be run into old moulds without detriment to its acceptableness to God and preciousness to men." (Alexander Maclaren)

A. God our refuge in older years.

1. (1-3) Trusting the LORD who delivers His people.

In You, O Lᴏʀᴅ, I put my trust;
Let me never be put to shame.
Deliver me in Your righteousness, and cause me to escape;
Incline Your ear to me, and save me.
Be my strong refuge,
To which I may resort continually;
You have given the commandment to save me,
For You *are* my rock and my fortress.

a. **In You, O Lᴏʀᴅ, I put my trust**: Many psalms begin with the description of the poet's need. The first line of Psalm 71 looks to God and declares the singer's trust in Yahweh, the Lᴏʀᴅ, the covenant God of Israel. The psalmist was confident that such trust in the Lᴏʀᴅ would lead to vindication and that he would **never be put to shame**.

i. "The Psalmist so often begins his prayer with a declaration of his 'faith' which is to the soul in affliction what an anchor is to a ship in distress." (Horne)

b. **Deliver me in Your righteousness**: Because the psalmist trusted in God, he boldly asked God to act righteously on his behalf, and to **deliver** him. He asked that the **righteousness** of God work on his behalf.

c. **Incline Your ear...save me...be my strong refuge**: In the previous line the psalmist established the basis of God's rescue: *deliver me in Your righteousness*. He then called on God to act righteously on behalf of His needy servant, to rescue and protect him.

i. **Be my strong refuge**: "Here we see a weak man, but he is in a strong habitation: his security rests upon the tower in which he hides and is not placed in jeopardy through his personal feebleness." (Spurgeon)

d. **You have given the command to save me**: Confident that it was God's will, even His **command**, the psalmist prayed with full confidence that God would be his **rock** and his **fortress**.

2. (4-6) Trusting in the constant care of God.

Deliver me, O my God, out of the hand of the wicked,
Out of the hand of the unrighteous and cruel man.
For You are my hope, O Lord Gᴏᴅ;
You are my trust from my youth.
By You I have been upheld from birth;
You are He who took me out of my mother's womb.
My praise *shall be* continually of You.

a. **Deliver me, O my God, out of the hand of the wicked**: The source of the psalmist's misery is revealed. There was a **wicked** man, **unrighteous**

and cruel who seemed to hold the psalmist in his grip. From this he needed God to **deliver** him.

>   i. **Out of the hand of the wicked**: "Ever remembering that wickedness is at least as dangerous when it tempts as when it persecutes; and can smile, as well as frown, a man dead." (Horne)

> b. **You are my hope, O Lord GOD**: The psalmist proclaimed his **hope** and **trust** in *Adonai Yahweh*, the Master and covenant God of Israel. It wasn't just that his hope was *in* Yahweh; He *was* his **hope**.

> c. **By You I have been upheld from birth**: Noting God's care and help to him from the earliest age, the psalmist appealed to God's continued care, and in turn he promised **praise** to God that was just as continual.

>   i. "As in the womb I lived upon thee, so from the womb." (Trapp)

>   ii. **My praise shall be continually of You**: "Where goodness has been unceasingly received, praise should unceasingly be offered." (Spurgeon)

3. (7-11) A strong refuge through a long life.

I have become as a wonder to many,
But You *are* my strong refuge.
Let my mouth be filled *with* Your praise
***And with* Your glory all the day.**
Do not cast me off in the time of old age;
Do not forsake me when my strength fails.
For my enemies speak against me;
And those who lie in wait for my life take counsel together,
Saying, "God has forsaken him;
Pursue and take him, for *there is* none to deliver *him*."

> a. **I have become a wonder to many, but You are my strong refuge**: Because of the many adversities and attacks, many people were amazed at the psalmist. They were in **wonder** that a man – especially one so committed to God – could be so afflicted. Despite it all, he found a **strong refuge** in God Himself.

>   i. "The believer is a riddle, an enigma puzzling the unspiritual; he is a monster warring with those delights of the flesh, which are the all in all of other men; he is a prodigy, unaccountable to the judgments of ungodly men; a wonder gazed at, feared, and, by-and-by, contemptuously derided." (Spurgeon)

>   ii. "Christ, in his state of humiliation upon earth, was a 'sign' everywhere 'spoken against,' as Simeon foretold he would be; Luke 2:34." (Horne)

iii. **But You are my strong refuge**: "Note, too, the pivotal effect of the phrase *but thou* (71:7b) in re-directing his attention from himself and the encircling enemy; an escape *to* reality rather than from it." (Kidner)

b. **Let my mouth be filled with Your praise**: Because God had been so faithful as a **strong refuge**, the psalmist was determined to speak **praise** unto God and speak of His **glory**.

i. "God's bread is always in our mouths, so should his praise be. He fills us with good; let us be also filled with gratitude. This would leave no room for murmuring or backbiting." (Spurgeon)

c. **Do not forsake me when my strength fails**: The psalmist knew the faithfulness of God through his younger years and now asked that God continue that faithfulness in his **old age** and as his **strength fails**. He knew that *man's* strength diminishes with old age, but *God's* strength does not.

i. "It is not unnatural or improper for a man who sees old age coming upon him to pray for special grace, and special strength, to enable him to meet what he cannot ward off, and what he cannot but dread; for who can look upon the infirmities of old age, as coming upon himself, but with sad and pensive feelings? Who would wish *to be* an old man?" (Barnes, cited in Spurgeon)

ii. The psalmist did not only speak of the loss of *physical* and *mental* strength, but also the potential loss of *spiritual* strength. Not every believer grows stronger in the Lord as he grows older. The Bible is filled with examples of those who sinned or fell away in the older years.

- David sinned against Bathsheba and her husband Uriah in his mature years (2 Samuel 11).
- Solomon was drawn away to idolatry in his later years (1 Kings 11).
- King Asa's trust in God greatly declined in his later years (2 Chronicles 16:7-12).

d. **For my enemies speak against me**: The psalmist knew what his adversaries said against him. He knew they claimed that **God has forsaken him** and **there is none to deliver him**. His adversity made them think God was no longer with him, so it was a good time to attack (**pursue and take him**).

i. Jesus knew what it was like for men to say against Him, "**God has forsaken him**" (Luke 23:35-37). "Our Lord felt this barbed shaft and it is no marvel if his disciples feel the same. Were this exclamation the truth, it were indeed an ill day for us; but, glory be to God, it is a barefaced lie." (Spurgeon)

4. (12-13) Help me by striking my enemies.

O God, do not be far from me;
O my God, make haste to help me!
Let them be confounded *and* consumed
Who are adversaries of my life;
Let them be covered *with* reproach and dishonor
Who seek my hurt.

a. **O my God, make haste to help me**: With determined enemies as described in the previous lines, the psalmist needed God's help *soon*. He felt as if delayed help was no help at all.

i. The psalmist had to deal with the fact that as his years advanced, his troubles did not go away. The problems remained. This is a significant test for some believers, but the psalmist understood it as compelling his constant and more personal trust in God.

ii. "Notice the still more intense grip of faith in the second clause. The psalmist first says, 'O God,' [and] then he says, 'O my God.' It is grand pleading when we so grasp God with the personal grip of faith that we cry, 'O my God, make haste for my help.'" (Spurgeon)

b. **Let them be confounded and consumed...Let them be covered with reproach and dishonor**: This was the help the psalmist asked for. He wanted God to strike his adversaries with confusion and consumption, with disapproval and dishonor. He not only wanted them defeated, but also discredited.

i. Adam Clarke regarded these **let them** statements more as prophecies than prayers: "They *shall* be confounded: these are *prophetic* denunciations." (Clarke)

B. Rising hope and praise.

1. (14-16) Continual hope, continual strength.

But I will hope continually,
And will praise You yet more and more.
My mouth shall tell of Your righteousness
***And* Your salvation all the day,**
For I do not know *their* limits.
I will go in the strength of the Lord God;
I will make mention of Your righteousness, of Yours only.

a. **I will hope continually, and will praise You yet more and more**: The psalmist was in a serious crisis and depended upon God for help. Yet in this psalm he does not slip into despair or seem to lose the sense of God's favor. Psalm 71 is a wonderful combination of both problems and praise.

 i. **I will hope continually**: "I shall expect deliverance after deliverance, and blessing after blessing; and, in consequence, I will praise thee more and more. As thy blessings abound, so shall my praises." (Clarke)

 ii. "When I cannot rejoice in what I have, I will look forward to what shall be mine, and will still rejoice." (Spurgeon)

 iii. **Praise You yet more and more**: "A dying hope would bring forth declining songs; as the expectations grew more dim, so would the music become more faint; but a hope immortal and eternal, flaming forth each day with intenser brightness, brings forth a song of praise which, as it shall always continue to arise, so shall it always gather new force." (Spurgeon)

b. **My mouth shall tell of Your righteousness and Your salvation all the day**: He was happy to testify of both God's **righteousness** and His **salvation**, and to do so all day long. He felt the entire day was needed because he did **not know** the **limits** of God's **righteousness** and **salvation**. They are limitless.

 i. **I do not know their limits**: "Lord, where I cannot count I will believe, and when a truth surpasses numeration I will take to admiration." (Spurgeon)

c. **I will go in the strength of the Lord GOD**: Looking forward, the psalmist was confident in God's **strength**, despite his sense of diminished personal strength with advancing years (Psalm 71:9).

 i. "He who goeth to the battle against his spiritual enemies should go, confiding not in his own 'strength,' but in that of the Lord God; not in his own 'righteousness,' but in that of his Redeemer. Such a one engageth with omnipotence on his side, and cannot but be victorious." (Horne)

d. **I will make mention of Your righteousness, of Yours only**: The psalmist was only interested in telling of *God's* **righteousness**, not of his own or the supposed righteousness of pagan gods.

 i. **Of Yours only**: "Man's righteousness is not fit to be mentioned – filthy rags are best hidden; neither is there any righteousness under heaven, or in heaven, comparable to the divine." (Spurgeon)

2. (17-18) The strength of God from youth to old age.

O God, You have taught me from my youth;
And to this *day* I declare Your wondrous works.
Now also when *I am* old and grayheaded,
O God, do not forsake me,
Until I declare Your strength to *this* generation,
Your power to everyone *who* is to come.

a. **You have taught me from my youth**: The psalmist had the blessed fortune to have followed God and learned of Him from his young years. It was something that benefited him to his older years, still declaring God's **wonderful works**.

i. To be **taught** from one's **youth** displays stability and consistency. There is no fluttering about from one fad to another, from one controversy to another.

ii. "He says, 'O God, thou hast taught me from my youth,' which implies that God had continued to teach him: and so indeed he had. The learner had not sought another school, nor had the Master turned off his pupil." (Spurgeon)

b. **When I am old and grayheaded, O God, do not forsake me, until I declare Your strength to this generation**: He prayed for the continued presence of God so that he could **declare God's** strength to a new **generation**.

i. "There is nothing more calculated to keep the heart of age young, than to stand by the young, sympathizing with their ambitions, heartening their endeavours, and stiffening their courage, by recounting the stories of the strength of God, the experiences of His might." (Morgan)

ii. "There is nothing more pitiful, or else more beautiful than old age. It is pitiful when its pessimism cools the ardours of youth. It is beautiful when its witness stimulates the visions and inspires the heroism of the young." (Morgan)

iii. **To everyone who is to come**: "To all succeeding generations, to whom I will leave a lasting monument of this glorious example of all-sufficiency, such as this Psalm is." (Poole)

3. (19-21) Revived by the God who does great things.

Also Your righteousness, O God, *is* very high,
You who have done great things;
O God, who *is* like You?
You, who have shown me great and severe troubles,
Shall revive me again,
And bring me up again from the depths of the earth.

You shall increase my greatness,
And comfort me on every side.

a. **Your righteousness, O God, is very high**: The psalmist considered the greatness of God, first in that His **righteousness** was of a different order than that of men, **very high** above that of men; and then, that God is the one who has **done great things**, beyond what men can do. The surpassing **righteousness** and power of God made him ask, **O God, who is like You?**

i. **Who is like You**: "God is alone, – who can resemble him? He is eternal. He can have none *before*, and there can be none *after*, for in the infinite *unity* of his *trinity* he is that eternal, unlimited, impartible, incomprehensible, and uncompounded ineffable Being, whose *essence* is hidden from all created intelligences, and whose *counsels* cannot be fathomed by any creature that even his own hand can form. WHO IS LIKE UNTO THEE! will excite the wonder, amazement, praise, and adoration of angels and men to all eternity." (Clarke)

b. **You who have shown me great and severe troubles, shall revive me again**: He understood that all things were in God's hands and that if he had experienced **great and severe troubles**, that too was **shown** to him by God. That same God could also **revive** him, bringing him **up again from the depths of the earth**.

i. "Never doubt God. Never say that He has forsaken or forgotten. Never think that He is unsympathetic. He will quicken again." (Meyer)

c. **You shall increase my greatness, and comfort me on every side**: More than a prayer, this was a confident proclamation. Though he was older in years, he still expected that God would **increase** his **greatness** and continue his **comfort**.

i. **You shall increase my greatness**: The idea is that as the years continued, the psalmist would see more and more of the **great things** (Psalm 71:19) God does. "The word 'greatness' alludes to 'great things' (71:19), i.e., Yahweh's saving acts." (VanGemeren)

4. (22-24) The music of praise.

Also with the lute I will praise You—
And Your faithfulness, O my God!
To You I will sing with the harp,
O Holy One of Israel.
My lips shall greatly rejoice when I sing to You,
And my soul, which You have redeemed.
My tongue also shall talk of Your righteousness all the day long;
For they are confounded,

For they are brought to shame
Who seek my hurt.

a. **With the lute I will praise You.... To You I will sing with the harp**:
The psalmist promised to praise God not only with his voice, but also with
his musical instruments. It would be a song celebrating God for what He
has done (**Your faithfulness**) and for who He is (**O Holy One of Israel**).

i. The psalmist was concerned about properly celebrating God's person
and work. "To celebrate it aright, with the melody of instruments,
voices, and affections, all in perfect concord, is the duty and delight
of the church militant; which, when thus employed, affords the best
resemblance of the church triumphant." (Horne)

ii. **O Holy One of Israel**: Kidner notes that this title for God is
uncommon outside of the Book of Isaiah and that it describes God
as "One in which 'unapproachable light' and covenant-love meet
together." (Kidner)

b. **My tongue also shall talk of Your righteousness all the day long**: His
lips and **soul** were already given to praise God in song. Now he added the
talk of his tongue to speak of God's **righteousness**, especially as it was seen
in triumph over his enemies (**they are brought to shame who seek my
hurt**).

i. "This is vindication, not vindictiveness. It will be part of the joy of
heaven (*cf.* Revelation 15:3; 18:20)." (Kidner)

Psalm 72 – The King and the King of Kings

The title of this psalm is **A Psalm of Solomon***. It is possible to translate the Hebrew here (and in almost all the psalms which reference an author) as "A Psalm to Solomon," and some have regarded it as David's psalm to and about his son Solomon and his Greater Son the Messiah. Yet, the most natural way to take the title is as it is given,* **A Psalm of Solomon** *with the understanding that the line about David in 72:20 refers to the collection of Book Two of Psalms, which is heavy with David's psalms, separating Book Two from Book Three, which begins with 11 psalms authored by Asaph.*

It is possible that Solomon compiled Book Two of Psalms (Psalms 42-72) and composed this psalm as a fitting conclusion for the collection of mostly David's psalms. It is a fitting conclusion, because it unexpectedly does not focus upon David himself, but on the Messiah – the King of Kings and the Son of David.

"The New Testament nowhere quotes it as Messianic, but this picture of the king and his realm is so close to the prophecies of Isaiah 11:1-5 and Isaiah 60-62 that if those passages are Messianic, so is this." (Derek Kidner)

A. Prayer for a king.

1. (1-4) The king's prayer for wisdom.

Give the king Your judgments, O God,
And Your righteousness to the king's Son.
He will judge Your people with righteousness,
And Your poor with justice.
The mountains will bring peace to the people,
And the little hills, by righteousness.
He will bring justice to the poor of the people;
He will save the children of the needy,
And will break in pieces the oppressor.

a. **Give the king Your judgments, O God, and Your righteousness to the king's Son**: Solomon began this psalm asking God to bless him as the monarch of Israel, and to bless him with wise **judgments** and a reign displaying God's **righteousness**. This was the same heart behind his great request to God in 1 Kings 3:5-9.

> i. These prayers "reflect the antique conception of a king as the fountain of justice, himself making and administering law and giving decisions." (Maclaren)

> ii. "As a royal psalm it prayed for the reigning king, and was a strong reminder of his high calling; yet it exalted this so far beyond the humanly attainable (*e.g.* in speaking of his reign as endless) as to suggest for its fulfillment no less a person than the Messiah, not only to Christian thinking but to Jewish." (Kidner)

> iii. "The Targum [an ancient Aramaic paraphrase of the Hebrew Bible] at verse 1 adds the word 'Messiah' to 'the king', and there are rabbinic allusions to the psalm which reveal the same opinion." (Kidner)

b. **He will judge Your people with righteousness**: Anticipating the blessing asked for, Solomon announced his intention to rule with **righteousness** and **justice**, even for the **poor** (who are often denied justice).

> i. "*Righteousness* dominates this opening, since in Scripture it is the first virtue of government, even before compassion (which is the theme of verses 12-14)." (Kidner)

c. **The mountains will bring peace to the people**: Sometimes **mountains** represent human governments in the Bible, and Solomon may have intended this allusion. He had in mind a national government (**mountains**) that blessed the people and local government (**the little hills**) that ruled with **righteousness**. This godly government would accomplish at least three things:

- **He will bring justice to the poor**: Though they are often denied justice, the king and his government will make sure that justice is administered fairly.

- **He will save the children of the needy**: The king and his government will rescue those most vulnerable in society.

- **And will break in pieces the oppressor**: The king and his government will protect Israel, keeping the people free from external domination and from internal corruption.

> i. **Mountains will bring peace**: We have connected the idea of **mountains** with human government, yet there are different understandings of this. Spurgeon quoted three different authors with three different ideas as to what these **mountains** speak of.

- Geddes wrote they spoke of messengers placed on a series of mountains or hilltops who distributed news through a land.

- Mollerus wrote that it spoke of the fertility of soil on the mountains.

- Caryl wrote that it speaks of the safety from robbers who often infested mountain passes.

- Maclaren wrote of another sense: "The mountains come into view here simply as being the most prominent features of the land."

ii. **Children of the needy**: "The phrase, *the children of the afflicted*, is put for *the afflicted*, an idiom quite common in Hebrew." (Calvin, cited in Spurgeon)

iii. **Break in pieces the oppressor**: "The tale bearer, saith the Greek; the slanderer, saith the Latin; the devil, say some. Over these he shall turn the wheel." (Trapp)

2. (5-7) Blessings upon such a well-governed kingdom.

They shall fear You
As long as the sun and moon endure,
Throughout all generations.
He shall come down like rain upon the grass before mowing,
Like showers *that* water the earth.
In His days the righteous shall flourish,
And abundance of peace,
Until the moon is no more.

a. **They shall fear You as long as the sun and moon endure**: The answer to the prayer in the previous lines would mean that the people of Israel – the king, his government, and the people – would **fear** the Lord forever, **throughout all generations**.

i. "As the psalmist pours out his petitions, they glide into prophecies; for they are desires fashioned upon promises, and bear, in their very earnestness, the pledge of their realisation." (Morgan)

b. **He shall come down like rain upon the grass**: God's presence would then be with His people as broad, as thick, and as good as **showers that water the earth**.

i. "The word *zggez*, which we translate *mown grass*, more properly means *pastured grass* or *pastured land*; for the *dew* of the night is intended to restore the grass which has been eaten in the course of the day." (Clarke)

ii. "Refreshing and salutary, as the drops of heaven, to the shorn and parched grass, is the mild administration of a wise and pious prince to his subjects. And what image can convey a better idea of those most beneficial and blessed effects which followed the descent of the Son of God upon the earth, and that of the Spirit, at the day of Pentecost? The prophets abound with descriptions of those great events, couched in terms borrowed from the philosophy of rain and dew. See Isaiah 44:3; 55:10; Hosea 14:5; Hebrews 6:7." (Horne)

iii. The Scriptures often connect the ideas of righteous and just government and blessing upon the ecology and produce of the land. "The Psalm as a whole, shows that what we call the 'moral realm' and the 'realm of nature' form one indivisible whole to the Israelites. A community which lives according to righteousness enjoys not only internal harmony, but also prosperity in field and flock." (Anderson, cited in VanGemeren)

iv. "Injustice has made Palestine a desert; if the Turk and Bedouin were gone, the land would smile again; for even in the most literal sense, justice is the fertilizer of lands, and men are diligent to plough and raise harvests when they have the prospect of eating the fruit of their labours." (Spurgeon)

c. **In His days the righteous shall flourish**: As God sends such a rich blessing, His people will **flourish** and there will be an **abundance of peace** (*shalom*) that will last beyond comprehension (**until the moon is no more**).

i. In a limited sense, this was true of Solomon. "In the kingdom of Solomon, through the influence of his wisdom, good men were encouraged, righteousness flourished, and the land enjoyed tranquility." (Horne)

ii. In a greater sense, it points to Jesus alone. The connection between the **righteous** and **peace** reminds us of Melchizedek, the One who was and is both the King of Righteousness and the King of Peace (Hebrews 7:1-3).

B. The Greater King.

1. (8-11) Looking to a greater King, a greater reign.

He shall have dominion also from sea to sea,
And from the River to the ends of the earth.
Those who dwell in the wilderness will bow before Him,
And His enemies will lick the dust.
The kings of Tarshish and of the isles
Will bring presents;

The kings of Sheba and Seba
Will offer gifts.
Yes, all kings shall fall down before Him;
All nations shall serve Him.

a. **He shall have dominion also from sea to sea**: Solomon began to lift his vision above a desire for his own reign to be blessed towards the anticipation of the reign of a greater Son of David, Messiah the King. This King would **have dominion** far greater than Solomon.

i. Under David and Solomon, Israel had its greatest extent of territory.

ii. "The messianic government spreads out over seas, rivers, and land. It is unnecessary to restrict the meaning to a particular sea or river because 72:8 speaks of his universal rule, encompassing seas, rivers, and lands." (VanGemeren)

b. **His enemies will lick the dust**: To oppose the King with such a great dominion meant certain defeat. His enemies would be brought low in a way associated with the curse upon the enemy in Genesis 3:14-15.

i. "Bear in mind that it was a custom with many nations that, when individuals approached their kings, they kissed the earth, and prostrated their whole body before them. This was the custom especially throughout Asia." (LeBlanc, cited in Spurgeon)

ii. "Tongues which rail at the Redeemer deserve to lick the dust." (Spurgeon)

c. **All kings shall fall down before Him**: Solomon sang of a king far greater than Solomon ever was. **All nations shall serve Him**, even those from faraway places and islands.

i. This was prophesied in a beautiful way by the prophet Nathan in 2 Samuel 7, which had in mind both David's immediate son and successor (Solomon) and David's ultimate Son and Successor (Jesus the Messiah). Both were in view in 2 Samuel 7:11-16, and both are in view in Psalm 72. The fulfillment in Solomon's day is described in 1 Kings 10:23-25.

ii. "The distant nations are the kings of the 'distant shores' (72:10): Tarshish (cf. Psalm 48:7), Sheba (modern Yemen), and Seba (an African nation: cf. Genesis 10:7; Isaiah 43:3, 45:14)." (VanGemeren)

iii. "*Tarshish* may have been Tartessus in Spain; it was in any case a name associated with long voyages; likewise *the isles* or 'coastlands' were synonymous with the ends of the earth: see, *e.g.* Isaiah 42:10." (Kidner)

2. (12-14) The compassionate rule of Messiah the King.

For He will deliver the needy when he cries,
The poor also, and *him* who has no helper.
He will spare the poor and needy,
And will save the souls of the needy.
He will redeem their life from oppression and violence;
And precious shall be their blood in His sight.

a. **He will deliver the needy when he cries, the poor also**: The justice and righteousness Solomon prayed for and aspired to regarding his own reign (Psalm 72:1-4) will be perfectly fulfilled in the Greater King.

i. "All helpless ones are under the especial care of Zion's compassionate King; let them hasten to put themselves in fellowship with him. Let them look to him, for he is looking for them." (Spurgeon)

b. **He will save the souls of the needy**: His work will go beyond what is thought of today as *social work*; the Greater King will also work to **save the souls** of the **poor and needy**.

c. **He will redeem their life from oppression and violence**: We can see this in both the **oppression and violence** they are targets of, and of that which they inflict upon others. Both are forms of slavery that require one to be set free from by purchase (**redeem their life**).

i. **Oppression and violence**: "Those two noted engines of all mischief to the poor, viz. privy deceit…and open violence, fraud and force, craft and cruelty." (Trapp)

ii. "The king is represented in Psalm 72:14 as taking on himself the office of Goel, or Kinsman-Redeemer, and ransoming his subjects' lives from 'deceit and violence.'" (Maclaren)

iii. Blessed as it was, Solomon's own reign did not live up to this fully. After his death they complained of his oppression (1 Kings 12:4). "Solomon continues to speak more wisely than he was ever to act." (Kidner)

d. **Precious shall be their blood in His sight**: The lives of the **poor and needy** are often considered to be of little value. The Messiah, the Greater King, will regard their lives as **precious**. This is especially meaningful when we consider the cheap regard for life outside of and before the world influenced by Christianity.

3. (15-17) The exaltation of the Greater King.

And He shall live;
And the gold of Sheba will be given to Him;

Prayer also will be made for Him continually,
And daily He shall be praised.
There will be an abundance of grain in the earth,
On the top of the mountains;
Its fruit shall wave like Lebanon;
And *those* of the city shall flourish like grass of the earth.
His name shall endure forever;
His name shall continue as long as the sun.
And *men* shall be blessed in Him;
All nations shall call Him blessed.

a. **He shall live**: Commentators debate if the **He** spoken of here refers to the ransomed man of the previous lines or of the King who ransomed him. Since the previous lines speak of a multitude redeemed and this **He** speaks of One, and because the following lines fit much better with the King, we regard **He shall live** as both a wish and a declaration for the King.

i. "How little this might mean is obvious from the address, 'O king, live forever', in the book of Daniel; yet also how much, can be seen from the Messianic prophecies and from the way these were understood in New Testament times." (Kidner)

ii. Inspired by the Holy Spirit, Solomon wrote things regarding Messiah the King that were perhaps beyond his own understanding. It's possible he never knew how wonderful it would be to say of the King of Kings who laid down His life as a sacrifice for sins that after three days in the tomb all would see and say, **He shall live**.

b. **The gold of Sheba will be given to Him**: The Greater King would receive gifts and honor and praise. In turn He would bestow great blessing on the earth (**an abundance of grain in the earth**) and upon His people (**those of the city shall flourish**).

i. "Poor as God's people usually are, the era will surely arrive when the richest of the rich will count it all joy to lay their treasures at Jesus' feet." (Spurgeon)

ii. **Its fruit shall wave like Lebanon**: "It shall yield such abundance of corn, that the ears, being thick, and high, and full of corn, shall, when they are shaken with the wind, make a noise not unlike that which the tops of the trees of Lebanon sometimes make upon the like occasion." (Poole)

iii. "Gold, grain, and fruit were ancient measures of prosperity. So this is a way of saying that under the reign of Jesus there will be prosperity of every conceivable kind." (Boice)

c. **Prayer also will be made for Him continually**: We can think of how prayer could and would be offered **for** an earthly king, but we don't often think of believers praying for Jesus Messiah.

i. We can say that we pray **for** Jesus when we pray for one of His people. There is a sense in which we pray **for** Jesus when we pray for the spread of His gospel.

d. **His name shall endure forever**: Solomon sensed that this Greater Son of David, the Greater King, would be more than a great man. He and His fame, and greatness of His character, would **endure forever**.

i. "We see on the shore of time the wrecks of the Caesars, the relics of the Moguls, and the last remnants of the Ottomans. Charlemagne, Maximilian, Napoleon, how they flit like shadows before us! They were and are not; but Jesus for ever is." (Spurgeon)

ii. "The perpetuity, which he conceived of as belonging to a family and an office, really belongs to the One King, Jesus Christ, whose Name is above every name, and will blossom anew in fresh revelations of its infinite contents, not only while the sun shines, but when its fires are cold and its light quenched." (Maclaren)

e. **Men shall be blessed in Him; all nations shall call Him blessed**: Solomon recognized that this King of Kings was not only the fulfillment of the promise made to David in 2 Samuel 7:11-16. He was also the fulfillment of the great promise made to Abraham in Genesis 12:1-3: *In you all the families of the earth shall be blessed.*

i. "Christ is all blessing. When you have written down his name, you have pointed to the fountain from which all blessings flow." (Spurgeon)

ii. "To us the song of this psalm is a prophecy of hope. We have seen the King, and we know the perfect Kingdom must come, for God cannot be defeated." (Morgan)

iii. Psalm 72 speaks powerfully of the kingdom of the King of Kings and speaks of it in terms of His *personal* rule, not ruling through an institution such as the Church. "In this Psalm, at least, we see a personal monarch, and he is the central figure, the focus of all the glory; not his servant, but himself do we see possessing the dominion and dispensing the government. Personal pronouns referring to our great King are constantly occurring in this Psalm; *he* has dominion, kings fall down before *him,:* and serve *him;* for *he* delivers; *he* spares, *he* saves, *he* lives, and daily is *he* praised." (Spurgeon)

4. (18-19) Closing doxology of praise.

Blessed *be* the Lord God, the God of Israel,
Who only does wondrous things!
And blessed *be* His glorious name forever!
And let the whole earth be filled *with* His glory.
Amen and Amen.

a. **Blessed be the Lord God, the God of Israel, who only does wondrous things**: Solomon was moved to praise when he considered the greatness of Messiah the King. The work in and through Jesus the Messiah is the work of **wondrous things**.

b. **Let the whole earth be filled with His glory**: The thought of the greatness of God and His work naturally led the heart to long that this blessing be extended through **the whole earth** and that it not only be touched by but **filled with His glory**.

i. "We pray that the atheist, the blasphemer, the hardened rebel, the prodigal, may each be filled with God's glory; and then we ask for mercy for the whole earth; we leave not out so much as one, but so hope and expect the day when all mankind shall bow at the Saviour's feet." (Spurgeon)

ii. There is also a tragedy in this psalm. As high as it soars with the concept of the king and his reign, we remember the sad disappointment of how quickly the monarchy in Israel declined after Solomon. There were certainly some good kings after him, but the glory of the kingdom went from Solomon's gold (1 Kings 10:16-17) to Rehoboam's bronze (1 Kings 14:25-28) in only about five years.

5. (20) End to the Second Book of Psalms.

The prayers of David the son of Jesse are ended.

a. **The prayers of David**: We take this as Solomon's postscript on the collection of psalms gathered into Book Two. David authored most of the psalms in Book Two, and Asaph composed the first 11 psalms of Book Three, so this is a good marking point. We also note that these are not only *songs*, but also **prayers**.

b. **David the son of Jesse**: Because this psalm so exalts the King of Kings, Solomon properly did not refer to David with any royal title, though deserved. David happily takes the lower place before the Greater Son of David and is simply **the son of Jesse**, a simple farmer of Bethlehem.

Psalm 73 – "My Feet Almost Slipped"

The title of this psalm (**A Psalm of Asaph**) *tells us that it was written by the great singer and musician of David and Solomon's era (1 Chronicles 15:17-19, 16:5-7, 25:6). 1 Chronicles 25:1 and 2 Chronicles 29:30 add that Asaph was a prophet in his musical compositions.*

This wonderful psalm may be best understood by the dominant pronouns within. When Asaph is troubled by the fate of the ungodly (verses 1-12), the dominant pronoun is they. *When he describes his own frustrated thinking leading to the resolution (verses 13-17), the dominant pronoun is* I. *When he finds resolution of the problem (verses 18-22), the dominant pronoun is* You, *in the sense of God. When He proclaims the assurance of his faith and fellowship with God (verses 23-28), the dominant pronouns are a mixture of* You *and* I.

A. The Problem Presented.

1. (1-3) The contradiction between the goodness of God and the prosperity of the wicked.

Truly God *is* good to Israel,
To such as are pure in heart.
But as for me, my feet had almost stumbled;
My steps had nearly slipped.
For I *was* envious of the boastful,
When I saw the prosperity of the wicked.

> a. **Truly God is good to Israel**: Asaph began this psalm with a simple declaration of the goodness of God to His people. By this he indicated that he understood not only that God was good, but that He actively showed that goodness **to Israel** and to the **pure in heart**.

> > i. Asaph was an organizer and leader for the temple choirs in the days of David, and presumably for Solomon after him. He was one who *prophesied according to the order of the king* (1 Chronicles 25:1-2).

ii. "The writer does not doubt this, but lays it down as his firm conviction. It is well to make sure of what we do know, for this will be good anchor-hold for us when we are molested by those mysterious storms which arise from things which we do not understand." (Spurgeon)

b. **But as for me, my feet had almost stumbled**: Asaph knew what he said about God in the first verse was true; yet there was another truth that disturbed him greatly. It made him **almost** stumble; it made his **steps** nearly slip.

i. "It shows that having doubts like Asaph's is not incompatible with responsible Christian living. It may have been true, as he says, that his feet 'had *almost* slipped.' But they had not actually slipped, or at least they had not slipped so far as to make him forget his responsibilities as a leader of God's people." (Boice)

c. **For I was envious of the boastful, when I saw the prosperity of the wicked**: This was another truth that seemed to contradict what Asaph knew of God as declared in the first verse. He knew that God was **good to Israel** and to the **pure in heart**, but it also seemed that God was good to the **boastful** and to the **wicked**. It all seemed so unfair to Asaph, and this made him **almost** stumble and slip.

i. Asaph saw the same troubling evidence that many see every day in their own lives. Many people cannot deny that God is good to them; but it also seems that God is good – perhaps *too good* – to the **boastful** and the **wicked**. It is then easy to envy the wicked and their **prosperity**.

ii. Such deep questions cause one to question the moral order of the universe. After all, one asks, what good is there in being good? If the wicked enjoy the same prosperity as the **pure in heart**, then what is the reward of godliness?

iii. "If God is in control of things, the plans of the wicked should flounder. They should even be punished openly. The godly alone should prosper. But that is not what Asaph saw, and it is not what we see either. We see scoundrels getting rich. Utterly degenerate persons, like particularly vile rock musicians or movie stars, are well paid and sought after. Even criminals get rich selling their crime stories." (Boice)

iv. "The faith in which he had been reared and to which he clung made his difficulties in this respect only the greater. He had been taught that the good always prosper and that the wicked always go to the wall." (Chappell)

v. We could say that this was the same faith believed so strongly by Job's friends – the same faith that prompted the question of the disciples, "Who sinned, this man or his parents, that he was born blind?" (John 9:2)

vi. "It is a pitiful thing that an heir of heaven should have to confess 'I was envious,' but worse still that he should have to put it, 'I was envious at the foolish.'" (Spurgeon)

2. (4-9) The good life of the wicked.

For *there are* no pangs in their death,
But their strength *is* firm.
They *are* not in trouble *as other* men,
Nor are they plagued like *other* men.
Therefore pride serves as their necklace;
Violence covers them *like* a garment.
Their eyes bulge with abundance;
They have more than heart could wish.
They scoff and speak wickedly *concerning* oppression;
They speak loftily.
They set their mouth against the heavens,
And their tongue walks through the earth.

a. **For there are no pangs in their death**: Perhaps Asaph had seen some of the wicked die agonizing and painful deaths; but he had seen enough wicked people die peaceful deaths to make him say, "**there are no pangs in their death**."

i. "Men may die like lambs and yet have their place for ever with the goats." (Matthew Henry, cited in Spurgeon)

ii. "'He fell asleep like a child,' say his friends; and others exclaim, 'He was so happy, that he must be a saint.' Ah! This is but their apparent end. God knoweth that the dying repose of sinners is but the awful calm which heralds the eternal hurricane." (Spurgeon)

b. **They are not in trouble as other men, nor are they plagued as other men**: Here Asaph developed his argument even further. Not only are the wicked rewarded equally to the righteous, they seem to be *more blessed* than the pure in heart. Their lives seem to have *less* **trouble** and are not as **plagued** as the average man.

i. "While many saints are poor and afflicted, the prosperous sinner is neither. He is worse than other men, and yet he is better off; he ploughs least, and yet has the most fodder. He deserves the hottest hell, and yet has the warmest nest." (Spurgeon)

c. **Therefore pride serves as their necklace**: In Asaph's analysis, because God did not punish the wicked as He should, they simply became *more* wicked, and even wore their **pride** as a prominent **necklace**. They therefore became more violent, greedy, and more likely to scoff and blaspheme.

i. "*Chains of gold*, and *golden rings*, were ensigns of magistracy and civil power. As these chains encompassed their necks, or the rings their wrists and fingers, as the signs of the *offices* in virtue of which they acted; so violence, oppressive conduct, encompassed them." (Clarke)

ii. We appreciate the poetic power of Asaph's description. We see the wicked man with an ostentatious **necklace** of **pride**. He is covered with an impressive **garment**, but that covering is **violence** towards others. He is so filled with good food that his **eyes bulge with abundance**, and he has **more than heart could wish**. His mouth always scoffs and speaks **wickedly**, and his **mouth** is **set...against the heavens**. Worst of all, *everyone* seems to hear about this wicked man and his prosperity, because it seems as if his **tongue walks through the earth**.

iii. "The whole passage is a masterly picture of these darlings of fortune: overblown, overweening; laughable if they were not so ruthless; their vanity egging them on to hector the very universe." (Kidner)

iv. Together with Asaph, we picture these rich, famous, proud, showy, violent, greedy, foul-speaking gangsters strutting about enjoying their wickedness. We are as troubled by their prosperity and the seeming indifference of God toward them as Asaph was.

v. **Their eyes bulge with abundance**: "By fatness, or corpulency, the natural lines of the face are *changed*, or rather *obliterated*. The characteristic distinctions are gone; and we see little remaining besides the *human hog*." (Clarke)

3. (10-14) The doubts of the godly.

Therefore his people return here,
And waters of a full *cup* are drained by them.
And they say, "How does God know?
And is there knowledge in the Most High?"
Behold, these *are* the ungodly,
Who are always at ease;
They increase *in* riches.
Surely I have cleansed my heart *in* vain,
And washed my hands in innocence.
For all day long I have been plagued,
And chastened every morning.

a. **Therefore his people return here**: This wicked man has associates who are just like him, and they take and take just as he does (**waters of a full cup are drained by them**).

> i. This is a difficult verse to translate and fit into the context. "Most modern versions find here the popular worship of success." (Kidner)

b. **They say, "How does God know?"** In the previous verses Asaph told us that the wicked man sets his mouth against heaven. Here, he tells us what the wicked man and his associates say against heaven. They claim that God is blind or ignorant; therefore, they can do as they please and God is unable to do anything against them.

c. **Behold, these are the ungodly**: In his frustration, Asaph saw the **ungodly** life as the *good* life. They are **always at ease**; they always **increase in riches**. They are rewarded for their wickedness by a God who seems to be as unknowing as the wicked say that He is.

d. **Surely I have cleansed my heart in vain**: The frustration kept building for Asaph. He felt that it was **vain** for him to be pure in heart, **vain** for him to have clean hands before God, **vain** for him to be innocent.

> i. "Poor Asaph! He questions the value of holiness when its wages are paid in the coin of affliction." (Spurgeon)

e. **For all day long I have been plagued, and chastened every morning**: Asaph felt that his life was much more difficult than the life of the ungodly man. While the wicked man enjoyed all his wealth and ease and pride, Asaph had to endure being **plagued** and **chastened**, and he had to endure it **all day long** and **every morning**.

> i. **Plagued** is bad, yet one might assign a plague to anonymous and natural causes. **Chastened** is even worse, because it implies that *God Himself* was afflicting Asaph with the difficulties. God was easy on the wicked and hard on Asaph.

> ii. As we would expect in a poetic outpouring, Asaph was exaggerating. The life of the wicked was not as good as he observed, nor was his life as bad as he felt it to be. Yet one cannot deny or contradict the *feeling* that prompted Asaph in this psalm, and we can instead strongly identify with that feeling.

B. The Problem Understood.

1. (15-17) The power of a new perspective.

If I had said, "I will speak thus,"
Behold, I would have been untrue to the generation of Your children.
When I thought *how* to understand this,

It *was* too painful for me—
Until I went into the sanctuary of God;
Then I understood their end.

a. **If I had said, "I will speak thus"**: Asaph caught himself from sliding further into despair over the perceived prosperity of the wicked. He did not want to be **untrue to the generation of Your children**, in the sense that he did not want to promote this sense of injustice and despair that he felt.

b. **When I thought how to understand this, it was too painful for me**: Asaph was caught in a trap. He could not deny the evidence that said that the wicked and ungodly often have good lives. He could not deny that his own life was often hard, leaving him feeling plagued and chastened by God. He felt all this to be true, but he also felt he could not talk about it because it would be **untrue** to others. Therefore, it was all **too painful** for him.

c. **Until I went into the sanctuary of God**: The crisis seemed to build and build for Asaph, **until** he went into the house of the Lord. There he gained a perspective on his problem that he did not have before. There he was able to see things from an *eternal* viewpoint, and he then **understood their end**.

i. "What then did the psalmist do? The answer to some will seem perfectly childish. He went to church.... Just what others got out of this service we are not told. But the psalmist came into possession of certain gripping convictions that steadied him and enabled him to walk in the after days with firmness and assurance." (Chappell)

ii. What did going to the house of God do for Asaph? There, he could gain understanding in several ways.

- By prayer and worship in the sanctuary, he understood that God was at the center of all things, and he gained a fresh appreciation of both God and eternity.

- By hearing the word of God in the sanctuary, he understood that there was a truth that went beyond what he saw and experienced in everyday life.

- By observing sacrifice at the sanctuary, he understood that God takes sin so seriously that it must be judged and atoned for, even if it is by an innocent victim who stands in the place of the guilty by faith.

iii. This is one of God's great purposes in establishing a *place* where His people come to meet with Him. It is never to imply that there is only one or only a few places where man can meet with God, or that they must be ornate or glorious buildings. It is to emphasize that it is good to have a place separate from other places where we focus on a heavenly, eternal perspective.

iv. For Asaph, this was **the sanctuary of God**. It was the temple in Jerusalem, or the tabernacle that existed before the temple. For us, it is the place where we meet with God's people for worship and fellowship and hearing the word of God.

v. When Asaph went to **the sanctuary of God**, he received *understanding*. It wasn't only a place to impact the senses and the feelings, but the *understanding* of a man. Asaph didn't remark on how he *felt* their end or even *experienced* their end; he **understood their end**. It isn't a bad thing to feel and experience the right things in the house of God, but there must also be *understanding* – the communication of truth in ways that can be received.

vi. When Asaph went to **the sanctuary of God**, it only did him good because he connected with *eternity*, something that made him understand **the end** of the wicked. He didn't need to go to the house of God to hear about the news of the day or the same talk one would hear in the marketplace or the business office. Asaph needed the ultimate relevance, the relevance of eternity.

vii. "*Their end* is literally 'their afterward', their future which will unmake everything they have lived for." (Kidner)

2. (18-20) The unsafe place of the wicked.

Surely You set them in slippery places;
You cast them down to destruction.
Oh, how they are *brought* to desolation, as in a moment!
They are utterly consumed with terrors.
As a dream when *one* awakes,
***So,* Lord, when You awake,**
You shall despise their image.

a. **Surely You set them in slippery places**: This is part of the understanding Asaph gained in the house of the Lord. He understood that the ease and security of the wicked was really only an illusion, and they were actually **set...in slippery places**, ready to fall at any time.

i. Earlier in the psalm, Asaph worried that his feet had almost slipped (verse 2). Now, with a perspective gained from the house of the Lord, he sees that the *wicked* are the ones **in slippery places**.

ii. "Sinner you may fall *now*, at once. The mountain yields beneath your feet, the slippery ice is melting every moment. Look down and learn your speedy doom. Yonder yawning gulf must soon receive you, while we look after you with hopeless tears. Our prayers cannot follow you; from your slippery standing place you fall and you are gone for ever. *Death* makes the place where you stand slippery, for it dissolves your life every hour. Time makes it slippery, for every instant it cuts the ground from under your feet. The *vanities* which you enjoy make your place slippery, for they are all like ice which shall melt before the sun. You have no foot-hold, sinner, you have no sure hope, no confidence. It is a melting thing you trust to." (Spurgeon)

b. **Oh, how they are brought to desolation, as in a moment**: Asaph could only understand this with the *eternal* perspective brought to him at the house of the Lord. In daily life he could only see what worked well for the wicked; with an eternal perspective he saw their **destruction**, their **desolation**, their **terrors**.

i. Earlier in the psalm, we had the feeling that Asaph would gladly trade places with the wicked man who seemed to be blessed. After gaining this eternal perspective, we see that Asaph would *never* trade places with them. Who wants **destruction**, **desolation**, and **terrors**?

c. **As a dream when one awakes**: With an eternal perspective from the house of God, Asaph understood that the good life of the ungodly is really as fragile as a dream, and they will soon wake to the reality of the **destruction**, **desolation**, and **terrors** that are their portion.

i. "Their happiness is like that in a dream, wherein a man seems to be highly pleased and transported with ravishing delights, but when he awakes he finds himself deceived and unsatisfied." (Poole)

ii. "Let them flaunt their little hour, poor unsubstantial sons of dreams; they will soon be gone; when the day breaketh, and the Lord awakes as a mighty man out of his sleep, they will vanish away. Who cares for the wealth of dreamland? Who indeed but fools?" (Spurgeon)

d. **So, Lord, when You awake**: Asaph admitted that it *seemed* as if God were asleep because one could not always see His active hand of judgment against the wicked. Using this idea, Asaph knew that God would not always sleep in His patience toward the wicked, and one day He would **awake** and judge them; He would **despise their image**.

3. (21-24) Confessing foolishness and receiving guidance.

Thus my heart was grieved,
And I was vexed in my mind.
I *was* so foolish and ignorant;
I was *like* a beast before You.

Nevertheless I *am* continually with You;
You hold *me* by my right hand.
You will guide me with Your counsel,
And afterward receive me *to* glory.

a. **Thus my heart was grieved.... I was so foolish and ignorant**: Asaph confessed before the Lord his sinful lack of understanding before he went into the house of the Lord. He felt **foolish** that he had forgotten the obvious truths of eternity and God's justice.

b. **I was like a beast before You**: Asaph rightly observed that animals seem to have no concept of eternity. They live their lives for momentary pleasures, satisfying natural urges. When Asaph forgot about eternity, he was truly **like a beast before** God.

i. "Hebrew, *beasts*, which may signify a great beast; a most stupid and sottish creature, like one not only void of grace, but of reason too.... I minded only present things, as the brutes do." (Poole)

ii. "This was as far as Job got in his struggles with Asaph's question. For when God finished interrogating Job, Job confessed that God's ways were entirely beyond his understanding, and he despised his pride and repented." (Boice)

c. **Nevertheless I am continually with You; You hold me by my right hand**: Asaph here declared both that *he* was **with** God, and that *God* was with him. It wasn't enough for Asaph to know and to say that God was with him; he also had to confess that he was with God.

d. **You will guide me with Your counsel, and afterward receive me to glory**: With the new perspective gained at the house of the Lord, Asaph knew that God would **guide** him in this life and ultimately **receive** him **to glory**.

i. Significantly, Asaph expected God to **guide** him with His **counsel**. He expected to hear God's wisdom and receive guidance through it. He didn't expect to be guided primarily through feelings, circumstances, or experiences, but to be guided through **counsel**.

ii. Asaph had the faithful expectation of an **afterward** of **glory**. This is a deliberate contrast with the *end* of the wicked mentioned in verses 17-19. As a godly man, Asaph has his **afterward** and the wicked will have quite another.

4. (25-28) The glory of a heavenly hope.

Whom have I in heaven *but You*?
And *there is* none upon earth *that* I desire besides You.

My flesh and my heart fail;
But God *is* the strength of my heart and my portion forever.
For indeed, those who are far from You shall perish;
You have destroyed all those who desert You for harlotry.
But *it is* good for me to draw near to God;
I have put my trust in the Lord God,
That I may declare all Your works.

a. **Whom have I in heaven but You?** This is the beautiful expression of a longing heart for God and for eternity. Intellectually, Asaph probably understood that there was much for him in heaven. There were angels and dwelling places and streets of gold and the companionship of the people of God throughout all generations. Yet all of that paled in the light of the presence of God.

i. "There is none in heaven, with all its stars and angels, enough for thee but Him." (Maclaren)

ii. "Let sinners have an earthly prosperity, I am satisfied with thee, and with thy favour. Since thou givest me support and conduct here, and carriest me safe from hence to eternal glory, what do I need more? Or what can I desire more?" (Poole)

iii. Boice notes, "Verse 25 is a particularly fine expression and has been a blessing to many over the ages. Charles Wesley (1707-1788), the great Methodist hymn writer, was thinking about it on his deathbed and actually composed a hymn based on it as his final testimony. Calling his wife to him, he dictated:

'In age and feebleness extreme,
What shall a sinful worm redeem?
Jesus, my only hope thou art,
Strength of my failing flesh and heart;
O, could I catch a smile from thee,
And drop into eternity.'"

b. **And there is none upon earth that I desire besides You**: For Asaph, God was not only a heavenly hope but an earthly desire as well. God was both his inheritance in heaven and his earthly **desire**.

c. **My flesh and my heart fail; but God is the strength of my heart and my portion forever**: Asaph recognized both his weakness and the strength of God, and the *enduring character* of God's strength.

i. "In ancient Israel the priests enjoyed a privileged status of having the Lord as their 'share' and 'inheritance' (Numbers 18:20). Though they were denied the privilege of land ownership, they, along with

the Levites, were taken care of by the Lord's tithes and offerings."
(VanGemeren)

ii. "Allusion is here made to the division of the promised land. I ask no
inheritance below; I look for one above." (Clarke)

d. **Indeed, those who are far from You shall perish**: Asaph no longer
had doubts about the destiny of the ungodly. With the eternal perspective
gained at the house of the Lord, he understood that they would indeed
perish.

i. "No human spirit that is not *united* to God can be saved. *Those who
are* FAR FROM THEE *shall perish* – they shall be *lost, undone, ruined*; and
that without remedy. Being *separated from God* by sin, they shall never
be *rejoined*; the great gulf must be between them and their Maker
eternally." (Clarke)

e. **It is good for me to draw near to God; I have put my trust in the
Lord GOD, that I may declare all Your works**: It is staggering to see how
much good Asaph's visit to the house of the Lord did for him. It gave him
understanding and an eternal perspective.

i. He saw the great benefit in drawing near to God, which he doubted
before (verse 13). "It may seem good in the worldling's eyes to go his
way to his wine cups, and to make merry in the dance; it may seem
good to yonder truster in an arm of flesh, to seek out his friends and
his kinsmen, and entrust his case to their discretion; it may seem good
to the desponding to retire in melancholy to brood over his sorrows,
and to the dissipated, to endeavor to drown all care in vanity, but to
me, says the psalmist, it is good, preeminently good, that I should
draw near unto God." (Spurgeon)

ii. He saw the value of putting his trust in God, now understanding
that God was reliable and could be trusted.

iii. He had a passion to **declare all** God's **works**. He would become a
messenger of God's goodness and of the eternal perspective he gained
in the house of the Lord.

Psalm 74 – Asking God to Remember His Destroyed Sanctuary

This psalm is titled **A Contemplation of Asaph**. *It is a plea and a prayer in great sorrow from the destruction of the sanctuary (Psalm 74:3, 7). The majority of commentators believe this psalm followed the destruction of the temple by the Babylonians. Some argue that it is even later, following the desecration of the temple in the days of Antiochus Epiphanes. If these later dates are true, this* **Asaph** *is not the great singer and musician of David and Solomon's era, unless* **Asaph** *composed this psalm prophetically, which was possible according to 1 Chronicles 25:1 and 2 Chronicles 29:30.*

James Montgomery Boice explains the thinking of a later Asaph: "Either this is a later Asaph, which is not unlikely since the name might have been perpetuated among the temple musicians, or, more likely, the name was affixed to many psalms produced by this body of musicians. We know that the 'descendants of Asaph' were functioning as late as the reign of Josiah (2 Chronicles 35:15)."

There is another option: the Asaph of David and Solomon's time composed this psalm on the occasion or the memory of the destruction of the tabernacle in Shiloh (1 Samuel 4). The word sanctuary *used in Psalm 74:3, 7 is also used of the tabernacle (Exodus 25:8; Leviticus 12:4, 21:12; Numbers 10:21, 18:1).*

A. The plea for help when the sanctuary is destroyed.

1. (1-2) Asking God to remember His people.

O God, why have You cast *us* off forever?
***Why* does Your anger smoke against the sheep of Your pasture?**
Remember Your congregation, *which* You have purchased of old,
The tribe of Your inheritance, *which* You have redeemed—
This Mount Zion where You have dwelt.

a. **O God, why have You cast us off forever?** Asaph lived and served during the reigns of David and Solomon, which were generally times of security

253

and blessing for Israel. Yet even within those generally good times, there were occasions of difficulty in the face of Israel's enemies. Asaph wrote during such a season, or possibly with such a difficult time in mind. He wrote of the terrible sense that God had **cast us off forever** and is no longer *for* us.

i. This is a desperate psalm, yet "this is not the song of an atheist, but the wail of a believer." (Morgan)

ii. "It is faith, more than doubt, that precipitates the shower of questions which begins and ends this half of the psalm." (Kidner)

iii. "The questioner asks how God can be angry with his own people forever. He does not question the correctness of his judgment but uses the question and the lament as the basis for an appeal to God's fatherly heart." (VanGemeren)

iv. "When the heart is hot and restless, and it seems as though God had forsaken His own, he is a wise man who turns to God in song, even though the song be only a complaint." (Morgan)

b. **Why does Your anger smoke against the sheep of Your pasture?** It wasn't just that Asaph felt that God had stopped caring for Israel (**cast us off**). Added to that was the sense that God was *angry* at them, and in some sense working *against* them.

i. "This is a fierce complaint, bordering just possibly on impropriety as an address to God. When we complain it is more often the case that we just complain, either to ourselves or to other people. It is better to complain to God." (Boice)

c. **Remember Your congregation**: From such despair Asaph asked God to change His apparent attitude toward Israel. It seems clear that Asaph understood that God's indifference and anger was more in appearance than in fact; otherwise, the following appeals would be of no use.

- Asaph asked God to **remember** that Israel belonged to Him, and was His **congregation**.

- Asaph asked God to remember that Israel was His **purchased** people, bought out of the slave market of the nations.

- Asaph asked God to remember that Israel was His **inheritance**, His valued treasure.

- Asaph asked God to remember that He had **purchased** and **redeemed** Israel, and that from times of **old**.

- Asaph asked God to remember that He had **dwelt** among His people in Jerusalem (**Mount Zion**) in a special way.

i. We sense that Asaph thought, "If God would only **remember** His special care and connection with Israel, He would rescue us." He therefore brought many reasons and appeals to God in prayer.

ii. "Pleading is wrestling: arguments are the grips, the feints, the throes, the struggles with which we hold and vanquish the covenant angel. The humble statement of our wants is not without its value, but to be able to give reasons and arguments why God should hear us is to offer potent, prevalent prayer." (Spurgeon)

iii. **Which You have purchased**: "What a mighty plea is redemption. O God, canst thou see the bloodmark on thine own sheep, and yet allow grievous wolves to devour them?" (Spurgeon)

iv. Poole believed that **the tribe of Your inheritance** referred to "the tribe of Judah, which thou hast in a special manner chosen for thine inheritance, and for the seat of the kingdom, and for the birth of the Messiah. And thus here is an elegant gradation from the general to particulars; first the *congregation*, consisting of all the tribes; then the *tribe* of Judah."

2. (3-7) The destruction of the sanctuary.

Lift up Your feet to the perpetual desolations.
The enemy has damaged everything in the sanctuary.
Your enemies roar in the midst of Your meeting place;
They set up their banners *for* signs.
They seem like men who lift up
Axes among the thick trees.
And now they break down its carved work, all at once,
With axes and hammers.
They have set fire to Your sanctuary;
They have defiled the dwelling place of Your name to the ground.

a. **Lift up Your feet**: Asaph asked God to *run* to their aid, because the sanctuary – the tabernacle or temple – had been invaded and ransacked. He hoped this would give God reason to move quickly for Israel's good.

i. "God is represented as having withdrawn himself, and departed afar off; he is therefore entreated to return without delay, to view the long-lasting desolations of the once highly favoured city." (Horne)

ii. We have no indication of the tabernacle or the temple being so abused by Israel's enemies in the days of David or Solomon. Not long before David's time, the tabernacle was overrun and ransacked at Shiloh when Eli was high priest (1 Samuel 4). There are a few different ways to explain Asaph's description of these **perpetual desolations**.

- Asaph wrote of the catastrophe at Shiloh described in 1 Samuel 4, either being alive at that time or writing in the memory of it.

- Asaph wrote prophetically of a catastrophe that was still in the future.

- The Asaph who wrote this psalm was not the same Asaph associated with the reigns of David and Solomon, or this psalm came from his "school" and was written many years later.

iii. Among the far less likely possibilities are the suggestions that Asaph had only a symbolic sanctuary in mind, or that there was a devastating attack on the tabernacle or temple in the days of David and Solomon that was not recorded.

b. **Your enemies roar in the midst of Your meeting place**: Asaph asked God to defend *His* sanctuary, *His* tent of meeting. Those who oppose God had come **with axes and hammers** to destroy, and **have set fire to Your sanctuary** – and they destroy with furious energy.

i. **Your enemies roar**: "Instead of hearing the priestly benediction (Numbers 6:24-26), they heard the roaring of enemy voices." (VanGemeren)

ii. **They set up their banners up for signs**: "The *signs* would be the military ensigns (*cf.* the same word in Numbers 2:2)." (Kidner)

iii. "As a Jew felt a holy horror when he saw an idolatrous emblem set up in the holy place, even so do we…when from pulpits, once occupied by men of God, we hear philosophy and vain deceit." (Spurgeon)

iv. **With axes and hammers they have set fire to Your sanctuary**: Spurgeon thought of how modern critics try to destroy the church today. Their use of pretended objectivity and love of truth, ridicule, and debating tricks are like the **axes and hammers** that destroy a beautiful building made unto God's glory.

3. (8-9) The destruction of places and prophets.

They said in their hearts,
"Let us destroy them altogether."
They have burned up all the meeting places of God in the land.
We do not see our signs;
***There is* no longer any prophet;**
Nor *is there* any among us who knows how long.

a. **Let us destroy them altogether**: Having successfully attacked the sanctuary of God, the enemies of the Lord wanted to **destroy** the people of God **altogether**. They hoped to do this when they **burned up all the meeting places of God in the land**.

i. The synagogue did not exist as an established institution until the Babylonian captivity. Yet it seems likely that there were **meeting places of God** throughout the land of Israel. When Israel was obedient, these were not places of sacrifice but places of prayer and hearing of the Scriptures. The Levites were commanded to teach Israelites the scriptures (Deuteronomy 17:9-12, 33:10; Leviticus 10:8-11). It makes sense that there might have been **meeting places of God** in many communities even before the synagogue became an established institution.

ii. "It is supposed that there were no synagogues in the land till after the Babylonish captivity. How then could the Chaldeans burn up any in Judea? The word *moadey*, which we translate *synagogues*, may be taken in a more general sense, and mean *any places* where *religious assemblies* were held: and that such places and assemblies did exist long *before* the Babylonian captivity, is pretty evident from different parts of Scripture." (Clarke)

iii. "Although there was only one place appointed for Israel's worship, because it alone housed the altar for the appointed burnt sacrifices, and although the formation of formal synagogues seems to date from a later time, there must, as Perowne says, 'surely have been some public worship beyond the limits of the family, and if so, houses for its celebration.'" (Boice)

b. **We do not see our signs; there is no longer any prophet**: The enemies of God and His people succeeded in gravely damaging the spiritual life of Israel.

i. In saying **no longer any prophet** and **any among us**, Poole thought this was some poetic hyperbole. "It is not unusual in Scripture, to say that there is none of a sort of persons or things, when there is a very great scarcity of them." (Poole)

ii. "Our problem is not an absence of God's Word or God's teachers. Our problem is that we do not value this Word. We do not cherish it and study it. We do not memorize its important passages. Instead we allow countless lesser things (like television) to take the Bible's place." (Boice)

4. (10-11) How long?

O God, how long will the adversary reproach?
Will the enemy blaspheme Your name forever?

Why do You withdraw Your hand, even Your right hand?
Take it **out of Your bosom and destroy** *them.*

a. **O God, how long will the adversary reproach?** Asaph saw the destruction of the spiritual institutions and life of Israel, and with heart and logic he asked how long this low and afflicted state would last.

b. **Why do You withdraw Your hand?** Asaph did not lose confidence in the power or ability of God. He knew that if God put forth His hand of power against these enemies, He would **destroy them.**

B. The demonstration of God's great power.

1. (12-17) Remembering the greatness of God.

For God *is* **my King from of old,**
Working salvation in the midst of the earth.
You divided the sea by Your strength;
You broke the heads of the sea serpents in the waters.
You broke the heads of Leviathan in pieces,
And **gave him** *as* **food to the people inhabiting the wilderness.**
You broke open the fountain and the flood;
You dried up mighty rivers.
The day *is* **Yours, the night also** *is* **Yours;**
You have prepared the light and the sun.
You have set all the borders of the earth;
You have made summer and winter.

a. **God is my King from of old**: Asaph meditated first on the royal authority of God and then upon His great power. The same God who **divided the sea by** His **strength** could rescue His people in the present crisis.

i. "Things could hardly be worse to the eyes of sight. Then came the declaration of what the eyes of faith beheld. In spite of all these apparent contradictions, God was seen as King, working for salvation." (Morgan)

ii. "The man of faith is never blind to the desolation. He sees clearly all the terrible facts. But He sees more. He sees God. Therefore his last word is never desolation: it is rather salvation." (Morgan)

b. **You broke the heads of the sea serpents in the waters**: In several places the Bible mentions **sea serpents** and **Leviathan**, and often in the context of creation. Usually **Leviathan** is considered to be a sea-monster or dragon that terrorized sailors and fishermen. Some consider these **sea serpents** and **Leviathan** real in history; others consider them to be legendary.

i. Most commentators see here remembrance of deliverance from Egypt (**You divided the sea**), and the references to **sea serpents** and **Leviathan** to be poetic references to Egypt. Yet this hymn of praise seems to have more references to creation (**day** and **night**, **light** and the **sun**). One can also see this as connected to creation rather than to the Exodus.

ii. In the ancient Middle East, there were many popular legends about the gods who combated different hostile deities in order to create the earth. Biblical authors showed that Yahweh is the hero. It is Yahweh who **divided the sea**, even though ancient legends said that Tiamat (the Deep) was the chaotic goddess defeated by the hero god Marduk (Bel), or Yam (the Sea) who was defeated by Baal. It is Yahweh who **broke the heads of Leviathan in pieces**, not Marduk or Baal.

iii. "The point here is that what Baal had claimed in the realm of myth, God had done in the realm of history – and done for His people, *working salvation*." (Kidner)

iv. "The psalmist chose the language of Canaanite mythology to celebrate Yahweh's victory over the nations." (VanGemeren)

v. The name **Leviathan** means *"twisting one"* and is also used in many interesting places in Scripture.

- Psalm 74:12-14 refers to Leviathan as a sea serpent, and relates that God broke the head of the Leviathan long ago, perhaps at creation.

- Psalm 104:26 also refers to Leviathan as a sea creature.

- Isaiah 27:1 speaks of the *future* defeat of Leviathan, also associating it with a *twisted serpent* that lives *in the sea.*

- Isaiah 51:9 and Psalm 89:8-10 speak of a serpent associated with the sea that God defeated as a demonstration of His great strength, and identifies this serpent with the name *Rahab*, meaning *proud one.*

- Job 26:12-13 also refers to God's piercing defeat of a fleeing serpent associated with the sea.

iv. Satan is often represented as a dragon or a serpent (Genesis 3; Revelation 12 and 13) and the sea is thought of as a dangerous or threatening place in the Jewish mind (Isaiah 57:20; Mark 4:39; Revelation 21:1). It's possible that Leviathan is another serpent-like manifestation of Satan, whose resistance to creation was overcome.

v. It is important to note that the Hebrew Scriptures do not simply believe or adopt this Canaanite mythology; they take it and transform it, using it to exalt Yahweh in a way that the Canaanite myths never did. Elmer B. Smick notes this in the *Expositor's Bible Commentary* on Job: "Here the sea that God subdues is not the deity Yam. Job depersonalized Yam by using the definite article (the sea), thus expressing his innate monotheistic theology.... Further, by his own wisdom, skill, and power he 'cut Rahab to pieces' and 'pierced the gliding serpent,' unlike Marduk who depended on the enablement of the father-gods."

c. **You broke open the fountain and the flood**: Asaph recounted examples of God's power and authority over nature. God has power over the waters, over **day** and **night**, and over all the seasons.

i. **You**: "The sevenfold repetition of the word brings forcibly into view the Divine personality and former deeds which pledge God to act now." (Maclaren)

2. (18-21) Asking God to remember and respect His covenant.

Remember this, *that* the enemy has reproached, O LORD,
And *that* a foolish people has blasphemed Your name.
Oh, do not deliver the life of Your turtledove to the wild beast!
Do not forget the life of Your poor forever.
Have respect to the covenant;
For the dark places of the earth are full of the haunts of cruelty.
Oh, do not let the oppressed return ashamed!
Let the poor and needy praise Your name.

a. **Remember this, that the enemy has reproached, O LORD**: After declaring the unmatched power of God, Asaph then called upon God to take vengeance upon His enemies and to protect His people (**do not deliver the life of Your turtledove to the wild beast**).

i. **Your turtledove**: "Fitly compared to a turtle-dove, because of the great resemblance of their dispositions and conditions, being simple, and harmless, and meek, and faithful, and mournful, and exposed to manifold injuries, and unable to defend itself from them." (Poole)

b. **Have respect to the covenant**: Asaph wisely and persuasively called upon God to act in view of His **covenant** with His people. In a dangerous world, **full of the haunts of cruelty**, God's people could rely on God's covenant promise.

i. "That which he mainly urgeth is the covenant, that hive of heavenly honey, as one calleth it." (Trapp)

ii. "In every trial, when desiring any blessing, when the crushing blows of the adversaries' hatchet are heard, turn to God, and say, 'Have respect unto the covenant, of which Jesus is the Mediator and his blood the seal.'" (Meyer)

3. (22-23) Asking God to act in His own cause.

Arise, O God, plead Your own cause;
Remember how the foolish man reproaches You daily.
Do not forget the voice of Your enemies;
The tumult of those who rise up against You increases continually.

a. **Arise, O God, pleadYour own cause**: Asaph approached God with concern for *His* **own cause**. He asked God to act not only out of compassion for His people, but also out of concern for His glory, to rebuke **the foolish man** who **reproaches You daily**.

i. "The Lord is begged to remember that he is himself reproached, and that by a mere man – that man a fool, and he is also reminded that these foul reproaches are incessant, and repeated with every revolving day. It is bravely done when faith can pluck pleas out of the dragon's mouth, and out of the blasphemies of fools find arguments with God." (Spurgeon)

b. **The tumult of those who rise up against You increases continually**: Asaph pressed the *urgency* of the plea. With wickedness on the increase, there was more reason for God to act sooner rather than later.

Psalm 75 – The Righteous Judge Exalts and Brings Low

The title of this psalm is **To the Chief Musician. Set to "Do Not Destroy." A Psalm of Asaph. A Song.** *Some suppose* **the Chief Musician** *to be the Lord* GOD *Himself, and others suppose the reference to be a leader of choirs or musicians, such as Heman the singer (1 Chronicles 6:33 and 25:6). The tune* **Do Not Destroy** *was also used in the Davidic Psalms 57, 58, and 59. The author* **Asaph** *was the great singer and musician of David and Solomon's era (1 Chronicles 15:17-19, 16:5-7; 2 Chronicles 29:13). 1 Chronicles 25:1 and 2 Chronicles 29:30 add that Asaph was a prophet in his musical compositions.*

A. God's rebuke of the proud.

1. (1) Thanks to the God who is near.

We give thanks to You, O God, we give thanks!
For Your wondrous works declare *that* Your name is near.

a. **We give thanks**: Asaph wrote this from the perspective of the congregation; they together say **we give thanks** unto God, and the thought is repeated for emphasis. The people of God gladly **give thanks** unto their God.

    i. "We should praise God again and again. Stinted gratitude is ingratitude. For infinite goodness there should be measureless thanks." (Spurgeon)

b. **For Your wondrous works declare that Your name is near**: Their gratitude toward God had a basis, a reason. They gave thanks to God not only for His **wondrous works**, but for what those works proclaimed: that God, in all His character and attributes (**Your name**), was **near** to His people.

    i. We are grateful for God's great works among us, but not only for the works themselves. They are constant reminders of the love, goodness, mercy, and wisdom of God toward and among His people. It is also a wonderful thing to know and experience that His **name is near.**

ii. "The *name of God* is said to be *near,* because it had come into public notice, and was in every mind and every tongue – opposed to what is *unknown* and *obscure,* which is said to be far remote." (Venema, cited in Spurgeon)

iii. "The reason for rejoicing lies in the manifest presence of God proclaimed and celebrated in the stories of God's mighty acts. In remembrance and retelling of the history of salvation lies the comforting affirmation of God's closeness to his people." (VanGemeren)

iv. "God's *name* is part of His self-giving: a revelation of who He is (Exodus 34:14-15) and an invitation to call upon Him (Acts 2:21)." (Kidner)

2. (2-3) God speaks of His judgment.

"When I choose the proper time,
I will judge uprightly.
The earth and all its inhabitants are dissolved;
I set up its pillars firmly. Selah

a. **When I choose the proper time, I will judge uprightly**: The previous lines of the psalm were spoken from the perspective of God's people. These are spoken from the perspective of God Himself. God declares that He **will judge,** and that He will **judge uprightly.** As Abraham understood, the Judge of all the earth will do right (Genesis 18:25).

b. **When I choose the proper time**: In His judgments God reserves the right to **choose the proper time.** We often feel that *we know* the proper time for God's judgments, and we are often troubled because God does not seem to share our perspective. The believer should have a humble trust in the uprightness of God's judgments *and* the **proper time** for them.

i. This "reveals the time and the method of the Divine activity. His time is 'the set time.' That is, He acts, never too soon and never too late. It is a great word." (Morgan)

ii. "If judgment were left in our hands, we would probably let it flash out against anything that displeases us whenever we see it. But God lets evil go unchecked sometimes for a rather long time, knowing that he has appointed a proper time when it will be brought down." (Boice)

c. **The earth and all its inhabitants are dissolved**: God declared the great power of His judgments. At His judgments people and things are either **dissolved** or they are established **firmly.**

i. "There may be apparent and indeed very real dissolution of all human organization and order; but the true pillars of the earth are God-established and cannot be broken down. This conviction is the citadel of the soul." (Morgan)

d. **Selah**: The rightness, the timing, and the power of God's judgments are all worthy of our deep consideration.

3. (4-5) God speaks to the proud.

"I said to the boastful, 'Do not deal boastfully,'
And to the wicked, 'Do not lift up the horn.
Do not lift up your horn on high;
Do *not* speak with a stiff neck.'"

a. **Do not deal boastfully**: From the previous lines of the psalm, it is best to regard this as Asaph recording God's words from His own perspective. In light of His great judgments, God warned the proud (**the boastful**) to no longer boast and exalt their own strength (**lift up the horn**).

i. "Lifting one's horn against heaven is the equivalent of shaking one's fist in God's face." (Boice)

ii. **Horn on high**: "A metaphor from untamed and stiff-necked oxen, which will not bow their heads to receive the yoke, but lift up their heads and horns to avoid it." (Poole)

b. **Do not speak with a stiff neck**: The figure of the **stiff neck** was taken from the world of agriculture, where ox or cattle might resist the yoke for plowing and other work. God cautioned the proud and wicked not to resist Him in the same way.

i. "Impudence before God is madness. The out-stretched neck of insolent pride is sure to provoke his axe. Those who carry their heads high shall find that they will be lifted yet higher, as Haman was upon the gallows which he had prepared for the righteous man." (Spurgeon)

B. Reasons for humility.

1. (6-7) Be humble because promotion comes from God.

For exaltation *comes* neither from the east
Nor from the west nor from the south.
But God *is* the Judge:
He puts down one,
And exalts another.

a. **Exaltation comes neither from the east nor from the west**: Asaph hoped to teach the proud ones whom he warned in the previous lines. They should first know that their **exaltation**, their success and standing did not come from earth and human initiative. They should stop their proud confidence in self.

i. "Ambitionists used to look this way and that way how to advance themselves, but all in vain." (Trapp)

ii. "The word '*promotion*' [**exaltation**] here is used in a very expressive way; it means the *desire of self-advancement*, (*harim*), and would teach us that all our inward schemes, and outward plans, cannot gain for us advancement, unless based upon the fear and love of God." (Bateman, cited in Spurgeon)

b. **But God is the Judge**: Every successful person, everyone exalted in some way, should humbly look to God with gratitude. It is God who **puts down one, and exalts another**. A humble mind and heart is the proper response, instead of boastful words, the celebration of one's own strength, or resistance against God.

i. "Promotions in any direction, to positions of credit, influence, or consideration, are the gift and the work of God." (Meyer)

ii. This is not to say that hard work, preparation, good habits, and other human aspects do not contribute to success – they clearly do. Yet even those things are gifts and abilities from God and should be regarded with humility and gratitude toward Him.

iii. "Empires rise and fall at his bidding. A dungeon here, and there a throne, his will assigns. Assyria yields to Babylon, and Babylon, to the Medes. Kings are but puppets in his hand; they serve his purpose when they rise and when they fall." (Spurgeon)

2. (8-9) Be humble because the wicked will be judged even as the righteous praise.

For in the hand of the LORD there is a cup,
And the wine is red;
It is fully mixed, and He pours it out;
Surely its dregs shall all the wicked of the earth
Drain *and* drink down.
But I will declare forever,
I will sing praises to the God of Jacob.

a. **In the hand of the LORD there is a cup**: Asaph here used the **cup** as a figure of God's judgment. The idea is that God demonstrates His judgment upon **the wicked**, and they are forced to **drain and drink down** the bitter cup.

i. "There is a grim contrast between the images of festivity and hospitality called up by the picture of a host presenting the wine cup to his guests, and the stern compulsion which makes the 'wicked' gulp down the nauseous draught held by God to their reluctant lips." (Maclaren)

ii. "They scoffed his feast of love; they shall be dragged to his table of justice, and made to drink their due deserts." (Spurgeon)

iii. "They who have drunk so willingly and freely of the cup of sin, shall be forced, whether they will or no, to drink the cup of judgment. And it is not a sip or two shall serve their turns; they must drink all, dregs and all, they shall drink it to the bottom, and yet they shall never come to the bottom; they have loved long draughts, and now they shall have one long enough; there is eternity to the bottom." (Caryl, cited in Spurgeon)

iv. **Fully mixed**: "*Well mixed* is a reference to the spices which might be added for pungency; so NEB, 'hot with spice'." (Kidner)

b. **I will sing praises to the God of Jacob**: In contrast to **the wicked of the earth**, Asaph spoke for the people of God who **declare** and *rejoice* in the judgments of God.

3. (10) Be humble because God Himself will bring the wicked low and raise the righteous high.

"All the horns of the wicked I will also cut off,
***But* the horns of the righteous shall be exalted."**

a. **All the horns of the wicked I will also cut off**: The symbol of the horn was used earlier in this psalm (verses 4-5) in the familiar sense as an expression of strength and domination (as with ox or cattle). This psalm ends with another word from God's own perspective, vowing to put down the proud and wicked one (as earlier in verse 7).

i. **The horns of the wicked**: "Their honour and power, which they made an instrument of mischief to oppress good men. A metaphor from horned and mischievous beasts." (Poole)

b. **The horns of the righteous shall be exalted**: God's work of judgment is not only *against* the proud and wicked; it is also *for* **the righteous**. As surely as He will **cut off** the arrogant pride of the wicked, He will also **exalt** the strength of the righteous.

i. "All their *power* and *influence*, will I cut off; and will exalt and extend the *power* of the righteous." (Clarke)

Psalm 76 – The Greatness of God and Man's Proper Response

This psalm is titled **To the Chief Musician. On stringed instruments. A Psalm of Asaph. A Song. Asaph** *was the great singer and musician of David and Solomon's era (1 Chronicles 15:17-19, 16:5-7; 2 Chronicles 29:13). 1 Chronicles 25:1 and 2 Chronicles 29:30 add that Asaph was a prophet in his musical compositions.*

This psalm celebrates a great victory of God on behalf of His people, and those who connect it with the defeat of Sennacherib (Isaiah 37:36) attribute Psalm 76 to a later Asaph, or to someone who was the literal or spiritual descendant of the Asaph of David and Solomon's time.

A. God's might shown in Zion.

1. (1-3) The greatness of God in Zion.

In Judah God *is* known;
His name *is* great in Israel.
In Salem also is His tabernacle,
And His dwelling place in Zion.
There He broke the arrows of the bow,
The shield and sword of battle. Selah

> a. **In Judah God is known**: Asaph happily proclaimed that God was **known** in Judah and that **His name is great in Israel**. God would get the praise due to Him among His people.
>
> > i. We notice that **God is known**, that He has revealed Himself. God is knowable, and our knowledge of God is not only subjective. We do not worship an unknown god as the ancient Athenians did (Acts 17:23).
> >
> > ii. We notice that **in Judah God is known**. The nations had their ideas of deity, but the true revelation of God came through the Jewish people – the covenant descendants of Abraham, Isaac, and Jacob. "In

those days, if you wanted to know who God was and what he was like, you had to turn to the Jews and their Bible." (Boice)

b. **In Salem also is His tabernacle**: God has a further connection with Israel; it is in their land that He chose to make **His dwelling place** and to establish **His tabernacle**.

> i. Asaph's mention of the **tabernacle** might be a reference to history, or perhaps it is poetic. Yet it is more likely that the **tabernacle** was brought to **Salem**, to the city of **Zion**, when David brought the ark of the covenant there (2 Samuel 6).

> ii. It seems that **Salem** was the ancient name for *Jerusalem* (Genesis 14:18, Hebrew 7:1-2).

> iii. "The Pilgrims also loved this psalm, and it was from verse 2 that they derived the name of one of the very first settlements in the New World: Salem, Massachusetts." (Boice)

> iv. The phrase **His dwelling place in Zion** uses an interesting word. "Not His '*abode*' but His 'covert' or 'lair' is the bold expression here, with its tacit comparison of the Lord to a lion (*cf.* Jeremiah 25:38, and see Psalm 27:5)." (Kidner)

> v. "This means that the picture of God in stanza one is of a lion crouching on Mount Zion, ready to pounce. In other words, he is to be reckoned with, to be feared." (Boice)

c. **There He broke the arrows of the bow**: Jerusalem became the center of Israel when David conquered the city and brought peace to the city of peace (2 Samuel 5:6-10). In many ways before and after, God breaks the weapons of those set against Him and His people.

> i. Asaph spoke of a fearsome weapon, **the arrows of the bow**: "The *fiery arrows*. Arrows, round the heads of which inflammable matter was rolled, and then ignited, were used by the ancients, and shot into towns to set them on fire; and were discharged among the towers and wooden works of besiegers." (Clarke)

> ii. God's ability to fight on behalf of His people "made the queen-mother of Scotland say, that she more feared the prayers of John Knox than an army of thirty thousand fighting soldiers. The king of Sweden, as soon as he set foot in Germany, fell down to prayer, and what great things did he in a little time!" (Trapp)

> iii. "Like many of the fighting psalms, this too has been a favorite of Christians during religious warfare. The embattled Huguenots sang it as they marched into battle at Cloigny. The Covenanters sang it

at Drumclog in 1679 when they defeated the government troops of 'Bloody Claverhouse'.... Psalm 76 was sung in thanksgiving services marking the defeat of the Spanish Armada in 1588." (Boice)

iv. "While the weapons of our warfare are spiritual, God is the same in might; and while He is in the midst our defense is sure. No weapon formed against the trusting people can prosper." (Morgan)

2. (4-6) Praise to the triumphant God.

You *are* more glorious and excellent
***Than* the mountains of prey.**
The stouthearted were plundered;
They have sunk into their sleep;
And none of the mighty men have found the use of their hands.
At Your rebuke, O God of Jacob,
Both the chariot and horse were cast into a dead sleep.

a. **You are more glorious and excellent than the mountains of prey**: Asaph thought of the beauty and the bounty of the **mountains of prey**, the places remote and wild enough to be home to wild animals. He knew that the Lord God was **more glorious and excellent than** these beautiful places.

i. We imagine Asaph hiking in the high mountains where the goats and ibex and other wild animals live. He is stunned by their beauty, but goes on to think: *Our God is* **more glorious and excellent** *than even these mountains.*

ii. "Thou art more illustrious and excellent than all the mountains of prey, i.e., where wild beasts wander, and prey on those that are more helpless than themselves." (Clarke)

iii. The Septuagint gives an alternative reading of **mountains of prey**. "*The everlasting mountains* is a reading borrowed from the LXX, probably rightly, in place of the somewhat obscure 'mountains of prey' (AV, RV)." (Kidner)

b. **None of the mighty men have found the use of their hands**: The God who is greater than the mountains also helped His people in battle. He helped them by confounding their enemies who were **sunk into their sleep**.

i. "The occasion that springs to mind here is the elimination of Sennacherib's army overnight by the angel of the Lord (Isaiah 37:36). The LXX brings in an allusion to it in its version of the title." (Kidner)

ii. **The stouthearted were plundered**: "They came to spoil, and lo! they are spoiled themselves. Their stout hearts are cold in death, the angel of the pestilence has dried up their life-blood, their very heart is taken from them." (Spurgeon)

iii. **Both the chariot and horse were cast into a dead sleep**: "The Israelites always had a special fear of horses and scythed chariots; and, therefore, the sudden stillness of the entire force of the enemy in this department is made the theme of special rejoicing." (Spurgeon)

B. Giving honor to the great God.

1. (7-9) The fear of the LORD.

You, Yourself, *are* to be feared;
And who may stand in Your presence
When once You are angry?
You caused judgment to be heard from heaven;
The earth feared and was still,
When God arose to judgment,
To deliver all the oppressed of the earth. Selah

a. **You, Yourself, are to be feared**: Asaph thought of the importance of giving honor and reverence – a healthy fear – to the great God. He emphasized the personal aspect of it – that God Himself is **to be feared**, more than the things He may do.

i. **You, Yourself are to be feared**: "The Hebrew is simple, but very emphatic: *attah nora attah*, 'Thou art terrible; thou art.' The repetition of the *pronoun* deepens the sense." (Clarke)

b. **Who may stand in Your presence when once You are angry**: Our respect and reverence for God goes beyond admiration of His greatness. It is also connected to our knowledge of His righteousness, His power, and His authority as Judge. We understand that God is the best friend and the worst enemy.

c. **When God arose to judgment, to deliver all the oppressed of the earth**: God uses His righteous might not primarily to defend Himself, but to **deliver all the oppressed**. He cares about the poor and needy, and every wrong will be set right or recompensed when God rises **to judgment**.

i. "Note the purpose of *judgment*, which is *to save* those who commit their cause to God. This is the chief aspect of justice in the Psalms, where the plight of those who either cannot or will not hit back at the ruthless is a constant concern." (Kidner)

2. (10-12) Honoring the God who rules over all.

Surely the wrath of man shall praise You;
With the remainder of wrath You shall gird Yourself.
Make vows to the LORD your God, and pay *them;*
Let all who are around Him bring presents to Him who ought to be feared.
He shall cut off the spirit of princes;
He is awesome to the kings of the earth.

a. **Surely the wrath of man shall praise You**: Asaph considered the judgments of God and how God uses His judgment to *deliver the oppressed* (verse 9). In this the psalmist sees the matchless wisdom and providence of God, who can work all things together so marvelously that He will make **the wrath of man** bring Him praise.

i. "Even the most hostile acts against his rule will bring him 'praise' (cf. Acts 2:23; Romans 8:28)." (VanGemeren)

ii. The Bible and history are filled with the fulfillment of this promise and principle. Haman was filled with wrath against Mordecai; God used the wrath of Haman to bring Himself praise. The religious leaders of Jesus' day were filled with wrath against God's own Son; God used the wrath of the religious leaders to bring Himself praise. We can see this principle fulfilled in history; by faith we should believe it to be so today when men show their wrath against God and His people.

iii. **The wrath of man** "shall not only be overcome but rendered subservient to thy glory. Man with his breath of threatening is but blowing the trumpet of the Lord's eternal fame." (Spurgeon)

iv. "This singer of the olden time had seen the wrath of man working havoc in human affairs, as we also have seen it. But he watched it closely, and he had seen God, surrounding all its activity by His own presence and holding it within His Own grasp, and so compelling it at last to work towards His praise." (Morgan)

b. **With the remainder of wrath You shall gird Yourself**: God will even *adorn* Himself with the "leftovers" of man's wrath against Him and His people. This in no way justifies the wrath of man, but it does show the surpassing greatness of God.

i. Other translations give a different sense of this difficult Hebrew phrase.

• *And the survivors of your wrath are restrained* (NIV).

• *The residue of wrath thou wilt gird upon thee* (RSV).

ii. If the Hebrew text is to be understood in this sense, then the idea is that God promises to *restrain* the wrath of man. First comes the promise to bring good out of even the wrath of man, and then the promise is to *restrain* that wrath.

iii. "Then he had seen God, when the limit was reached, restrain this wrath, in the pictorial language of the singer, girding it upon Himself, and so preventing its further action under the will of man." (Morgan)

iv. "The wrath of man had been allowed up to a certain point, to bring into clear evidence the greater power of God; and then He had quietly put a term to its further manifestation." (Meyer)

c. **Make vows to the LORD your God, and pay them**: Asaph brought a logical conclusion to the facts presented. If God is this great, then we owe our vows to *Him*, and vows made should be paid.

i. "To vow or not is a matter of choice, but to discharge our vows is our bounden duty. He who would defraud God, his own God, is a wretch indeed." (Spurgeon)

d. **Let all who are around Him bring presents to Him**: We can and should honor God with more than our vows. In humble submission we should **bring presents to Him**, giving to Him our first and our best.

i. "If such should have been the gratitude and devotion of Israelites, for a temporary deliverance from the fury of an earthly tyrant, how much higher ought that of Christians to rise, for eternal redemption from the great oppressor!" (Horne)

e. **He is awesome to the kings of the earth**: Even the **princes** and the **kings of the earth** can and should see the awe of this great God. They should keep their vows to Him and bring presents to honor Him. No one is excluded from the reverence and praise of the great God and King.

i. "None are great in his hand. Caesars and Napoleons fall under his power as the boughs of the tree beneath the woodman's axe." (Spurgeon)

Psalm 77 – The Troubled Heart Remembers God's Great Works

This psalm is titled **To the Chief Musician. To Jeduthun. A Psalm of Asaph**.

The Chief Musician *is thought by some to be the* LORD *God Himself, and others suppose him to be a leader of choirs or musicians in David's time, such as Heman the singer or Asaph (1 Chronicles 6:33, 16:5-7, and 25:6). "The notation 'For the director of music'* [**Chief Musician**] *appears in fifty-five psalms (also in Habakkuk 3:19) and serves probably as a musical addition, marking the psalm to be a part of temple worship or to be recited by the leader of the choir." (Willem VanGemeren)*

Jeduthun *(mentioned also in the titles of Psalm 39 and 62) was one of the musicians appointed by David to lead Israel's public worship (1 Chronicles 16:41; 25:1-3). Charles Spurgeon wrote regarding Jeduthun: "The sons of Jeduthun were porters or doorkeepers, according to 1 Chronicles 16:42. Those who serve well make the best of singers, and those who occupy the highest posts in the choir must not be ashamed to wait at the posts of the doors of the Lord's house."*

Asaph *was the great singer and musician of David and Solomon's era (1 Chronicles 15:17-19, 16:5-7; 2 Chronicles 29:13). 1 Chronicles 25:1 and 2 Chronicles 29:30 add that Asaph was a prophet in his musical compositions.*

"The message of this psalm is that to brood on sorrow is to be broken and disheartened, while to see God is to sing on the darkest day. Once we come to know that our years are of His right hand, there is light everywhere." (G. Campbell Morgan)

A. Comfort and anguish in remembering the works of God.

1. (1-3) Seeking God and remaining troubled.

I cried out to God with my voice—
To God with my voice;
And He gave ear to me.
In the day of my trouble I sought the Lord;
My hand was stretched out in the night without ceasing;
My soul refused to be comforted.

I remembered God, and was troubled;
I complained, and my spirit was overwhelmed. Selah

a. **I cried out to God with my voice**: This psalm begins with a thought common in the psalms, with the psalmist describing his cry to God. He **cried out** to God, and he knew that God heard him (**He gave ear to me**).

> i. "Days of trouble must be days of prayer; in days of inward trouble, especially when God seems to have withdrawn from us, we must seek him, and seek till we find him. In the day of his trouble he did not seek for the diversions of business or recreation, to shake off his trouble that way, but he sought God, and his favour and grace. Those that are under trouble of mind, must not think to drink it away, or laugh it away, but pray it away." (Henry, cited in Spurgeon)

b. **In the day of trouble**: His cry to God was urgent (**in the day of trouble**), active (**stretched out**), and persistent (**without ceasing**).

> i. "In Oriental fashion he 'stretched out' his hands in prayer (Psalm 143:6) and continued to lift up his hands 'at night'." (VanGemeren)

c. **My soul refused to be comforted**: Encouraging thoughts came to mind but were immediately put away. Friends spoke of God's goodness in the present and brighter future, but the **soul refused** any comfort.

> i. Sometimes comfort is refused because it is superficial. One may say to the person in despair, "Go to a movie and have some fun," or other advice that treats his despair lightly. Sometimes we are in such despair that seeking God and God alone can help, and nothing superficial.

> ii. "He refused some comforts as too weak for his case, others as untrue, others as unhallowed; but chiefly because of distraction, he declined even those grounds of consolation which ought to have been effectual with him. As a sick man turns away even from the most nourishing food, so did he. It is impossible to comfort those who refuse to be comforted." (Spurgeon)

> iii. "There may be a further hint of this tenacity by an echo of Jacob's refusal to be comforted over Joseph (Genesis 37:35)." (Kidner)

d. **I remembered God, and was troubled**: The psalmist earnestly and sincerely cried out to God and knew that God heard him – yet was **troubled**, and felt his **spirit was overwhelmed**. The sense is, "God, I know you are there – why won't You help me the way I need to be helped?"

> i. Most often when the believer cries out to God and senses he or she is heard, it brings the peaceful assurance of faith. This is not always the case. Sometimes – especially when we remain in our difficulty instead

of being delivered from it – the sense that God has heard us yet our trouble remains brings *more* frustration and not less.

ii. Perhaps this was some of what Paul felt regarding his thorn in the flesh described in 2 Corinthians 12:7-10. At first he felt the frustration of unanswered prayer; then he felt the challenge of prayer answered, but not according to previous expectation.

iii. This is the kind of struggle with God known by those somewhat further along in their relationship with God. The depth and complexity of this struggle is worthy of meditation – thus, **Selah** is here inserted.

2. (4-6) The diligent search.

You hold my eyelids open;
I am so troubled that I cannot speak.
I have considered the days of old,
The years of ancient times.
I call to remembrance my song in the night;
I meditate within my heart,
And my spirit makes diligent search.

a. **You hold my eyelids open**: Asaph considered the *intensity* of his cry to God. With weary eyes and a troubled heart, he sincerely sought God.

i. "Sorrow, like a beast of prey, devours at night; and every sad heart knows how eyelids, however wearied, refuse to close upon as wearied eyes, which gaze wide opened into the blackness and see dreadful things there. This man felt as if God's finger was pushing up his lids and forcing him to stare out into the night." (Maclaren)

ii. **I cannot speak**: "This shows an *increase* of sorrow and anguish. At *first* he felt his misery, and *called aloud*. He receives more light, sees and feels his deep wretchedness, and then his words are swallowed by excessive distress. His woes are too big for utterance." (Clarke)

b. **I have considered the days of old**: Asaph considered the *extent* of his cry to God, considering what God had done even in **ancient times**. He wondered why God seemed to answer those in the past with more satisfaction than He does in the present.

c. **I call to remembrance my song in the night**: Asaph's seeking after God remembered better times (**song in the night**), and it was deep (**I meditate within my heart**) and **diligent**.

3. (7-9) The searching questions.

Will the Lord cast off forever?
And will He be favorable no more?

Has His mercy ceased forever?
Has *His* promise failed forevermore?
Has God forgotten to be gracious?
Has He in anger shut up His tender mercies? Selah

a. **Will the Lord cast off forever?** With these questions Asaph spoke his fear that the season of dryness and frustration might last **forever**. He feared that never again would he see the favor of God, the mercy of God, and the fulfillment of God's **promise**.

i. "Very wisely this good man argued with himself, and sought to cure his unbelief. He treated himself homeopathically, treating like with like. As he was attacked by the disease of questioning, he gave himself questions as a medicine. Observe how he kills one question with another, as men fight fire with fire. Here we have six questions, one after another, each one striking at the very heart of unbelief." (Spurgeon)

ii. "Beloved, if we were sometimes thus to school ourselves and cross-question our own unbelief, the Holy Spirit would give us comfort." (Spurgeon)

b. **Has God forgotten to be gracious?** With two more questions Asaph wondered if God's grace and mercy were no longer available to him; that they were **forgotten** or blocked toward him.

i. Many a beloved saint has felt the agony of these questions; we could wish that each of them would ask these questions as boldly and honestly as Asaph did.

ii. "Spurgeon's studies of the psalms were produced between 1865 and 1885, and during those twenty years he experienced much ill health, which continued to deteriorate until his death in 1892. He had neuralgia and gout, which left him with swollen, red, painful limbs, so that he frequently could not walk or even write. He had debilitating headaches, and with these physical ills came frightful bouts of depression, leading almost to despair." (Boice)

iii. Therefore, Spurgeon would write of this psalm: "Alas, my God, the writer of this exposition well knows what thy servant Asaph meant, for his soul is familiar with the way of grief. Deep glens and lonely caves of soul depressions, my spirit knows full well your awful glooms!" (Spurgeon)

iv. **Has He in anger shut up His tender mercies**: "The *tender mercies* of God are the *source* whence all his kindness to the children of men flows. The metaphor here is taken from a *spring*, the mouth of which is closed, so that its waters can no longer run in the same channel." (Clarke)

v. "If you are a child of God, yet never had to ask these questions, you ought to be very grateful; but if you have to ask them, be very thankful that Asaph asked them before you; and believe that, as he had a comfortable answer to them, so shall you. It is always a comfort when you can see the footprints of another man in the mire and the slough, for if that man passed through unharmed, so may you, for his God shall also be your Helper." (Spurgeon)

c. **Selah**: Asaph spoke things that believers rarely feel safe to speak about. Many believers won't risk this kind of honesty. Asaph's honest anguish is worthy of contemplation.

B. The greatness of God.

1. (10-12) Anguish turns to remembering.

And I said, "This *is* my anguish;
***But I will remember* the years of the right hand of the Most High."**
I will remember the works of the LORD;
Surely I will remember Your wonders of old.
I will also meditate on all Your work,
And talk of Your deeds.

a. **This is my anguish**: We appreciate the honest **anguish** of Asaph in this psalm. For him, the apparent gap between what he believed and what he felt was painful.

b. **But I will remember**: In the midst of the painful anguish between what he believed and what he felt, Asaph spoke to himself and declared what he would *do*. He was determined to **remember** something, to keep it in mind.

i. "To the insinuations of distrust, faith now begins to reply." (Horne)

ii. "Memory supplies the colours with which Hope paints her truest pictures." (Maclaren)

iii. "Memory is a fit handmaid for faith. When faith has its seven years of famine, memory like Joseph in Egypt opens her granaries." (Spurgeon)

c. **But I will remember the years of the right hand of the Most High**: Asaph was determined to remember the better seasons when God's power seemed unhindered, when His symbolic hand of strength and skill (**the years of the right hand**) were evident. In discouraging times he decided to remember better times and take firm hope for the future.

i. "If no good was in the present, memory ransacked the past to find consolation. She fain would borrow a light from the altars of yesterday to light the gloom of to-day. It is our duty to search for comfort, and not in sullen indolence yield to despair." (Spurgeon)

d. **I will remember...I will also meditate...and talk of Your deeds**: Asaph presented a three-step process to encouragement and healing. It begins with remembering God's great works, His **wonders of old**. Then we should **meditate** on those works, and what they may have to teach us today. The third step is to **talk** of these great things with others.

i. **I will remember the works of the LORD**: Kidner indicated that this was a public *remembrance*. "Strictly speaking, 'I will make mention of'; *i.e.*, it is a public recounting of these deeds."

2. (13-15) The greatness of God in His sanctuary.

Your way, O God, is in the sanctuary;
Who is so great a God as our God?
You are the God who does wonders;
You have declared Your strength among the peoples.
You have with Your arm redeemed Your people,
The sons of Jacob and Joseph. Selah

a. **Your way, O God, is in the sanctuary**: In the first part of the psalm, Asaph explained the goodness of remembering, meditating, and speaking of God's greatness. He begins the second part of the psalm by actually describing God's good works, beginning **in the sanctuary** – either of the temple or tabernacle.

i. The **way** of God was in the sanctuary in the sense that the tabernacle or the temple and its rituals clearly spoke of the way to God through the blood of an innocent sacrifice, ultimately pointing to the person and work of Jesus Christ.

b. **You are the God who does wonders; You have declared Your strength among the peoples**: Asaph spoke of the miraculous works that displayed the strength of God, as He had done time and again in the history of Israel.

c. **You have with Your arm redeemed Your people**: Many times through their history, Israel saw God's faithful strength rescue them from all kinds of trouble.

i. **The sons of Jacob and Joseph**: "The coupling of *Jacob* and *Joseph* as ancestors of the people redeemed from the Egyptians may be due to the insistence of both of them that the Promised Land, not Egypt, must be their final rest (Genesis 47:29ff; 50:24f)." (Kidner)

3. (16-20) The greatness of God at the Red Sea.

The waters saw You, O God;
The waters saw You, they were afraid;
The depths also trembled.
The clouds poured out water;
The skies sent out a sound;
Your arrows also flashed about.
The voice of Your thunder *was* in the whirlwind;
The lightnings lit up the world;
The earth trembled and shook.
Your way *was* in the sea,
Your path in the great waters,
And Your footsteps were not known.
You led Your people like a flock
By the hand of Moses and Aaron.

a. **The waters saw You, O God**: In this last portion of the psalm, Asaph most likely had in mind the parting and crossing of the Red Sea as an example of one of the great works of God that he would remember, meditate upon, and tell of. He began by poetically describing the waters of the Red Sea as **afraid** of Yahweh, and ready to flee at His presence.

i. "The waters of the Red Sea are here beautifully represented as endued with sensibility, as seeing, feeling, and being confounded, even to the lowest depths, at the presence and power of their great Creator." (Horne)

b. **The clouds poured out water**: We are not told of a mighty thunderstorm that accompanied the parting of the Red Sea, but Asaph described the rain, **thunder**, and lightning (**Your arrows also flashed about**). It's hard to know at this point if Asaph described something not included in Exodus 14 or simply spoke of the presence and power of God in poetic terms.

i. It seems more favorable to take this literally. The ancient Jewish historian Josephus did: "As soon as ever the whole Egyptian army was within it, the sea flowed to its own place, and came down with a torrent raised by storms of wind and encompassed the Egyptians. Showers of rain also came down from the sky, and dreadful thunders and lightning, with flashes of fire. Thunder-bolts also were darted upon them; nor was there anything which used to be sent by God upon men, as indications of his wrath, which did not happen at this time; for a dark and dismal night oppressed them. And thus did all these men perish, so that there was not one man left to be a messenger of this calamity to the rest of the Egyptians." (Josephus, cited in Spurgeon)

ii. "Either these are details missing from the original account but preserved in the historical memory of the people or they are a poetic embellishment of the incident. Whatever the case, there is nothing improbable about these additional manifestations of God's power on that great night of nights for Israel." (Boice)

iii. **Your arrows**: "Either hail-stones, or rather lightnings or thunderbolts, which are called God's *arrows*, Psalms 18:14, 144:6." (Poole)

c. **The earth trembled and shook**: Asaph described the presence of God as being so manifest at the parting of the Red Sea that the earth itself shook. Again, since this is not recorded in the Exodus 14 account, either he adds information or is simply giving a poetic description.

d. **Your way was in the sea, Your path in the great waters**: When God miraculously parted the waters of the Red Sea, it was as if He cleared a great road or **path** for Himself that He also gave to His people to use.

i. **Your path in the great waters**: "It is a true picture of God's sway over nature. Even when He was incarnate, the winds and waves would obey Him and the sea provide a path for Him." (Kidner)

ii. **Your footsteps were not known**: "God is described as wading through mighty oceans as a man might ford some tiny stream. The Atlantic with fathomless depths is no more to Him than a brook to us." (Meyer)

e. **You led Your people like a flock**: As a final description of God's mighty work at the Red Sea, Asaph noted that God led His people on the path through the sea, as well as by His servants Moses and Aaron.

i. We see that God works *both* in great wonders (as at the Red Sea) and in the normal leading of His people through human instruments (**Moses and Aaron**). One never excludes the other.

ii. "The smiter of Egypt was the shepherd of Israel. He drove his foes before him, but went before his people." (Spurgeon)

iii. "The loving-kindness of God towards Israel did not stop at the Red Sea, but he conducted his chosen flock, by the guidance of faithful pastors, through all the perils of the wilderness, to the land of promise." (Horne)

iv. "This mighty God has the tender heart of a shepherd. He leads His people like a flock; not overdriving, but carrying the lambs in His bosom, and gently leading those that are with young. Mightier than the mightiest, but meeker than the meekest!" (Meyer)

Psalm 78 – Learning from God's Faithfulness to His Rebellious People

This psalm is titled **A Contemplation of Asaph**. *The author* **Asaph** *was the great singer and musician of David and Solomon's era (1 Chronicles 15:17-19, 16:5-7; 2 Chronicles 29:13). 1 Chronicles 25:1 and 2 Chronicles 29:30 add that Asaph was a prophet in his musical compositions.*

"Psalm 78 is the longest of the historical psalms. Its lesson is that history must not repeat itself. The people must never again be unbelieving." (James Montgomery Boice)

A. Introduction: Learning from the past, teaching for the future.

1. (1-4) Gaining the attention of the people of God.

> **Give ear, O my people, *to* my law;**
> **Incline your ears to the words of my mouth.**
> **I will open my mouth in a parable;**
> **I will utter dark sayings of old,**
> **Which we have heard and known,**
> **And our fathers have told us.**
> **We will not hide *them* from their children,**
> **Telling to the generation to come the praises of the LORD,**
> **And His strength and His wonderful works that He has done.**

a. **Give ear, O my people, to my law**: Psalm 78 is a *wisdom* psalm, written to instruct God's people. The theme is the goodness and kindness of God to His stubborn and rebellious people. Asaph began by asking for the attention of God's people so they could hear the wisdom he would speak.

i. Psalm 78 begins with a principle sometimes neglected among those who would speak wisdom to others: you must first gain the *attention* of your listeners if you would teach them and reach them.

ii. **Incline your ears**: "Inclining the ears does not denote any ordinary sort of hearing, but such as a disciple renders to the words of his master, with submission and reverence of mind, silent and earnest, that whatever is enunciated for the purpose of instruction may be heard and properly understood, and nothing be allowed to escape. He is a hearer of a different stamp, who hears carelessly, not for the purpose of learning or imitation, but to criticise, to make merry, to indulge animosity, or to kill time." (Musculus, cited in Spurgeon)

b. **I will open my mouth in a parable**: Psalm 49 is another wisdom psalm with reference to a proverb or **parable** and the **dark sayings**. The phrase **dark sayings** does not have in mind hidden or mystical knowledge, but things that can simply be difficult to understand – *riddles* that are good topics for instruction.

> i. **In a parable**: "The word for *parable* (*masal*) gives the book of Proverbs its title. Basically this means a comparison, *i.e.*, a saying which uses one realm of life to illuminate another." (Kidner)

> ii. Matthew 13:35 quotes Psalm 78:2 as a prophecy of the way Jesus would teach.

c. **Which we have heard and known, and our fathers have told us**: Asaph will not bring up *new* things for discussion, but things already within the mind of Israel.

d. **Telling to the generation to come the praises of the Lord**: Asaph knew what followed in this psalm came from events and themes received from their **fathers**. He also knew that what they had received, they had to pass on to the next **generation**; they had a responsibility to **not hide them from their children**.

> i. "For the classic passage on teaching this faith to one's *children* see Deuteronomy 6:6-9, for Scripture has no room for parental neutrality." (Kidner)

> ii. "The more of parental teaching the better; ministers and Sabbath-school teachers were never meant to be substitutes for mothers' tears and fathers' prayers." (Spurgeon)

e. **The praises of the Lord, and His strength and His wonderful works that He has done**: Asaph was concerned about passing on at least three things to the next generation.

- The **praises of the Lord** – teaching them that God was worthy of our adoration and gratitude.

- God's **strength** – His power and greatness above and beyond all.

- **His wonderful works** – that is, God's power and greatness in active assistance to His people.

i. It is *still* good and necessary for us to pass these things on. We should speak often about them and tell the continually unfolding story of how God has done **wonderful works** in and through His people.

ii. This speaks to the importance of seeing and understanding the hand of God as He moves in and through history. "History should ever be the record of the works of God. That is to emphasize the important factor. History thus written, and thus taught, will so affect hope and memory in youth, as to constrain it to obedience to the God revealed; and this is the way of life for man and nation." (Morgan)

iii. This psalm emphasizes the **strength** and the **wonderful works** of God – not the strength or wonderful works of His people. This psalm is remarkably honest about the failings of God's people. "The supreme quality of this psalm is that throughout all its measures, over against the repeated failure of His people, God's persistent patience is set forth in bold relief." (Morgan)

iv. "Those who forget God's works are sure to fail in their own." (Spurgeon)

2. (5-8) Teaching one generation to avoid the errors of previous generations.

For He established a testimony in Jacob,
And appointed a law in Israel,
Which He commanded our fathers,
That they should make them known to their children;
That the generation to come might know *them,*
The children *who* **would be born,**
That **they may arise and declare** *them* **to their children,**
That they may set their hope in God,
And not forget the works of God,
But keep His commandments;
And may not be like their fathers,
A stubborn and rebellious generation,
A generation *that* **did not set its heart aright,**
And whose spirit was not faithful to God.

a. **He established a testimony in Jacob, and appointed a law in Israel**: Using poetic repetition for style and emphasis, Asaph began by describing one of the greatest of God's *wonderful works* (verse 4) – the giving of God's word to **Israel**.

i. Centuries later the Apostle Paul would explain that one of the great advantages God gave to Israel was that He committed to them His word, *the oracles of God* (Romans 3:2).

b. **That they should make them known to their children**: Then and now, God gives His word so that it will be *transmitted* to following generations. In theory, the revelation of God's word can perish or become utterly irrelevant if not passed on to the next generation.

> i. "Through Moses he had commanded all Israelites, regardless of tribal descent, to instruct their children at home (Deuteronomy 6:6-9, 20-22; cf. Exodus 10:2; 12:26-27; 13:8)." (VanGemeren)

c. **That they may arise and declare them to their children**: Not only should our children be taught, they should be taught to teach **their children** so that the word and the work of God will continue throughout the generations.

> i. "*Five* generations appear to be mentioned above: 1. Fathers; 2. Their children; 3. The generation to come; 4. And their children; 5. And their children. They were never to lose sight of their history throughout all their generations." (Clarke)

d. **That they may set their hope in God, and not forget the works of God**: The purpose of communicating to the next generation is that they would learn to trust God for themselves, never forgetting His wonderful works.

e. **But keep His commandments; and may not be like their fathers**: To the psalmist, losing trust in God and forgetting His works would lead to disobedience. If the younger generation is well instructed, they would be more likely to be obedient, avoiding many of the errors of **their fathers**.

f. **A stubborn and rebellious generation**: Asaph described the sins of previous generations in Israel. They were **stubborn and rebellious**; they did not **set** their **hearts aright**, and their **spirit was not faithful to God**. Asaph's focus was on heart and attitude more than on *action*.

3. (9-11) Preview and overview: losing the spiritual battle.

The children of Ephraim, *being* armed *and* carrying bows,
Turned back in the day of battle.
They did not keep the covenant of God;
They refused to walk in His law,
And forgot His works
And His wonders that He had shown them.

a. **The children of Ephraim**: The tribe of **Ephraim** was one of the larger tribes of Israel, and sometimes God called Israel "**Ephraim**." In 2 Chronicles 25:7 God used the phrase *children of Ephraim* to refer to the people of Israel as a whole.

i. "As the largest of the breakaway tribes, their subsequent history was to make them almost a symbol of backsliding and apostasy." (Kidner)

ii. "The prophetic writings (especially Hosea) show that Ephraim became the leader in the rebellion and disloyalty that cursed the nation, and so, figuratively and standing for the rest, Ephraim is here addressed." (Morgan)

b. **Being armed and carrying bows, turned back in the day of battle**: Because it is difficult to match this with a known instance in Israel's history, perhaps the sense here is of a *spiritual* battle. Spiritually speaking, God equipped Israel for conflict. They were **armed** and had **bows**. Yet they often failed in **the day of battle**, because **they did not keep the covenant of God**.

i. "The incident referred to is not known. It was a time when 'Ephraim, though armed with bows, turned back on the day of battle' (Psalm 78:9). Nothing exactly like this is found anywhere in the Old Testament." (Boice)

ii. Yet, "The psalmist's description 'armed with bows' fits well with their aggressiveness as portrayed in the Book of Judges (Judges 8:1-3; 12:1-6)." (VanGemeren)

iii. "The reference to Ephraim in Psalm 78:9-11 is not to be taken as alluding to any cowardly retreat from actual battle. Psalm 78:9 seems to be a purely figurative way of expressing what is put without a metaphor in the two following verses. Ephraim's revolt from God's covenant was like the conduct of soldiers, well armed and refusing to charge the foe." (Maclaren)

iv. God makes spiritual resources available to His people for the spiritual conflicts they face (Ephesians 6:10-18). However, the effectiveness of those resources depends in some regard on their decision to actually make use of them. Ultimately, God's people are assured of victory in Jesus. Day to day there may be defeats and setbacks – being **turned back in the day of battle** – because available resources are not used.

v. Spiritually considered, there are many who are **turned back in the day of battle**, though in different ways.

• Some turn back before the battle begins.

• Some turn back as soon as the battle is engaged.

• Some turn back when the first injury is received.

• Some turn back when the battle becomes long.

c. **They refused to walk in His law, and forgot His works and His wonders**: Disobedience and ignorance among God's people were examples of being **turned back in the day of battle**. This is a warning to all generations: the spiritual battle may be lost.

i. **And forgot His works**: "It would seem almost past belief to us as we read that a people so led could forget. Yet is not this sin of forgetfulness with us perpetually? In some day of danger and perplexity we become so occupied with the immediate peril as utterly to fail to think of past deliverances. Such forgetfulness is of the nature of unbelief in its worst form." (Morgan)

ii. **Forgot His works**: "Not historically, but practically. They did not so remember them, as to love, and serve, and trust that God of whose infinite power and goodness they had such ample experience." (Poole)

iii. "Ere we condemn them, let us repent of our own wicked forgetfulness, and confess the many occasions upon which we also have been unmindful of past favours." (Spurgeon)

B. Stubborn, rebellious Israel in the Exodus from Egypt.

1. (12-16) God brought Israel out of Egypt, through the sea, and gave the people water in the wilderness.

Marvelous things He did in the sight of their fathers,
In the land of Egypt, *in* **the field of Zoan.**
He divided the sea and caused them to pass through;
And He made the waters stand up like a heap.
In the daytime also He led them with the cloud,
And all the night with a light of fire.
He split the rocks in the wilderness,
And gave *them* **drink in abundance like the depths.**
He also brought streams out of the rock,
And caused waters to run down like rivers.

a. **Marvelous things He did in the sight of their fathers, in the land of Egypt**: Asaph remembered how God helped His people as described in the first part of the Book of Exodus. Through a series of miraculous plagues and demonstrations of God's power, Pharaoh was compelled to let Israel go from slavery, and the people left rewarded with riches from the Egyptians (Exodus 5-13).

i. "*Zoan* is better known as Tanis, in the north-east of the Nile Delta, a city which was either identical with Rameses II's capital (Raamses, which the Israelites helped to build: Exodus 1:11) or not many miles from it." (Kidner)

b. **He divided the sea and caused them to pass through**: As Pharaoh's armies pursued Israel, God miraculously brought the people through the sea on dry ground as God **made the waters stand up like a heap** (Exodus 14).

c. **In the daytime also He led them with the cloud, and all the night with a light of fire**: When the Israelites came into the wilderness of Sinai, God assured them and guided them with the two demonstrations of His presence – the **cloud** by day and the **fire** by night (Exodus 40:36-38).

> i. "**A cloud;** which was very comfortable, both for a shadow from the scorching heat of the climate and season, and for a companion and director in their journey." (Poole)

d. **He split the rocks in the wilderness, and gave them drink**: Often in the wilderness the nation of Israel needed water, and many times God miraculously provided. One occasion was at Meribah where Moses struck the rock and it presumably split, bringing forth water (Numbers 20:10-13, Isaiah 48:21).

> i. "**Rocks;** he useth the plural number, because it was twice done; once in Rephidim, Exodus 17:6, and again in Kadesh, Numbers 20:1,11." (Poole)

2. (17-20) Israel's stubborn, rebellious response to God's wonderful works.

But they sinned even more against Him
By rebelling against the Most High in the wilderness.
And they tested God in their heart
By asking for the food of their fancy.
Yes, they spoke against God:
They said, "Can God prepare a table in the wilderness?
Behold, He struck the rock,
So that the waters gushed out,
And the streams overflowed.
Can He give bread also?
Can He provide meat for His people?"

a. **But they sinned even more against Him**: God repeatedly did great and amazing things for Israel in taking the people out of Egypt and preserving them in the wilderness. Yet Israel's response was to sin **even more** and to rebel **against the Most High**.

b. **They tested God in their heart by asking for the food of their fancy**: God provided Israel's needs in the wilderness, but sometimes the people demanded more. He gave them manna, but they soon wanted meat – **the**

food of their fancy (as in Numbers 11:4-10, 18-23, and 31-34). This **tested** God.

i. God promises to provide our needs. He never promised to give us **the food of** our **fancy**.

ii. "Nothing is more provoking to God, than our quarrelling with our allotment, and indulging the desires of the flesh." (Henry, cited in Spurgeon)

iii. We could say that the people of Israel were guilty of at least two sins.

- They were dissatisfied with what God provided.
- They thought the reason why God didn't give them what they wanted was because He *couldn't* – that it was beyond His power.

c. **Can God prepare a table in the wilderness?** With these words they **spoke against God**; they **tested** Him, expressing their lack of faith in His power and lack of trust in His care. They didn't believe that God could give them a banquet in the wilderness.

i. "Israel had seen the wonderful works of God, cleaving the sea, lighting the night, and giving water from rocks. Yet they questioned God's ability to give bread, and to spread out a table in the wilderness." (Meyer)

ii. "It was no sin to be hungry and thirsty; it was a necessity of their nature. There is nothing living that does not desire and require food: when we do not we are dead, and that they did so was no sin. Their sin was *to doubt that God could or would support them in the wilderness, or allow those who followed his leadings to lack any good thing.* This was their sin." (North, cited in Spurgeon)

iii. "The expression, *spread a table,* uses the same words as Psalm 23:5, whose serenity is a shining contrast to this." (Kidner)

iv. In 1933 – the middle of the Great Depression – a young Irishman named J. Edwin Orr left a good paying job and, with no fixed source of income, he trusted that God would provide for him and his mother. He planned to travel around Great Britain with the message of prayer, salvation, and revival. He left Belfast with 2 shillings and 8 pence – about 65 cents. He had a bicycle, a change of clothes, and a Bible. He spent the next year travelling to every county in Great Britain and organizing some 300 prayer groups dedicated to pray for revival. He wrote a book about it all and finally convinced a publisher to take it – after being rejected 17 times. That first book, titled *Can God–?,* was based on Psalm 78:19 and published in 1934. It sold hundreds of thousands of copies and was a tremendous inspiration to Christians in that day. Orr's book and his life were a remarkable demonstration of the fact that God *can* **prepare a table in the wilderness**.

v. "Though behind us lay the gift of the Cross, the miracles of the Resurrection and Ascension, the care exercised by God over our early years, the goodness and mercy of our after lives, we are disposed to say, 'Can God?'.... Fetch arguments for faith from the days that have gone." (Meyer)

vi. "The words are wrongly placed. Never say again, 'Can God?' but God can." (Meyer)

d. **Can He give bread also? Can He provide meat for His people?** Repeatedly, God showed Israel that He could do all this and more. The people asked these doubting questions with the miraculously provided manna in their stomachs.

i. "Who will say that a man is thankful to his friend for a past kindness, if he nourishes an ill opinion of him for the future?" (Gurnall, cited in Spurgeon)

3. (21-25) God's anger with the unbelief and mistrust of Israel.

Therefore the LORD heard *this* and was furious;
So a fire was kindled against Jacob,
And anger also came up against Israel,
Because they did not believe in God,
And did not trust in His salvation.
Yet He had commanded the clouds above,
And opened the doors of heaven,
Had rained down manna on them to eat,
And given them of the bread of heaven.
Men ate angels' food;
He sent them food to the full.

a. **Therefore the LORD heard this and was furious**: God blessed and provided for Israel in the escape from Egypt and in the wilderness; Israel responded with complaining and unbelief. God did not ignore this; He **heard** it and He **was furious** with their sin against Him.

i. Keep in mind that the sins Asaph had in mind were the sins of ingratitude, testing God, and doubting His power and His care. These were sins God was **furious** with. We often think God takes little account of such sins.

ii. "He was not indifferent to what they said. He dwelt among them in the holy place, and, therefore, they insulted him to his face. He did not hear a report of it, but the language itself came into his ears." (Spurgeon)

b. **So a fire was kindled against Jacob**: Asaph may have had in mind what happened at Taberah, where in judgment *the fire of the LORD burned among* Israel (Numbers 11:1-3).

c. **Because they did not believe in God, and did not trust in His salvation**: In case we didn't get it before, Asaph stated it clearly for emphasis. These were the sins that made God **furious** and made His judgment burn like **fire** against Israel. Unbelief and mistrust toward God are counted as small sins by many today.

i. "In the text it appears as if all Israel's other sins were as nothing compared with this; this is the peculiar spot which the Lord points at, the special provocation which angered him. From this let every unbeliever learn to tremble more at his unbelief than at anything else. If he be no fornicator, or thief, or liar, let him reflect that it is quite enough to condemn him that he trusts not in God's salvation." (Spurgeon)

d. **Yet He had commanded the clouds above, and opened the doors of heaven**: Their dark sin is set against the white background of God's goodness and constant care for them. He gave them and *kept* giving them **bread of heaven** and **angels' food**, and they ate **to the full**.

i. There have been many attempts to understand manna as a known natural phenomenon. It's possible that there is a link to something along these lines, such as the sugary substance modern Arabs call *mann*; yet the sense of verses 24-25 is that there was something *supernatural* and even *other-worldly* about manna.

ii. "'Tis called 'angels' food,' not because the angels do daily feed upon it, but because it was both made and ministered by the ministry of angels, and that phrase sets forth the excellency of it." (Ness, cited in Spurgeon)

e. **And given them of the bread of heaven**: John records in his Gospel that in trying to persuade Jesus to keep providing miraculous bread, those who had been fed quoted this line from verse 24 (*Our fathers ate the manna in the desert; as it is written, "He gave them bread from heaven to eat,"* John 6:31). In quoting this psalm to Jesus, they fulfilled it in a negative way, showing the same ingratitude and willingness to test God that Israel showed in the wilderness.

i. "In appealing to this very psalm, the arguers [those contesting with Jesus in John 6] were handling too sharp a weapon." (Kidner)

ii. In verse 24, **bread of heaven** is more literally *grain of heaven* – or, *corn* in the King James Version. "The manna was round, like coriander seed, and hence was rightly called corn; it did not rise from the earth, but descended from the clouds, and hence the words of the verse are literally accurate." (Spurgeon)

4. (26-31) The sending of fowl for meat.

He caused an east wind to blow in the heavens;
And by His power He brought in the south wind.
He also rained meat on them like the dust,
Feathered fowl like the sand of the seas;
And He let *them* fall in the midst of their camp,
All around their dwellings.
So they ate and were well filled,
For He gave them their own desire.
They were not deprived of their craving;
But while their food *was* still in their mouths,
The wrath of God came against them,
And slew the stoutest of them,
And struck down the choice *men* of Israel.

a. **He also rained meat on them like the dust**: Numbers 11:31-33 describes how God sent quail to Israel when they complained about the manna. He literally **let them fall in the midst of their camp**, bringing the meat they craved to them.

b. **So they ate and were well filled, for He gave them their own desire**: Asaph wrote this with a strong sense of irony. Israel was **well filled**, but not with good quail meat in their stomachs. God **gave them their own desire**, but because **their craving** was rooted in their self-will, the result was not good.

i. **He gave them their own desire**: "The Lord shewed them that he could 'provide flesh for his people,' even enough and to spare. He also shewed them that when lust wins its desire, it is disappointed." (Spurgeon)

ii. "Consider that there is more real satisfaction in mortifying lusts than in making provision for them or in fulfilling them: there is more true pleasure in crossing and pinching our flesh than in gratifying it; were there any true pleasure in sin, hell would not be hell, for the more sin, the more joy. You cannot satisfy one lust if you would do your utmost, and make yourself never so absolute a slave to it; you think if you had your heart's desire you would be at rest: you much mistake; they had it." (Carmichael, cited in Spurgeon)

c. **While their food was still in their mouths, the wrath of God came against them**: Numbers 11:33 stated it like this: *But while the meat was still between their teeth, before it was chewed, the wrath of the LORD was aroused against the people, and the LORD struck the people with a very great plague.* God gave a disobedient and rebellious Israel all they desired and craved, and the quail turned to a plague of judgment among them.

5. (32-39) A merciful response to great sin.

In spite of this they still sinned,
And did not believe in His wondrous works.
Therefore their days He consumed in futility,
And their years in fear.
When He slew them, then they sought Him;
And they returned and sought earnestly for God.
Then they remembered that God *was* their rock,
And the Most High God their Redeemer.
Nevertheless they flattered Him with their mouth,
And they lied to Him with their tongue;
For their heart was not steadfast with Him,
Nor were they faithful in His covenant.
But He, *being* full of compassion, forgave *their* iniquity,
And did not destroy *them.*
Yes, many a time He turned His anger away,
And did not stir up all His wrath;
For He remembered that they *were but* flesh,
A breath that passes away and does not come again.

a. **In spite of this they still sinned**: In some ways this is the most tragic line of this psalm. Despite all the blessings and the strongest of corrections, **they still sinned**. Israel didn't learn either from God's goodness or from His wrath.

b. **Therefore their days He consumed in futility and their years in fear**: God said that the generation of unbelieving people could not enter the Promised Land; that generation would be **consumed** in the wilderness (Numbers 14:22-24). The **futility** was expressed in the idea that they came out of Egypt, but never into Canaan. The **fear** was expressed in their unwillingness to take the land by faith (Numbers 14:1-4).

c. **When He slew them, then they sought Him**: It took the most extreme correction from God, but eventually a generation of people grew and **sought earnestly for God** – but even their seeking was somewhat insincere.

i. "But such seeking after God, which is properly not seeking Him at all, but only seeking to escape from evil, neither goes deep nor lasts long." (Maclaren)

ii. "As iron is very soft and malleable while in the fire, but soon after returneth to its former hardness; so many, while afflicted, seem very well affected, but afterwards soon show what they are." (Trapp)

d. **Nevertheless they flattered Him with their mouth**: Their seeking of God was sincere but short-lived. Soon they came to God only with flattering, insincere words. Strange to think a man could think he could lie to God, yet **they** (and often *we*) **lied to Him with their tongue**.

i. "False on their knees, liars in their prayers. Mouth-worship must be very destestable to God when dissociated from the heart: other kings love flattery, but the King of Kings abhors it." (Spurgeon)

e. **But He, being full of compassion, forgave their iniquity**: God's response to their stubborn rebellion, to their insincere seeking, to their failure to be **faithful in His covenant**, was surprising. God showed His **compassion**, He **forgave**, and **many a time He turned His anger away**.

i. "It is indeed a great song of God's patience, and there is no story more fruitful than if men will but learn it." (Morgan)

ii. "Though not mentioned in the text, we know from the history that a mediator interposed, the man Moses stood in the gap." (Spurgeon)

f. **He remembered that they were but flesh, a breath that passes**: In part, God's understanding of the weakness of humanity prompted His compassion and forgiveness. One reason He was merciful to them was because of their frail nature.

i. "His compassion found expression in his forgiveness (cf. Psalm 65:3) of their sins, his forbearance with their stubborn spirits, and his empathy with the human condition, so that the full brunt of his anger did not destroy them." (VanGemeren)

ii. "How gracious on the Lord's part to make man's insignificance an argument for staying his wrath." (Spurgeon)

6. (40-55) From Egypt to Canaan, Israel's failure to remember the power of God.

How often they provoked Him in the wilderness,
***And* grieved Him in the desert!**

Yes, again and again they tempted God,
And limited the Holy One of Israel.
They did not remember His power:
The day when He redeemed them from the enemy,
When He worked His signs in Egypt,
And His wonders in the field of Zoan;
Turned their rivers into blood,
And their streams, that they could not drink.
He sent swarms of flies among them, which devoured them,
And frogs, which destroyed them.
He also gave their crops to the caterpillar,
And their labor to the locust.
He destroyed their vines with hail,
And their sycamore trees with frost.
He also gave up their cattle to the hail,
And their flocks to fiery lightning.
He cast on them the fierceness of His anger,
Wrath, indignation, and trouble,
By sending angels of destruction *among them.*
He made a path for His anger;
He did not spare their soul from death,
But gave their life over to the plague,
And destroyed all the firstborn in Egypt,
The first of *their* strength in the tents of Ham.
But He made His own people go forth like sheep,
And guided them in the wilderness like a flock;
And He led them on safely, so that they did not fear;
But the sea overwhelmed their enemies.
And He brought them to His holy border,
This mountain *which* His right hand had acquired.
He also drove out the nations before them,
Allotted them an inheritance by survey,
And made the tribes of Israel dwell in their tents.

a. **How often they provoked Him in the wilderness**: Asaph just explained God's compassionate response to Israel's sin. Yet he did not want to ignore Israel's sin, their great debt of ingratitude, and their rebellion against God.

b. **Again and again they tempted God, and limited the Holy One of Israel**: Not only did Israel's stubborn disobedience provoke and tempt God, there was a real sense in which it **limited the Holy One of Israel**. In one sense it is impossible for the creature to limit the Creator. Yet, when

God ties His work to man's faith and/or obedience, there is a sense in which man can and does limit God.

i. Matthew 13:58 says of the ministry of Jesus in Nazareth, *Now He did not do many mighty works there because of their unbelief.* As long as God chooses to work in concert with human agency, developing our ability to partner with Him, our unbelief can and may hinder the work of God.

ii. It's possible that **limited the Holy One of Israel** isn't the best translation of the Hebrew. "The rare verb in 41b probably means hurt or *provoked* (LXX and most moderns) rather than AV's 'limited', appropriate though the latter might seem." (Kidner)

c. **They did not remember His power, the day when He redeemed them from the enemy**: Asaph had in mind the great power God showed in setting Israel free from their 400 years of slavery in Egypt. The exodus redemption is often presented in the Hebrew Scriptures as a demonstration of the **power** of God.

i. In the New Testament we have a new and ultimate demonstration of the power of God: the resurrection of Jesus Christ (Romans 1:4, Ephesians 1:19-20, Philippians 3:10). Paul might have rephrased Psalm 78:42, *They did not remember His power, the day when He raised Jesus from the dead.*

ii. "The psalmist traces Israel's sin to forgetfulness of God's mercy, and thus glides into a swift summing up of the plagues of Egypt, regarded as conducing to Israel's deliverance. They are not arranged chronologically, though the list begins with the first." (Maclaren)

d. **When He worked His signs in Egypt**: Asaph recounted how God demonstrated His power for Israel and against Pharaoh by sending the plagues upon Egypt. The plagues were special demonstrations of God's power because they were focused against Egyptian deities.

- When God **turned their rivers into blood**, He showed He was greater than the Egyptian gods *Khnum* (said to be the guardian of the Nile), *Hapi* (supposedly the spirit of the Nile), and *Osiris*, said to have the Nile as his bloodstream (Exodus 7:17-20).

- When God **sent swarms of flies** and lice, He showed that He was greater than the Egyptian god *Imhotep* (believed to be the god of medicine), and that He was able to stop the whole worship of the Egyptian gods with loathsome lice and swarms of insects (Exodus 8:20-32).

- When God sent **frogs**, He showed that He was greater than the Egyptian goddess *Heqt*, believed to be the frog-goddess of fertility (Exodus 8:1-8:15).

- When God gave **their labor to the locust**, He showed that He was greater than the Egyptian god *Set*, thought to be the protector of crops (Exodus 10:1-20).

- When God destroyed their agriculture with **hail** and **frost** and their **flocks to fiery lightning**, He showed that He was greater than the Egyptian goddess *Nut*, the supposed sky goddess (Exodus 9:13-35).

- When God **gave up their cattle to the hail**, He showed that He was greater than the Egyptian goddess *Hathor*, believed to be a cow-like mother goddess (Exodus 9:1-7).

  i. "The psalm omits the plague of gnats, the disease inflicted on the livestock, the boils visited on the people, and the days of darkness. There is no discernible reason either for the choice of the six judgments or the omission of the other four." (Boice)

e. **By sending angels of destruction among them**: The worst of all the plagues was the last, the death of the firstborn. Egypt and Pharaoh would not give God *His* firstborn – Israel (Exodus 4:22-23); so God took the firstborn of Egypt (Exodus 11:1-12:30).

  i. "His last arrow was the sharpest. He reserved the strong wine of his indignation to the last. Note how the psalmist piles up the words, and well he might; for blow followed blow, each one more staggering than its predecessor, and then the crushing stroke was reserved for the end." (Spurgeon)

f. **He made His own people go forth like sheep**: After the death of the firstborn, the Egyptians begged the Israelites to leave and sent them away with gifts, happy to be rid of them. Asaph then summarized the next many years.

- **He led them on safely**: God protected them all the way.

- **The sea overwhelmed their enemies**: God destroyed the pursuing Egyptian army when the waters of the sea came crashing down upon them.

- **He brought them to His holy border**: The border of His holy land of promise.

- **He also drove out the nations before them**: Many of the Canaanite peoples were cleared away before Israel ever came to the land.

- He **allotted them an inheritance by survey**: The land was divided among those to whom He had made an eternal promise of the land.

  i. "The contrast is striking, and ought never to have been forgotten by the people. The wolves were slain in heaps, the sheep were carefully gathered, and triumphantly delivered. The tables were turned, and the poor serfs became the honoured people, while their oppressors were humbled before them." (Spurgeon)

C. Stubborn, rebellious Israel in the Promised Land.

1. (56-64) The terrible tragedy at Shiloh.

Yet they tested and provoked the Most High God,
And did not keep His testimonies,
But turned back and acted unfaithfully like their fathers;
They were turned aside like a deceitful bow.
For they provoked Him to anger with their high places,
And moved Him to jealousy with their carved images.
When God heard *this,* **He was furious,**
And greatly abhorred Israel,
So that He forsook the tabernacle of Shiloh,
The tent He had placed among men,
And delivered His strength into captivity,
And His glory into the enemy's hand.
He also gave His people over to the sword,
And was furious with His inheritance.
The fire consumed their young men,
And their maidens were not given in marriage.
Their priests fell by the sword,
And their widows made no lamentation.

a. **Yet they tested and provoked the Most High God**: The previous long section of this psalm (verses 40 through 55) recounted God's great faithfulness while in Egypt and as they went to Canaan. Yet once Israel came into the Promised Land, they **did not keep His testimonies, but turned back and acted unfaithfully.**

i. **Turned aside like a deceitful bow**: "In this they were unreliable, like a 'faulty bow' that springs wrongly when needed (cf. Psalm 78:9; Hosea 7:16)." (VanGemeren)

ii. "The figure of a 'deceitful bow,' in Psalm 78:57, well describes the people as failing to fulfil the purpose of their choice by God. As such a weapon does not shoot true, and makes the arrow fly wide, however well aimed and strongly drawn, so Israel foiled all Divine attempts, and failed to carry God's message to the world, or to fulfil His will in themselves." (Maclaren)

iii. "Israel boasted of the bow as the national weapon, they sang the song of the bow, and hence a deceitful bow is made to be the type and symbol of their own unsteadfastness; God can make men's glory the very ensign of their shame." (Spurgeon)

b. They provoked Him to anger with their high places, and moved Him to jealousy with their carved images: When Israel came into the Promised Land, they often worshiped the gods of the Canaanites, setting up altars on the **high places** and worshipping gods of **carved images**.

i. "The characteristic sin is no longer discontent (the paradox of the wilderness years with their daily miracles) but idolatry – the paradox of the years in Canaan, whose idolaters God had used Israel to judge." (Kidner)

c. He forsook the tabernacle of Shiloh: Asaph remembered the tragedy at **Shiloh**, where the Philistines overran the tabernacle, killed the priests, and captured the ark of the covenant (1 Samuel 4).

d. Delivered His strength into captivity, and His glory into the enemy's hand: When the ark of the covenant was captured at Shiloh, the daughter-in-law of Eli the high priest also learned that her husband, her brother-in-law, her father-in-law, and 30,000 Israeli soldiers were killed.

i. She was pregnant and the news was so overwhelming that she went into labor and died giving birth. With her last words she said to name the child born on such a tragic day, *Ichabod* – meaning, *the glory has departed* (1 Samuel 4:20-22). There certainly was a sense in which the glory had departed from Israel, but it wasn't the glory of the ark of the covenant. The glory that departed was the glory of God's blessing upon and presence with an obedient Israel.

e. The fire consumed the young men.... Their priests fell by the sword: Asaph reminded Israel that the losses at Shiloh were more than just the ark of the covenant. There was also a great loss of life, including the priests (1 Samuel 4:10-22).

i. **Their maidens were not given in marriage**: "They had not been honoured with nuptial songs according to the customs of those times, see Jeremiah 7:34; 16:9; 25:10. The meaning is, they had not been honourably married, because men were grown scarce by reason of the wars, Isaiah 4:1; Jeremiah 31:22. Or, they had been married without any solemnity, like poor bond-women; or privately, as in the time of public calamities." (Diodati, cited in Spurgeon)

2. (65-66) God's triumph after Shiloh.

Then the Lord awoke as *from* sleep,
Like a mighty man who shouts because of wine.
And He beat back His enemies;
He put them to a perpetual reproach.

a. **Then the Lord awoke as from sleep**: When the Philistines captured the ark of the covenant, they placed it as a trophy in the temple of their pagan god Dagon. Even while the symbol of His presence was captive in a pagan temple, God demonstrated His glory (1 Samuel 5).

i. **Like a mighty man**: "The renewal of his acts of mercy to Israel was so overwhelming that the psalmist likens God to a 'hero' (*gibbor*, NIV, 'man') who feels himself more heroic when intoxicated with wine (Psalm 78:65)." (VanGemeren)

ii. "One who, going forth to meet his enemy, having taken a sufficiency of wine to refresh himself, and become a proper stimulus to his animal spirits, *shouts* – gives the *war-signal* for the *onset*, impatient to meet the foe, and sure of victory. The idea is not taken from the case of a *drunken man*. A person in such a state would be very unfit to meet his enemy, and could have little prospect of conquest." (Clarke)

b. **He beat back His enemies**: The story of how God exalted Himself over the Philistines and **put them to a perpetual reproach** is found in 1 Samuel 5. In it all, God demonstrated that He was able to guard His glory when His people neglected His glory.

i. The King James Version translates the line from verse 66 *he smote his enemies in the hinder parts*. "**Smote his enemies in the hinder part,** with the disease of the emerods, which was both painful and shameful. He caused them to perpetuate their own reproach by sending back the ark of God with their golden emerods, the lasting monuments of their shame." (Poole)

3. (67-72) The hopeful choice of Jerusalem and David.

Moreover He rejected the tent of Joseph,
And did not choose the tribe of Ephraim,
But chose the tribe of Judah,
Mount Zion which He loved.
And He built His sanctuary like the heights,
Like the earth which He has established forever.
He also chose David His servant,
And took him from the sheepfolds;
From following the ewes that had young He brought him,

To shepherd Jacob His people,
And Israel His inheritance.
So he shepherded them according to the integrity of his heart,
And guided them by the skillfulness of his hands.

a. **But chose the tribe of Judah**: Asaph explained how God did not choose the other tribes to be the home of **His sanctuary**. **He rejected the tent of Joseph**, and instead chose Jerusalem (**Mount Zion**) to be the spiritual center of Israel.

i. "There are always new beginnings with God. Ephraim is rejected, but here Judah is chosen. Shiloh is abandoned, but the ark is brought to Mount Zion." (Boice)

b. **He also chose David His servant**: In some ways Jerusalem was an unlikely choice to be the center of Israel. In the same pattern, **David** – the humble shepherd boy **following the ewes that had young** – was God's choice **to shepherd Jacob His people and Israel His inheritance**.

c. **So he shepherded them according to the integrity of his heart, and guided them by the skillfulness of his hands**: Psalm 78 ends on a hopeful note. It concludes with recognition of and gratitude for the goodness of God in the **integrity** and **skillfulness** of David's rule.

i. **According to the integrity of his heart**: "David was upright before God, and never swerved in heart from the obedient worship of Jehovah. Whatever faults he had, he was unfeignedly sincere in his allegiance to Israel's superior king; he shepherded for God with honest heart." (Spurgeon)

ii. Like many aspects of David's rule, this was fulfilled in a much greater way in David's Greater Son, Jesus the Messiah. David's heart *mostly* had integrity; the heart of Jesus was perfect in integrity. David guided Israel with great skill; Jesus leads His people with perfect skill.

iii. "If Israel's record is her shame, God's persistent goodness emerges as her hope (and ours) for the unfinished story." (Kidner)

Psalm 79 – A Prayer from Conquered Exiles

Psalm 79 is titled **A Psalm of Asaph**, *though it was clearly written after the destruction of Jerusalem by the Babylonian armies. This event was so traumatic and important in the scope of Jewish history that it is described four times in the Hebrew Scriptures: 2 Kings 25, 2 Chronicles 36:11-21, Jeremiah 39:1-14, and Jeremiah 52. Since the Asaph most prominent in the Old Testament lived and served during the reigns of King David and King Solomon, this is likely a later Asaph.*

James Montgomery Boice (writing regarding Psalm 74) explains the concept of a later Asaph: "Either this is a later Asaph, which is not unlikely since the name might have been perpetuated among the temple musicians, or, more likely, the name was affixed to many psalms produced by this body of musicians. We know that the 'descendants of Asaph' were functioning as late as the reign of Josiah (2 Chronicles 35:15)."

A. The devastation of Jerusalem.

1. (1-4) Jerusalem destroyed, the temple defiled.

O God, the nations have come into Your inheritance;
Your holy temple they have defiled;
They have laid Jerusalem in heaps.
The dead bodies of Your servants
They have given *as* food for the birds of the heavens,
The flesh of Your saints to the beasts of the earth.
Their blood they have shed like water all around Jerusalem,
And *there was* no one to bury *them.*
We have become a reproach to our neighbors,
A scorn and derision to those who are around us.

> a. **The nations have come into Your inheritance**: The army that conquered Judah and destroyed Jerusalem was under the command of the king of Babylon. Yet like the armies of many ancient empires, it was made up of soldiers of many **nations** conquered by the Babylonians.

i. "It is the cry of amazement at sacrilegious intrusion; as if the poet were struck with horror. The stranger pollutes thine hallowed courts with his tread." (Spurgeon)

b. **Into Your inheritance**: The psalmist had the *land* of Israel in mind with the words, **Your inheritance**. The conquering Babylonians came against the people of Judah, but **into** the land of Israel. That particular land was important to God, and therefore Asaph noted the crisis of that land being invaded by the pagan King Nebuchadnezzar and his armies.

c. **Your holy temple they have defiled**: The temple was **holy**, but now was **defiled**. Jerusalem once prospered, but now was **laid** in **heaps**. The **servants** of God were dead, and their corpses disgraced (**given as food for the birds of heaven...** with **no one to bury them**).

i. **Your servants...Your saints**: "Though famine, war, death, and exile were deserved punishments for Judah's sins (Lamentation 1:8-9), the people are still spoken of as the people of God. They are called 'your servants' and 'your saints.'" (VanGemeren)

ii. "To lie unburied was the final humiliation, as though one had departed unloved and of no account, as disposable as an animal." (Kidner)

iii. "Either they denied them the honour of burial or else they mangled their dead bodies, and exercised their rage upon them, as the Papists did upon Huss and Zwinglius, and many of the English martyrs. A barbarous practice." (Trapp)

d. **We have become a reproach to our neighbors**: The shocking and brutal fall of Jerusalem and Judah made the Israelites a disgrace, contemptible to the surrounding nations.

i. **A scorn and derision**: "To find mirth in others' miseries, and to exult over the ills of others, is worthy only of the devil and of those whose father he is. Thus the case is stated before the Lord, and it is a very deplorable one." (Spurgeon)

2. (5-7) A prayer to turn away the anger of God.

How long, Lord?
Will You be angry forever?
Will Your jealousy burn like fire?
Pour out Your wrath on the nations that do not know You,
And on the kingdoms that do not call on Your name.
For they have devoured Jacob,
And laid waste his dwelling place.

a. **How long, LORD**: In the midst of the catastrophe of the conquest of Judah and Jerusalem, Asaph asked the question that many sufferers among God's people ask. **How long** does not question the *why* of suffering, but in faith asks the *when* of suffering, and if it will last forever.

> i. The disaster made Asaph question, but it did not make him an atheist. The question was still asked of God. "It was not easy to hold fast by the reality of God's special relation to a nation thus apparently deserted, but the psalmist's faith stood even such a strain, and is not dashed by a trace of doubt. Such times are the test and triumph of trust." (Maclaren)

> ii. "The very fact of the song is a revelation of the underlying confidence in God. In distress the heart seeks its way back to some hiding place, and finds it in the name of God." (Morgan)

b. **Will you be angry forever?** Asaph expressed the heart of the devastated people of Judah after the fall of Jerusalem. In the years of Jeremiah's ministry many false prophets had told them that deliverance would come. Because they ignored God's true messenger (Jeremiah), judgment came upon His people and they were completely unprepared for it.

> i. The good news was that God's anger and jealousy would not burn against His people forever. Jeremiah foretold the judgment to come, but he also told of restoration that would follow.

c. **Pour out Your wrath on the nations that do not know You**: God would answer Asaph's prayer in time, when judgment came upon the Babylonian Empire and they were conquered by the Medes and Persians. Babylon **devoured Jacob** and was in turn devoured.

> i. Verses 6 and 7 are remarkably similar to Jeremiah 10:25. It's possible that Jeremiah influenced the author of this psalm.

> ii. **His dwelling place**: Some take this as a reference to the temple, which was certainly destroyed in the conquest of Jerusalem. Yet it is more likely that it refers to the land of Israel itself, previously referred to as God's *inheritance* (verse 1).

B. The plea for rescue.

1. (8-10) Rescue us for Your glory.

Oh, do not remember former iniquities against us!
Let Your tender mercies come speedily to meet us,
For we have been brought very low.
Help us, O God of our salvation,
For the glory of Your name;

And deliver us, and provide atonement for our sins,
For Your name's sake!
Why should the nations say,
"Where *is* their God?"
Let there be known among the nations in our sight
The avenging of the blood of Your servants *which has been* shed.

a. **Do not remember former iniquities against us**: Speaking on behalf of the exiled survivors, Asaph humbled himself before God and admitted their sin against Him. They could no longer deny their sin; instead they could plead for forgiveness and for God's **tender mercies** to **come speedily**.

i. "The people were suffering the destruction of their entire civilization – politically, economically, socially, and religiously. Yet there is not the slightest suggestion that they did not actually deserve it, or that they did not deserve it continuing as long as it had." (Boice)

ii. The concept of **former iniquities** suggests a principle. "Sins accumulate against nations. Generations lay up stores of transgressions to be visited upon their successors; hence this urgent prayer." (Spurgeon)

b. **For we have been brought very low**: *Before* they were **brought very low**, they did not humbly repent. Now they were in the place to do it.

c. **For the glory of Your name**: Asaph wisely appealed to the **glory** of God in his prayer for help. The glory of Judah and Jerusalem had been shattered, yet God might move for His people in the interest of His own glory.

d. **Provide atonement for our sins**: This was another appropriate and wonderful confession of sin and dependence upon God for *His* **atonement**. Asaph knew that any man-made atonement would be useless; God must **provide atonement for our sins**.

i. **Provide atonement for our sins**: When the psalmist prayed this, the temple and the altar were destroyed. The normal sacrifices were impossible. He looked for a greater **atonement** that God Himself would provide (Genesis 22:8-14).

e. **Where is their God?** Asaph made a slightly different appeal, still with an eye to God's glory. Asaph considered the custom of the **avenging of the blood** in his ancient culture, where the murder of a family member would be answered by the work of the *goel*, the avenger of blood. He asked God to put the nations to silence and display His active presence by acting as the avenger of blood on behalf of His people.

i. **Where is their God?** "So Turks at this day (when they have the better of Christians) cry, Where is the Christian's God?" (Trapp)

ii. "The singer sees God reigning and working salvation, but the nations cannot see this. Their only proof of God is that of the prosperity of His people. In the hour of their adversity the nations will say, Where is their God?" (Morgan)

iii. "Prayer is therefore here made by the faithful, that God, not to gratify any vindictive spirit of theirs, but to vindicate his own attributes, would break the teeth of the oppressor, and work a public and glorious salvation for his chosen." (Horne)

2. (11-12) Have mercy on the condemned.

Let the groaning of the prisoner come before You;
According to the greatness of Your power
Preserve those who are appointed to die;
And return to our neighbors sevenfold into their bosom
Their reproach with which they have reproached You, O Lord.

a. **Let the groaning of the prisoner come before You**: Asaph considered the misery of his many countrymen who were prisoners in Babylon, asking God to hear their **groaning** and to act on their behalf.

i. "At the time of the Exodus, God had seen the affliction of his people and had heard their groanings (Exodus 2:24; 6:5). The people in exile were not unlike those in Egypt. They too groaned for the moment of their deliverance." (VanGemeren)

b. **Preserve those who are appointed to die**: Asaph then considered those among the exiles in Babylon who were condemned to death, and asked that God **preserve** them.

i. Clarke says **those who are appointed to die** is literally "'...sons of death.' Either those who were condemned to death because of their crimes, or condemned to be destroyed by their oppressors. Both these senses apply to the Israelites: they were sons of death, i.e., worthy of death because of their sins against God; they were condemned to death or utter destruction, by their Babylonish enemies." (Clarke)

c. **Return to our neighbors sevenfold into their bosom**: Asaph's final request was that God deal with their conquerors with both justice and vengeance, returning to them **sevenfold** the agony they inflicted upon Judah and the same **reproach** they directed towards God Himself.

i. Sometimes **sevenfold** is simply a way of saying *abundantly* or *in great measure* (Genesis 4:15, Isaiah 30:26).

ii. "They denied thine existence, mocked thy power, insulted thy worship, and destroyed thy house; up, therefore, O Lord, and make them feel to the full that thou art not to be mocked with impunity. Pour into their laps good store of shame because they dared insult the God of Israel." (Spurgeon)

3. (13) A vow to give thanks.

So we, Your people and sheep of Your pasture,
Will give You thanks forever;
We will show forth Your praise to all generations.

a. **Your people and sheep of Your pasture**: After praying for rescue, protection, and vengeance, Asaph ended this psalm with grateful dependence upon God. He properly recognized God's place as Shepherd over His **people and sheep**.

b. **We will give You thanks forever**: As grateful sheep, they would declare their **thanks** and **praise** both now and in the future.

i. "This is rather a faith-filled anticipation of a brighter, future day when God's people will once again praise him with full hearts and with fresh memories of what he has done for them." (Boice)

Psalm 80 – Restoring Israel, the Sheep and Vineyard of the LORD

This psalm is titled **To the Chief Musician. Set to "The Lilies." A Testimony of Asaph. A Psalm.** *As with Psalms 45, 60 and 69, this psalm is* **Set to "The Lilies."** *The phrase may refer to the general beauty of the composition, to the tune, or even to a six-stringed instrument known as the Shoshannim (the literal translation of the Hebrew).*

As with several of the Asaph psalms, this one is often attributed to a later Asaph. "Here not only the southern kingdom but also the northern kingdom – it calls God the 'Shepherd of Israel' and speaks of Ephraim and Manasseh, two of the major northern tribes – and since it asks for Israel's deliverance, it is best seen as a plea for the deliverance of the northern kingdom sometime before its fall to the Assyrian armies in 721 B.C." (James Montgomery Boice)

"A later Asaph we should suppose, who had the unhappiness to live, like the 'last minstrel,' in evil times. If by the Asaph of David's day, this Psalm was written in the spirit of prophecy, for it sings of times unknown to David." (Charles Spurgeon)

A. Israel's Shepherd and sorrow.

1. (1-3) A prayer to Israel's Shepherd for restoration.

Give ear, O Shepherd of Israel,
You who lead Joseph like a flock;
You who dwell *between* the cherubim, shine forth!
Before Ephraim, Benjamin, and Manasseh,
Stir up Your strength,
And come *and* save us!
Restore us, O God;
Cause Your face to shine,
And we shall be saved!

   a. **Give ear, O Shepherd of Israel**: The image of a king or ruler over a people being regarded as the *shepherd* was common in the ancient world.

307

Asaph rightly understood that in a special and wonderful way, Yahweh was the **Shepherd of Israel**. It was He who had and would **lead Joseph like a flock**.

> i. "Although appearing frequently elsewhere, the idea of God being Israel's shepherd occurs in the Psalter only twice, here and in Psalm 23." (Boice)

> ii. "The name is full of tenderness, and hence is selected by the troubled Psalmist: broken hearts delight in names of grace." (Spurgeon)

> iii. **Shepherd of Israel**: "Thou that feedest thy people, watchest over them, defendest, redeemest, reducest them; thou that handlest them, curest them, washest them, drivest them as they are able to go, carryest them in thy bosom, doest all the offices of a good shepherd for them." (Trapp)

> iv. "'Shepherd of Israel' reminds us of Jacob's blessing of Ephraim and Manasseh in which he invoked 'the God who shepherded me all my life long' to 'bless the lads,' and of the title in Genesis 49:24, 'the shepherd, the stone of Israel.'" (Maclaren)

> v. Because of the prominence of Joseph among his brothers, and because of the size of the tribes of the sons of Joseph (Ephraim and Manasseh), sometimes the Scriptures refer to all of Israel as **Joseph** (Ezekiel 37:16,19; Amos 5:6, 5:15, 6:6; Zechariah 10:6; Psalm 81:5; Obadiah 1:18).

b. **You who dwell between the cherubim**: This refers to two aspects. The lesser aspect is the presence of God as connected with the ark of the covenant and the institution of the tabernacle/temple. The greater aspect is the recognition that in heaven and its reality, God does **dwell between the cherubim**.

c. **You who dwell between the cherubim, shine forth**: Asaph asked that the God of this majesty and glory would **shine forth** on behalf of His people. When God does **shine forth**, darkness and gloom vanish and He is magnified.

d. **Before Ephraim, Benjamin, and Manasseh**: In the order of arrangement around the tabernacle and in the order of march, these three tribes were grouped together on the east side of the tabernacle (Numbers 2 and 10).

> i. "These three tribes went next after the ark, when it removed, Numbers 2:18-24; Numbers 10:22-24." (Trapp)

e. **Stir up Your strength, and come and save us**: The God mighty enough to shepherd Israel and bring the people from Egypt to Canaan was strong enough to deliver them in their present crisis – *if* His **strength** was stirred. This was a prayer of faith, understanding, and dependence.

f. **Restore us, O God**: This begins a refrain that is repeated three times in this psalm (verse 3, 7, and 19). It expressed trust and dependence upon God, and confidence that His favor (shown by His shining **face**) was all that was needed for Israel's restoration and blessing.

> i. "It is not so much said, '*turn* our captivity' but turn '*us.*' All will come right if we are right. The best turn is not that of circumstances but of character. When the Lord turns his people he will soon turn their condition." (Spurgeon)

> ii. Spurgeon saw in this line and the following a description of the factors in revival. First there is the restoration or turning of the people to God, and then there is the radiant face of God, shining in all the goodness of His presence. In those two combined we see the work of true revival happen.

> iii. "I want to see those times again, when first the refreshing showers came down from heaven. Have you never heard that under one of Whitfield's sermons there have been as many as two thousand saved? He was a great man; but God can use the little, as well as the great to produce the same effect; and why should there not be souls saved here, beyond all our dreams?" (Spurgeon)

g. **Cause Your face to shine**: This goes back to the blessing the priests were commanded to proclaim to the people of Israel (Numbers 6:24-26). It has the idea of God's presence, pleasure, and favor.

> i. "The psalmist must have heard this blessing a thousand times. So he prays here, 'Make your face shine upon us, that we may be saved.'" (Boice)

> ii. "Our greatest dread is the withdrawal of the Lord's presence, and our brightest hope is the prospect of his return. In the darkest times of Israel, the light of her Shepherd's countenance is all she needs." (Spurgeon)

> iii. **We shall be saved**: "To be 'saved' means here to be rescued from the assaults of hostile nations. The poet was sure that Israel's sole defence was God, and that one gleam of His face would shrivel up the strongest foes." (Maclaren)

2. (4-7) God's anger makes His people sorrowful.

O LORD God of hosts,
How long will You be angry

Against the prayer of Your people?
You have fed them with the bread of tears,
And given them tears to drink in great measure.
You have made us a strife to our neighbors,
And our enemies laugh among themselves.
Restore us, O God of hosts;
Cause Your face to shine,
And we shall be saved!

a. **O LORD God of hosts, how long will You be angry?** Asaph's heart poured out in sorrow before God. It is a terrible thing to sense that God is **angry** and that He is **against the prayer** of His people. The sorrow is deeper when it is recognized that it is the God of heavenly armies, the **LORD God of hosts**, who has in some way set Himself against His people.

i. "The rendering 'wilt Thou be angry?' is but a feeble reproduction of the vigorous original, which runs 'wilt Thou smoke?' Other psalms (*e.g.,* Psalm 74:1) speak of God's anger as smoking but here the figure is applied to God Himself." (Maclaren)

ii. **Against the prayer**: "That God should be angry with us when sinning seems natural enough, but that he should be angry even with our prayers is a bitter grief." (Spurgeon)

b. **Tears to drink in great measure**: Asaph used the metaphor of drinking tears to express the great sorrow of God's people. Psalm 42:3 uses a similar image: *My tears have been my food day and night.*

i. "There cannot be a more striking picture of Sion in captivity. Her bread is dipped in tears, and her cup is filled to the brim with them: no time is free from grief and lamentation." (Horne)

c. **Our enemies laugh among themselves**: The mocking and taunting of Israel's enemies were painful for Asaph and the people of God in their low condition. It stung to be **strife** to their neighbors, and to hear their mocking laugh.

i. **A strife to our neighbors**: "Always jealous and malicious, Edom and Moab exulted over Israel's troubles, and then fell to disputing about their share of the spoil." (Spurgeon)

ii. "The psalmist points to an angry God, a weeping nation, and mocking foes, a trilogy of woe." (Maclaren)

d. **Restore us, O God**: Asaph repeats and strengthens the refrain from verse 3, adding **of hosts**, emphasizing His power and authority. Fresh expression of their misery made for a fresh prayer for restoration and rescue by the shining, approving face of God.

B. Israel as a vine.

1. (8-11) The vine of Israel is planted in the Promised Land.

You have brought a vine out of Egypt;
You have cast out the nations, and planted it.
You prepared *room* for it,
And caused it to take deep root,
And it filled the land.
The hills were covered with its shadow,
And the mighty cedars with its boughs.
She sent out her boughs to the Sea,
And her branches to the River.

a. **You have brought a vine out of Egypt**: The **vine** is a familiar picture of Israel in the Old Testament. This vine was transplanted from **Egypt** and brought into the Promised Land. In Canaan, God **planted it**, making **room** by casting out the Canaanite nations.

i. Many passages of the Old Testament speak of Israel as **a vine**: Deuteronomy 32:32-33, Isaiah 5:1, Jeremiah 2:21, Ezekiel 17:5-6, Hosea 10:1, and Joel 1:7. The New Testament also applies the figure to Israel (Matthew 20:1, Matthew 21:33, Mark 12:1), and then more broadly to the people of God in general.

ii. "The vine is a plant weak and lowly, and needing support; when supported, wild and luxuriant, unless restrained by the pruning-knife; capable of producing the most valuable fruit, but if barren, the most unprofitable among trees, and fit only for the flames." (Horne)

b. **Caused it to take deep root, and it filled the land**: The vine of Israel was blessed in the Promised Land. Under God's blessing they took **deep root** and **filled the land** in a way that the variety of Canaanite tribes had not. It grew so strong and secure in the land that it did what was botanically impossible in a literal sense: the vine grew big as **the mighty cedars** and cast its **shadow** upon the hills.

i. "The figure is carried out with much beauty in detail. The Exodus was the vine's transplanting; the destruction of the Canaanites was the grubbing up of weeds to clear the ground for it; the numerical increase of the people was its making roots and spreading far." (Maclaren)

c. **She sent out her boughs to the Sea, and her branches to the River**: At its height under King David and King Solomon, Israel's domination stretched from the Mediterranean Sea (**the Sea**) to the Euphrates **River**.

i. This broad dominion of Israel was promised in Exodus 23:31 and Deuteronomy 11:24. 1 Kings 4:21 shows it was fulfilled by the reign of Solomon, who inherited David's dominion.

2. (12-13) The unprotected vineyard.

Why have You broken down her hedges,
So that all who pass by the way pluck her *fruit*?
The boar out of the woods uproots it,
And the wild beast of the field devours it.

a. **Why have You broken down her hedges?** In ancient Israel a vineyard was often surrounded by a thick and thorny hedge that kept out thieves and wild animals. Asaph looked at Israel's troubled state and could see that the symbolic **hedges** were **broken down** by the hand of God.

b. **All who pass by the way pluck her fruit**: Without protection of God's **hedges**, the land of Israel was ready to be plundered and devoured by her enemies.

c. **The boar out of the woods uproots it**: Wild boars are noted for their destruction, and can quickly lay waste to a vineyard. The enemies of God are pictured as such wild, destructive beasts.

i. "No image of a destructive enemy could be more appropriate than that which is used. We have read of the little foxes that spoil the vines, but the *wild boar* is a much more destructive enemy, breaking its way through fences, rooting up the ground, tearing down the vines themselves, and treading them under its feet. A single party of these animals will sometimes destroy an entire vineyard in a single night." (Wood, cited in Spurgeon)

ii. In 1520, as Martin Luther rose in prominence as a reformer, Pope Leo X published a condemnation of Luther and his work known as *Exsurge domini*. In the opening paragraph, he used this image from Psalm 80: "At thy ascension into heaven thou hast commanded the care, rule and administration of this vineyard to Peter as head and to thy representatives, his successors, as the Church triumphant. A roaring boar of the woods has undertaken to destroy this vineyard, a wild beast wants to devour it."

3. (14-16) A prayer for God to take pity upon the desolate vine.

Return, we beseech You, O God of hosts;
Look down from heaven and see,
And visit this vine
And the vineyard which Your right hand has planted,
And the branch *that* You made strong for Yourself.

It is burned with fire, *it is* cut down;
They perish at the rebuke of Your countenance.

a. **Return, we beseech You**: With an earnest plea Asaph prayed on behalf of the nation, begging God to **return** to them, to **look** upon the greatness of their need and to **visit this vine** that He Himself had planted.

i. "The suffering of the people is due to their own sin in turning away from God as Shepherd, Husbandman, and King. Their restoration can come only as He turns them back to Himself." (Morgan)

ii. **Visit this vine...and the branch that You made strong**: "A prayer for the leader whom the Lord had raised up, or for the Messiah whom they expected." (Spurgeon)

b. **It is burned with fire, it is cut down**: The great desolation of this vine came from the **rebuke** of God Himself, **the rebuke of Your countenance**.

4. (17-19) Restoration in the Man of God's Right Hand.

Let Your hand be upon the man of Your right hand,
Upon the son of man *whom* You made strong for Yourself.
Then we will not turn back from You;
Revive us, and we will call upon Your name.
Restore us, O Lord God of hosts;
Cause Your face to shine,
And we shall be saved!

a. **Let Your hand be upon the man of Your right hand**: In Israel's low place, Asaph knew that the nation needed *leadership*. He asked God to be with and to bless (**Let Your hand be upon**) a particular man – the **man** of God's right hand. Perhaps Asaph had first in mind the present king of Israel; but ultimately the Man of God's Right Hand is Jesus Christ (Ephesians 1:20, Hebrews 8:1).

i. "Nations rise or fall largely through the instrumentality of individuals: by a Napoleon the kingdoms are scourged, and by a Wellington nations are saved from the tyrant. It is by the man Christ Jesus that fallen Israel is yet to rise, and indeed through him, who deigns to call himself the Son of Man, the world is to be delivered from the dominion of Satan and the curse of sin." (Spurgeon)

ii. **The man of Your right hand**: "The only person who can be said to be at the right hand of God as intercessor, is Jesus the Messiah. Let him become our Deliverer: appoint him for this purpose, and let his strength be manifested in our weakness! By whom are the Jews to be restored, if indeed they ever be restored to their own land, but by Jesus

CHRIST? By HIM alone can they find mercy; through HIM *alone* can they ever be reconciled to God." (Clarke)

b. **Upon the son of man whom You made strong for Yourself**: Again, this was likely prayed with reference to the present king of Israel. Yet the ultimate **Son of Man** was Jesus Christ, who received God's strength as a submitted Son to His Father in heaven.

c. **Then we will not turn back from You**: In the strength of this Son of Man made strong, this Man of God's Right Hand, God's people would be restored to faithfulness. They would be revived and once against call upon His name.

   i. **Revive us**: "Only the Lord can 'revive' (Psalm 80:18) the people by forgiveness of their sins, by renewal of the covenant, and by driving out the enemies. This is not merely a prayer for deliverance from the enemy but an urgent petition for the blessings of God." (VanGemeren)

d. **Restore us, O LORD God of hosts**: The refrain is repeated a third and final time, yet this time adding Yahweh, the covenant name of God (**LORD God of hosts**). Under the leadership of God's great Messiah, God's people *would* be restored and once again know the shining radiance of God's face. They would be rescued.

   i. **Cause Your face to shine**: "Both for Israel and the Church this prayer has been answered in Christ. In Him we may be restored to God. In Him, the face of God is shining upon us in grace." (Morgan)

Psalms 41-80 – Bibliography

Adams, Reverend John *The Lenten Psalms* (New York: Charles Scribner's Sons, 1912)

Boice, James Montgomery *Psalms, Volume 1 – Psalms 1-41* (Grand Rapids, Michigan: Baker Books, 1994)

Boice, James Montgomery *Psalms, Volume 2 – Psalms 42-106* (Grand Rapids, Michigan: Baker Books, 1996)

Chappell, Clovis G. *Sermons from the Psalms* (Nashville, Tennessee: Cokesbury Press, 1931)

Clarke, Adam *The Holy Bible, Containing the Old and New Testaments, with A Commentary and Critical Notes, Volume III – Job to Song of Solomon* (New York: Eaton and Mains, 1827?)

Harris, Arthur Emerson *The Psalms Outlined* (Philadelphia: The Judson Press, 1925)

Horne, George *Commentary on the Psalms* (Audubon, New Jersey: Old Paths Publications, 1997 reprint of a 1771 edition)

Kidner, Derek *Psalms 1-72, A Commentary* (Leicester, England: Inter-Varsity Press, 1973)

Kidner, Derek *Psalms 73-150, A Commentary* (Leicester, England: Inter-Varsity Press, 1975)

Maclaren, Alexander *The Psalms, Volume I – Psalms 1-38* (London: Hodder and Stoughton, 1892)

Maclaren, Alexander *The Psalms, Volume II – Psalms 39-89* (London: Hodder and Stoughton, 1892)

Meyer, F.B. *Our Daily Homily* (Westwood, New Jersey: Revell, 1966)

Morgan, G. Campbell *Searchlights from the Word* (New York: Revell, 1926)

Morgan, G. Campbell *An Exposition of the Whole Bible* (Old Tappan, New Jersey: Revell, 1959)

Poole, Matthew *A Commentary on the Holy Bible, Volume 2* (London: The Banner of Truth Trust, 1968)

Spurgeon, Charles Haddon *The Treasury of David, Volume 1 – Psalms 1-57* (Peabody, Massachusetts: Hendrickson, 1988)

Spurgeon, Charles Haddon *The Treasury of David, Volume 2 – Psalms 58-110* (Peabody, Massachusetts: Hendrickson, 1988)

Spurgeon, Charles Haddon *The New Park Street Pulpit, Volumes 1-6* and *The Metropolitan Tabernacle Pulpit, Volumes 7-63* (Pasadena, Texas: Pilgrim Publications, 1990)

Trapp, John *A Commentary on the Old and New Testaments, Volume 3 – Proverbs to Daniel* (Eureka, California: Tanski Publications, 1997)

VanGemeren, Willem A. "Psalms," *The Expositor's Bible Commentary, Volume 5: Psalms-Song of Songs* (Grand Rapids, Michigan: Zondervan, 1991)

As the years pass I love the work of studying, learning, and teaching the Bible more than ever. I'm so grateful that God is faithful to meet me in His Word.

Mary Osgood is doing a wonderful work in proofreading and with editorial suggestions for these volumes of commentary on Psalms. Mary, thank you for helping me to write clearer and better!

Thanks to Brian Procedo for the cover design and the graphics work.

Most especially, thanks to my wife Inga-Lill. She is my loved and valued partner in life and in service to God and His people.

David Guzik

David Guzik's Bible commentary is regularly used and trusted by many thousands who want to know the Bible better. Pastors, teachers, class leaders, and everyday Christians find his commentary helpful for their own understanding and explanation of the Bible. David and his wife Inga-Lill live in Santa Barbara, California.

You can email David at
david@enduringword.com

For more resources by David Guzik,
go to www.enduringword.com

CPSIA information can be obtained
at www.ICGtesting.com
Printed in the USA
FFHW021859171219
57051522-62644FF